7/24/03

Dearest Ian —

This is to thank you for all that you have taught us. We are so very deeply proud of you —

With much, much love —

Cynthia
& Therese ♡

Praise for *Stories of the Courage to Teach*

"A book for troubled times in teaching. This powerful and moving collection of essays argues that we must join the values of the heart if teaching is to transcend the punishing pressures of the one-size-fits-all juggernaut of school-reform mania. A must-read for teacher educators, principals, and school board members!"
—Jay Casbon, dean, Graduate School of Education, Lewis & Clark College

"[This book] is a must-read for educators who often feel depleted from the demands of teaching and isolated from colleagues. Rediscover your purpose and passion for making a difference in the lives of children through stories of real people who teach with courage and integrity. There is something essentially human in these pages that speaks to the hearts of teachers who are disillusioned, depleted, and discouraged. You simply must reconnect with your identity, your true self, that spiritual being who felt called to teach children. It is powerful because it is the truth, spoken from the hearts of teachers who share a common experience."
—Paula Naegle, Nevada Teacher of the Year

"Teacher voices must be heard, and teacher wisdom about the needs of children must be heeded. It has always been from the teachers who speak from their hearts that we find the best solutions to improving our schools. Our job as policymakers is to listen."
—James B. Hunt, Jr., governor of North Carolina for four terms

"The core relationship in learning is between the student and the teacher. [This] book reminds us just how vital the forces of heart and spirit are to teaching and learning."
—Wendy D. Puriefoy, president, Public Education Network

STORIES OF
The Courage to Teach

Honoring the Teacher's Heart

Sam M. Intrator

Foreword by Parker J. Palmer

JOSSEY-BASS
A Wiley Company
www.josseybass.com

Published by

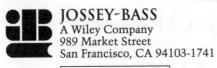

JOSSEY-BASS
A Wiley Company
989 Market Street
San Francisco, CA 94103-1741

www.josseybass.com

Jossey-Bass books and products are available through most bookstores. To contact Jossey-Bass directly, call (888) 378-2537, fax to (800) 605-2665, or visit our
website at www.josseybass.com.

Substantial discounts on bulk quantities of Jossey-Bass books are available to cor-
porations, professional associations, and other organizations. For details and dis-
count information, contact the special sales department at Jossey-Bass.

We at Jossey-Bass strive to use the most environmentally sensitive paper stocks available to us. Our publications are printed on acid-free recycled stock whenever possible,
and our paper always meets or exceeds minimum GPO and EPA requirements.

Credits are on p. 339.

Library of Congress Cataloging-in-Publication Data
   Stories of the courage to teach: honoring the teacher's heart / [edited by] Sam M. In-
trator; foreword by Parker J. Palmer.—1st ed.
      p.   cm.
   Includes bibliographical references and index.
   ISBN 0-7879-5632-5 (alk. paper)
   1. Teachers—Anecdotes. 2. Teaching—Anecdotes. I. Intrator, Sam M.
   LB1775 .S72 2002
371.1—dc21   2001007502

FIRST EDITION
HB Printing   10   9   8   7   6   5   4   3   2

Contents

Contents

CONTENTS

Gratitudes

In the middle of writing this book, our whole team was devastated by the death of Sarah Polster, our remarkable and visionary Jossey-Bass editor. Sarah championed the concept of this book and, like every great teacher I've ever known, helped guide the ideas along with keen questions and careful feedback. Her vision was that the courage stories told in this book by teachers would help beat back the forces that deform and deplete the teacher's heart and integrity. She believed in books that could make a difference in people's lives.

This book owes so much to the grace, intelligence, and wonderful spirit of Megan Scribner. She has a special, near-magical gift: what she touches becomes better. Her editor's hand made the writing in this book stronger and clearer, her good humor and companionship made the process more enjoyable, and her wisdom lifted the ideas higher.

My special thanks to Marcy and Rick Jackson, whose work at the Center for Teacher Formation on behalf of teachers is a blessing for the profession. Their courage and commitment to teachers is fierce, but their way in the world, gentle and kind. In their work as facilitators of the Courage to Teach retreats, they speak of the importance of "holding a space" where community can flourish—they hold this space wherever they are. I'm grateful for their friendship in my life. I would also like to thank Robin Gaphni for her support and good cheer in organizing the effort to seek a broad range of submitters.

Parker J. Palmer's Foreword and Afterword begin and close this volume, and his wise and generous presence is palpable throughout. To all of us who have the heart of a teacher, I know of no more compassionate or fervid defender of our integrity. Since I can't resist sports metaphors, I have to add that in my all-star lineup of teachers, I've penciled Parker in at the clean-up position. I also honor Sharon Palmer, whose caring support and gentle strength were so reassuring to me at various times in this project. I also want to recognize Sally Hare and Marianne Houston, two other leaders in the Courage to Teach movement whose contributions pushed this book ahead. On behalf of teachers everywhere, thanks to the Fetzer Institute for supporting this essential work.

I thank the Jossey-Bass family for its commitment to this work: Sheryl Fullerton, Mark Kerr, Chandrika Madhavan, Andrea Flint, and Jessica Egbert. A special thank you to Naomi Lucks Sigal for her careful reading of the manuscript, and to Bruce Emmer for his copyediting.

During the spring semester of 2001, I was fortunate enough to have a student in my class whose intelligence, grace, and spirit pushed all of us to learn more. I was thrilled when she agreed to help out with the book. Helen Lee's effort in researching sources, editing my writing, and supporting the ideas in this book was truly remarkable. In the early stages of the project, Lauren McDonald, another Smith student, supported me. Lauren's keen ability to understand the human dimension of this project and her ability to sensitively read and size up the submissions were of great help during the early stages of this work. These same qualities will leave an enduring mark on our world. They both, in my opinion, embody the very best hopes that Sophia Smith had for the college she founded.

For the past seventeen years, I've been blessed by a steady stream of wonderful and uplifting young people who have inspired me with their resilience, creativity, and energy. From New York City to Vermont to California and now Massachusetts, I am heartened by the resolute commitment of those who have passed through my classrooms to do good deeds and find ways to respect, understand, and honor our differences as people.

My life is filled with teachers. It is to these friends, colleagues, and mentors that I turned seeking constructive criticism, support, and patience while I floated scratchy drafts and half-baked ideas. In recollections of past conversations over coffee, in hallways, through e-mail, and in the other ways we come together, I was, and always will be, learning. These people include my colleagues at Morgan and Gill Halls, Deb Altman, Robert Bernheim, Jim Burke, Mike Copland, Joe Greenwald, Robert Kunzman, André LaChance, Noreen Likins, Jim Mangano, Connie Metz, Christine O'Donnell, Wendy Rosov, and Larry Thomas. I'm also thankful for Christine Barbuto, whose calm and kind presence sets the tone at Morgan Hall.

To my mentors at Stanford: this is my first book project, and it is forever clear how your habits and ethics as scholars live on in the way I try to do my work. Edwin Bridges, Elliot Eisner, and Robert Roesser—thank you. I suffered a profound personal loss when Alan "Buddy" Peshkin passed away. He dedicated his last book to "his battalion." It will forever be a source of honor to have been part of his people.

To my trio—Jake, Kaleigh, and Casey—who make my life thrilling: there is nothing that I exult in more than watching you teach and tend each other. And to the teachers of my children, thank you. Val Gardner, the indomitable principal of Champlain

Valley Union High School in Vermont, told me on the day my first child was born, "Now that you're a parent, you'll truly appreciate how important teachers are in our world." She, as always, knows the heart of the matter.

Finally, to my wife Jo-Anne: Jo, you have the heart of a teacher and the courage of a hero. Your strength sustains us all.

Northampton, Massachusetts Sam M. Intrator
February 2002

To Mom and Dad:
I honor their teachers' hearts,
hearts I shared with thousands
of New York City children
who were their students

Foreword

Listening to Teachers

Parker J. Palmer

TEACHERS AS CULTURE HEROES

America's teachers are the culture heroes of our time. Daily they are asked to solve problems that baffle the rest of us. Daily they are asked to work with resources nowhere near commensurate with the task. And daily they are berated by politicians, the public, and the press for their alleged failures and inadequacies.

This scenario may apply with special force to K–12 teachers in our public schools, but people who choose to teach in colleges and universities are often caught in a similar bind. In higher education, the choice to teach—that is, to care for students—frequently comes at considerable personal cost, because academic culture supports and rewards people who devote their energies to research and publication. "Don't worry about teaching," young faculty are often advised. "Worry about the research and publications you'll need to get tenure."

What Jacques Barzun said about teaching fifty years ago remains true today, at every level of education: "Teaching is not a lost art, but the regard for it is a lost tradition."[1]

It is bad enough that we lack regard for our teachers. It is even worse that we blame them, as we often do, for causing the very problems we want them to solve! "If you people would only teach values (or let the children pray in class or get back to basics or keep their noses to the grindstone), there wouldn't be so much crudity and crime in our society." It would be laughable—if it were not so cowardly, stupid, and cruel—that we, as a society, create private and public situations that breed vulgarity, violence, and neglect of the young and then lay the blame on a group of professionals who are more devoted to our children than many of us are!

If you are not a teacher and are skeptical either about their plight or their dedication, I have a suggestion to make: visit a public school near you and shadow a couple of teachers for a couple of days. Almost certainly you will witness for yourself the challenges teachers face, their lack of resources, and the deep demoralization they feel about serving as scapegoats for our nation's ills.

But you will also witness teacher after teacher transcending these conditions and caring for young people in remarkable ways. You will see teachers who bring sandwiches from home for youngsters who arrive at school hungry; who use their own money to buy unbudgeted classroom materials that students need to take next steps; who offer solace and encouragement to children and young adults who, for good reason, sometimes feel helpless and hopeless. They do all this in spite of everything, because they have a deep passion to help children learn and grow.

Caught in an anguishing bind between the good work they do and public misperceptions that surround them, hundreds of thousands of teachers somehow keep the faith and keep going— and we can be grateful that they do. Barzun got it right: though regard for teaching is a lost tradition, teaching, miraculously, is not a lost art. Every day in classrooms across the land, good people are working hard, with competency and compassion, at reweaving the tattered fabric of society on which we all depend.

But understandably, these good people are also leaving the

profession at record rates these days (50 percent of new teachers depart within five years), and we are paying the price. We need to stem this outgoing tide, and we might do so if we gave teachers what they deserve: something more fitting than endless demands and mindless criticism. We who depend on their efforts owe our teachers a gift—not another empty "teacher appreciation" day or "teacher of the year" award but a gift of real substance that will help them renew their spirits so they can continue to serve our children and our world well.

LEARNING TO LISTEN

I wish we could give our teachers better pay, better materials, and better working conditions, and do it all today. I wish we could give them wise leaders and an informed citizenry who are less obsessed with the scores students make on standardized tests and more concerned with helping teachers give children what they need to become fulfilled and contributing adults.

Someday we will need to give teachers all those things if we want our schools, and our society, to succeed. Sadly, that day is not near at hand. But we can hasten its coming by giving our teachers a gift that can commence this instant—the gift of listening openly and deeply to what they have to tell us about the reality of their work and the passions of their hearts.

You do not even have to lay this book down to start listening to teachers, for the book you are holding was conceived to give teachers a voice. In it, you will hear them speaking honestly and openly about what teaching is really like, telling stories that—if we will only try to understand them—can energize us to reform education in ways that really matter.

Listening may not seem like much of a gift to give another person, but it is at least a starting point—and, I would argue, much more. Listening is what the human self most yearns for: to be received, to be heard, to be known, and in the process to be honored. And listening, deep listening, is what gives rise to the impulse toward personal and social change.

We could heal many of this world's wounds if we were willing to listen. Think what might happen if white and black and Latino and Asian Americans were to listen with respect to one another. Think what might happen if mutual listening were to be practiced by men and women, young and old, religious and secular, rich and poor. But too many of us have stopped listening. We spend our time either ignoring or shouting claims and counterclaims at each other: witness the low quality of public discourse around most of our major issues—including education, where everyone has an answer but no one has an honest question for anyone else!

Why is it that we do not like to listen, or want to listen, or know how to listen? I think the answer is simple: we fear hearing something we don't want to hear, something that might compel us to reflect on ourselves and, in consequence, change our hearts and minds and behaviors. If we can keep talking, not listening, we can define our own reality and will not have to deal with the complexities and ambiguities that lie beyond our simplistic definitions. Listening too carefully might end up confusing us, and we would rather live with clear falsehoods than with complex and challenging truths!

Examples of this point abound—from the insistence of some religious leaders that we would eliminate school violence by posting the Ten Commandments on every classroom wall to the insistence of some political leaders that we would eliminate school dysfunction by posting standardized test results in the newspapers. Both proposals are cut from the same cloth, for both appeal to our primitive need for simplistic "solutions" in a complex world.

It is ludicrous to imagine that a heavily armed young sociopath is going to be turned around by words taped to a wall. It is equally ludicrous to imagine that correct answers to a set of multiple-choice questions prove that a student knows what one needs to know about history or literature or math—let alone about being a citizen and a civilized person. If we started listening to teachers and to what they know about the young, the inanity of both of these "solutions" would quickly be revealed, and we would need to move beyond sloganeering to engage the complexity of real thinking and real life.

WHEN WE LISTEN WELL

If we are to cut through our fear of the world's complexity so that we can start to hear its truth, we first need to listen to ourselves.

Paradoxically, our failure to hear what the world is trying to tell us begins in our failure to hear our own inner teacher. Somewhere deep within, we understand the truth about the world—but we keep that truth tucked safely away in a dark corner of the mind, where we can pretend that we do not know it and thus do not need to deal with it.

Suppose that more of us started paying attention to our built-in bunk detectors that know the difference between complex truths and simplistic, self-imposed delusions. Suppose that our political leaders were to do this before they start working on an education bill that will mindlessly force upon overburdened teachers testing requirements that cannot possibly benefit our children.

I can imagine their inner reveries—for I have heard some of them say such things aloud in moments of clarity and candor:

> Looking back on my life, it is clear that one or two teachers made the difference. Without them, I would not be where I am today. They knew how to encourage a kid whose life chances seemed limited—and they were given the time and resources to do it. As I help craft this education bill, I must make sure it supports those kinds of teachers and the conditions in which they flourish.

I send my children to private schools in Washington, D.C. I can't imagine sending any child of mine to a public school here, now or in the future. Why? Because the public schools here are a mess—and what we are proposing to do by way of educational reform is not going to change them for the better, today or tomorrow. We are not working for the kids. We are working to get reelected, and that's not the right way to go

Listening to oneself can be dangerous. It can create inner dissonance and even precipitate personal change. But inner listening is the most reliable way to get reconnected with what is real in the world. When we receive the world's news from within, we are much more likely to believe what we hear from without. So in this book you will find tales of teachers who learned to listen to their own inner truth, fortifying both their own souls and their ability to hear what other souls are saying.

Here you will also find tales of teachers who, having heard the needs of others—whether students, parents, fellow teachers, or administrators—reached out to connect with them, making both common cause and a difference in the world. Reaching out in this way is especially important in an educational culture infamous for its individualism. Teachers at every level walk into their classrooms and literally close the door on their work, isolating themselves in ways that make collegial connections unlikely.

Of course, self-isolation takes a great personal toll. But when teachers reach out, they find themselves less lonely, less afraid, less exhausted, less bored, and more alive. And the fruits of reaching out are professional as well as personal; a teacher who connects more deeply with students and colleagues is likely to find his or her work life transformed. Connecting with the needs of our students leads us to challenge all the ways in which "business as usual" fails to serve them well. Connecting with our colleagues gives us the collective courage necessary to make our teaching less responsive to arbitrary rules and more responsive to the truth of our students' lives.

Pedagogical practice has been so slow to turn toward the needs that today's students bring to school, and it is no wonder: when teachers are isolated from one another, few will be willing to take the risks and endure the failures that professional transformation requires. But when teachers come together as a community of colleagues—reminding each other that their ultimate accountability is not to the system but to their students' best interests—they find the courage to devote themselves to change.

As teachers learn to listen to themselves and to others, they find new ways of relating to the educational institutions in which they work. They become advocates for a new kind of institution, one that listens to the people within it and that encourages those people to listen to each other. In this book you will find stories of teachers who have done exactly that and become advocates for educational reform. Listening—openly, deeply, and faithfully—has consequences that are not just personal and professional but political as well.

The kind of institution we now need in our society has been called a "learning organization." This is an organization that is designed to grow from experience, to adjust quickly to rapid change, and to involve all its stakeholders in the process. Ironically, this concept is better known and more widely practiced in the corporate world than in the world of education, which is ostensibly devoted to learning! But in every realm, people who are trying to create this new organizational form have discovered that at bottom, a learning organization must be a listening organization. If it were not, it would not be able to learn anything.

Learning to listen is hard enough for us as individuals, given the challenge of what we may hear. But it is harder still for organizations, with their deep devotion to the status quo and their deep fear of acknowledging anything that might require them to alter it. To overcome this resistance, we need leaders who have the courage to walk into the fear of change—and help others develop the courage to come along with them. Deeper still, we need patterns of leadership that do not rely merely on elected and appointed leaders but also invite all who hear the truth to step forward, make their case, and invite others to follow.

One of the major challenges in educational reform is for teachers—who see themselves as working in service to the young—to see themselves also as leaders in service to our schools and our society. By embracing a larger leadership role, teachers would not dilute but deepen their commitment to children and youth. If more and more educational leaders were to rise from the ranks of teachers—transforming both our schools and the way our society supports them—the ultimate beneficiaries would be our young people, the most precious asset any society has.

NOTE

1. Barzun, J. *Teacher in America.* Boston: Little, Brown, 1945, p. 12.

Introduction

Honoring the Teacher's Heart

Sam M. Intrator

I am the son of two recently retired New York City Board of Education public school teachers. Combined, they racked up sixty-five years of service. We once sat down and figured out that between them, they had taught more than sixty thousand classes and five thousand students. They were lifers, as were most of their friends. I grew up with grade books, Delaney books, student papers, and the United Federation of Teachers newspaper on the kitchen table.

Though chalk may not course through my veins, teaching is in my blood. It is in some ways the family business. So when I came home one day and told my parents that I had just applied for a provisional teaching license at the New York City Board of Education headquarters at 65 Court Street, I didn't anticipate their reaction. "*What?* Why did you do that? You should look at other options," my father said, clearly dismayed at my decision. "You don't know what you're getting into," my mother said quite ominously.

From the vantage point of a son, teaching had been good to my parents. We traveled every summer as a family, and in the eyes of a freshly graduated college student, returning as a teacher to the schools of my youth seemed a virtuous channel to direct my brimming-over-the-top idealism. Curious about my parents' disappointment and chagrin but blithely undaunted, I quit my job as an editorial assistant in a plush Manhattan high rise and began itinerant day-to day subbing in New York City schools.

Sixteen years later, I better understand their response. In fact, most teachers I know have told me something similar. "Maybe I would do this job again, but I hope my son or daughter does something different." It's not a question I've ever heard asked in a survey about teachers' job satisfaction, but if you ask teachers, you'll be surprised at how many will answer something similar. As my dad told me, "This job can wear you down. There's a lot of gratuitous clucking about how we must value and support teachers. Then you get in there and it's pretty lonely and tough. You wish your son might find something easier—find something that has more prestige, status, and honor."

When I asked him years later why he felt so strongly about my decision to teach, he answered like the middle school social studies teacher he is. "Throughout history, sons followed in their fathers' occupational footsteps. Sons of carpenters became carpenters. Sons of tailors became tailors. Sons of artists became artists. There was honor in passing the family trade across generations. The father was honored to have the son follow in his stride because society cherished the work of the father. But our society and the system I worked in offers only lip-service honor—false honor. There's not a lot of honor in the way schools work and the way society treats and compensates teachers. . . . What's sad is that you come to the job eager to do wonderful things, but it's hard to sustain your heart. If a teacher doesn't have energy and if a teacher's heart is not in his work, everybody loses and nothing will get better."

After thirty-three years, my dad will tell you about cherished moments and wounds still raw. He'll tell you about the ethereal days when he believed he left an enduring impact on the world. My dad will also tell you that there were days when he could barely heft the chalk to the board and describe classes so demanding that they reduced his knees to quaking knick-knocks. If you ask, he'll tell you about how even after teaching the Gettysburg Address 150 times, watching Lincoln's words settle in young minds would still bring a tear to his eye. If you ask, he'll also tell you about how, midway through his more than three decades in the classroom, resentment and anger with the system left him in the doldrums and he could barely summon the strength to come back one September. But most of all, he'll tell you that the best teachers he knew—the colleagues in the trenches he most admired—had heart, soul, energy, and a special effervescence that allowed them to "reach kids." I'd pick him up at after school some days, and we'd pass one of his colleagues and he'd turn to me and nod: "She's good," he'd say. "She reaches kids."

My dad has more to say, as do so many of our veteran teachers long accustomed to being left out of the conversations, on what it takes to improve schools. Once you've given thirty-plus years of your life to something as absorbing as teaching, you come to know it well. If you ask my dad over a beer what he thinks should happen, he'll tell you bluntly, "We'd better figure out how to get good people into our classrooms and then figure out how to keep them fresh and alive. We don't recognize how hard teaching is on the spirit. We think it's about little techniques and tricks, but techniques only take you so far. We need teachers who care about kids, who care about what they teach, and who can connect with their students. On top of that, they need to have faith in the importance of their work. Keeping that faith over time hasn't been easy for me."

I share these snippets of my father's commentary—his thoughts and feelings on the "teacher's heart," because they represent to me the backdrop for this book. For some fathers and sons, the source of strength in a relationship can be baseball. For others, it might be the anatomy of a carburetor or the habits of a steelhead trout. For my dad and me over the past seventeen years, it's been, more often than not, the state of education and the role of the teacher in America.

Our conversations roam broadly, but there's a touchstone idea, a principle that calls us back no matter where the discussion wanders. It came to us one day while we were listening to some political pundits talk about President Bill Clinton's first campaign for the White House. They described how Clinton's advisers hung up a placard to remind them of the key and most critical issue of their campaign and to help them retain clarity in their deliberations. The placard read: "It's the economy, stupid." We laughed when we heard it and quickly turned to talking about how educational reformers, politicians, parents, philanthropists, and others concerned with improving schools should etch in granite or hang in gaudy, flashing neon from the White House a placard that reads: "It's the teachers, stupid!"

In other words, if schools are to be places that promote academic, social, and personal development for students, everything hinges on the presence of intelligent, passionate, caring teachers working day after day in our nation's classrooms. Teachers have a colossal influence on what happens in our schools, because day after day, they are the ultimate decision makers and tone setters. They shape the world of the classroom by the activities they plan, the focus they attend to, and the relationships they nurture.

If we want to attract and retain intelligent, passionate, caring teachers, we had better figure out what will sustain their vitality and faith in teaching. Education depends on what teachers do in their classrooms, and what teachers do in their classrooms is shaped by who they are, what they believe, and how vital and alive they are when they step before their students.

Before you turn to the essays in this book, I'd like to share one other exchange my father and I had after he read an earlier draft of this manuscript. In the draft, I concluded this section of the book by describing a memory of clutching tight to my father's shoulders as he walked the picket line during the 1968 strike by New York City teachers. I used this poignant memory as evidence of how, in the last three decades, through hard work and determined activism, teachers have successfully raised their professional status and improved their working conditions. After reading this draft, he paused and then replied with an edge to his voice. "Listen, I know you're writing a book about renewal, revitalization, and rejuvenation of the spirit, but we need remuneration too. We need our spirit, but we need to make a fair living. This society pays rainmakers—it pays the people who generate money. Teachers don't generate money. You can't forget this truth. It's hard for teachers to feel valued and honored in this society, when your worth is often measured in what you're paid. Paying teachers what they're worth to society is a way to honor the teacher's heart. You can't forget that."

My dad's point here is that teachers get mixed and disturbing messages about what they're worth to the communities they serve. Even amid the tremendous prosperity of the 1990s, many teachers saw their incomes stagnate, school building improvement plans denied, and proposals for providing more professional development time demeaned as crafty plots by teachers to work less. Honoring the teacher's heart must mean more than flowers, cards, and cookies, no matter how well intentioned and well meaning. Honor implies being accorded respect and distinction. Even as we become caught up in questions of meaning, my dad rightfully reminds us that "paying teachers what they're worth to society is a way to honor the teacher's heart."

But there are other ways, too. If we believe in the touchstone idea that teachers are the heart of the work—or more crudely, "It's the teachers, stupid!"—we must ask several questions: Why should we care about the heart of our teachers? What undermines the energy and vitality of our teachers? How can we care for the teacher's heart?

WHY SHOULD WE CARE ABOUT
THE HEART OF A TEACHER?

"One of the first things I learned when I started college was which teachers to take and which to avoid," a student of mine, Helen Lee, told me. "There are two lists that students circulate to each other: teachers with heart and teachers without. Teachers with heart are passionate, caring, alive, present, inspiring, and real. I am drawn to these teachers because they possess a love for what they are teaching and for their students. Teachers without heart are simply going through the motions and appear disinterested and bored with what they are teaching and with their students. There is no meaningful connection with the material or with us. . . . Relationships are important to me, and so I am drawn to teachers who are open, who are not afraid to be themselves, and who will treat me as an individual and pay attention to who I am."

Over the past few years, a spate of high-profile blue-ribbon reports have lifted up an elemental truism intuitively known by every parent who has trundled off a child to school and by every student who, like Helen, has spent time in the classroom: the teacher is the pivot on which all else turns in education.

Showcasing recent research on how the quality of the teacher dramatically affects student achievement, the report "What Matters Most: Teaching for America's Future" asserts, "What teachers know and can do is the most important influence on what students learn."[1] The American Council on Education synthesizes a slew of research to arrive at a similar conclusion in its report "To Touch the Future": "The success of the student depends most of all on the quality of the teacher. We know from empirical data what our intuition has always told us: Teachers make a difference. We now know that teachers make *the* difference."[2]

The evidence is compelling. Teachers represent the dominant factor in the educational equation. The quality of the teacher is the most important in-school factor for improving student achievement. In other words, both good and bad teaching leaves a legacy. Lee Shulman, president of the Carnegie Foundation for the Advancement of Teaching, writes, "The teacher must remain the key. . . . Debates over educational policy are moot, if the primary agents of instruction are incapable of performing their functions well. No microcomputer will replace them, no scripted lesson will direct and control them, no voucher system will bypass them."[3]

The prominence of these findings, combined with concerns over teacher shortages, have stirred educational policy officials, school district leaders, principals, and other influential figures to respond by funneling resources into a series of initiatives focused on improving the quality of the teaching corp. On the surface this should be good news for teachers. Yet teachers are wary. Historical precedent has taught teachers that when politicians and "civic-minded" captains of industry start waving around blue-ribbon reports calling for improvements in education, they will experience a series of mandates that attempt to narrow their discretion and constrain their autonomy.

The most recent calls for educational reform represent the fourth crisis in American education in the past century. The first occurred during the mid-1910s during the second Industrial Revolution and in the midst of a period of mass immigration to America. The second came during the depths of the Cold War in the 1950s when the Soviet Union beat us to space, and the third in the 1980s when our economy was listing. The present crisis coincides with the onset of the technological and information revolution.

Each of these events follows a generally familiar pattern in how they unfold. First, the crisis comes to public attention during times of unrest and anxiety about America's future. When there is uncertainty about the course of our collective destiny, we look at our schools with careful attention. Second, the scrutiny of education typically leads to a high-profile indictment that "the schools are failing," which subsequently erodes public confidence in education. Third, when there is a crisis of public confidence, calls for reform lead to implementing policies that seek to clarify objectives, engineer processes, and more closely monitor the performance of the people involved. The approach is very rational.

In education, the roots of rationalized policymaking and management can be traced to the 1910s, when educators became enchanted with the notion of scientific management as championed by Frederick Taylor, a forerunner of today's industrial consultants. Taylor's approach was to break down the production process into detailed and discrete steps. Ultimate efficiency was pursued by identifying unambiguous objectives and then prescribing standardized methods for achieving those outcomes. Individual creativity and personal discretion were viewed as sources of potential error and inefficiency in the production process.

Educational leaders focused on explicitly articulating curriculum objectives, mandating textbooks, developing batteries of tests aligned with curriculum objectives, mandating scripted pedagogical methods for teachers to use, and developing administrative systems that evaluated teachers based on objectified standards and methods.

Calls to improve education generally result in an array of efforts to control teachers. Working under the premise that teachers are defective, educational change efforts attempt to fix teachers, standardize their methods, employ programs that seek to hold them more explicitly accountable, and subject them to step-by-step programs designed to train them in methods that limit their professional and creative discretion. It is for these reasons that teachers are often wary of blue-ribbon reports and claims of investment in education.

This view of teaching discounts how so much of what is done in the classroom is what Arlie Hochschild describes as "emotional labor,"[4] where success and failure ride less on the specific methods adopted and more on the humanity of the connection teachers can weave in their face-to-face, voice-to-voice, and heart-to-heart interactions among themselves, their students, and the subjects they teach.

Teachers need technique, and they need subject matter expertise, but these matter little without the presence of heart and inspiration. The dictionary tells us that to do something "with heart" means to inspire with confidence, to embolden, to encourage, and to animate. To teach with heart means to be a genuine human presence in the lives of students. A teacher whose heart has not been engaged or has been extinguished is there only as a hazy, smothered presence: a cardboard cutout, a stiff, flat character playing the role of the teacher.

The reclamation of the teacher's heart as a legitimate subject for dialogue on what constitutes good teaching is the idea that galvanized the spirit and imagination of readers of Parker J. Palmer's book *The Courage to Teach: Exploring the Inner Landscape of a Teacher's Life*. Palmer's premise in the book unfolds from a simple insight: "Good teaching cannot be reduced to technique; good teaching comes from the identity and integrity of the teacher."[5]

For Palmer, teachers who ignite learning and growth in students ply their craft through myriad forms. The mode of pedagogy and technique matters less than the capacity to be fully present and engaged with students and subject. He explains, "In every class I teach, my ability to connect with my students and to connect them with the subject depends less on the method I use than on the degree to which I know and trust my own selfhood—and am willing to make it available and vulnerable in the service of learning."[6]

He likens teachers to weavers whose shuttle fervidly flies back and forth, threading together a fabric of student, teacher, and subject matter. "The methods used by these weavers vary widely: lectures, Socratic dialogues, laboratory experiments, collaborative problem solving, creative chaos. The connections made by good teachers are held not in their methods but in their hearts, meaning *heart* in the ancient sense, as the place where intellect and emotion and spirit will converge in the human self."[7]

Palmer's words, forged and burnished on the poet's anvil, affirm my father's own more straightforward observation hammered clear on the scuffed, gum-pocked junior high school teacher's desk: "We think it's about little techniques and tricks, but techniques only take you so far. We need teachers who care about kids, who care about what they teach, and who can communicate with kids. We, real-live teachers, are what make methods come alive. On top of that, we need to have faith in the importance of our work."

Together these two wise men point out a profound and elemental truth: methods, techniques, educational philosophies, and competencies are important, but even the most creative and imaginative teaching concept will drift along inertly until it becomes vitalized by the presence of a living, breathing, energized teacher.

Longtime teacher and literacy researcher Mem Fox amplifies this point:

> The plain fact of the matter is that teacher and children have heart, and those hearts play an enormous part in the teaching-learning process.
>
> Although I am a passionate advocate of whole language, I believe it perfectly possible for whole language to fail in the hands of a rude, thoroughly nasty teacher who hates children. Similarly, although I believe the teaching of phonics outside meaningful texts is the least efficient way to teach reading, I believe absolutely that a joyful, enthusiastic, experienced teacher who uses phonics and only phonics will nevertheless have a large measure of success in teaching his or her students to read.[8]

For years, I've asked students of all ages to talk and write about their teachers as part of classroom assignments, discussions, and formal research projects. Invariably, I hear about teachers whose pedagogy and practice defy any classification system. They talk about Mr. Smith as being funny and interesting or Ms. Gomez as being eccentric and creative or Mrs. James as being a confidant and a good listener.

Though disparate in some ways, several strands in particular run through these reflections. In fact, if you mine your own memories of good teachers, those individuals who left an enduring mark on your own growth and development, you'll probably discern similar themes.

First, students talk about teachers who recognized their special gifts, talents, and aptitudes. They describe teachers who encouraged them. As one student said, "I remember the day Mr. X. handed back a composition and he stopped next to me and bent over. He said, 'Bill you've got a real flair for describing things.' Nobody had ever said that to me. I can't tell you how much I still remember that moment." Second, students talk about teachers who made subject matter come alive. Very often these testimonials begin: "Mrs. X. awakened in me a love for English/history/math/science." Third, students talk about teachers who listened to them with deep respect. "Mr. Y. was interested not only in me but in all of us. He wanted us to share our struggles, our triumphs, our stories, and we yearned to tell him." Fourth, students talk about teachers who truly enjoyed teaching. They talk about a teacher's energy, zest, enthusiasm, and aliveness. They note that some teachers loved what they were doing so much that this love was infectious. "Ms. B.'s passion for Shakespeare was like the flu. You can't hang around her for very long without catching it," said a student about her eleventh-grade English teacher.

It's worth reviewing the common themes twining through the reflections by Palmer, my father, Fox, and the students when they talk about teaching: joy, passion, caring, heart, exuberance, energy, vitality, aliveness, and spirit. There's something ineffable and even "touchy-feely" about these words. This can be an issue for some educators who believe that characterizing teaching as work of the heart diminishes its gravitas. Others are uncomfortable with the idea of teaching being connected with inwardness because many of us in the profession have become accustomed to heaping blame only on external forces. Embracing the idea that teaching is an expression of our own selfhood means we must shoulder an important responsibility for our own successes and failures. There are many bitter teachers, long worn down by the real indignities of the job, who have a difficult time attributing success and failure to anything other than "those kids," "that bastard in the principal's office," "that damn test," or "that hellish certification office."

Being open to a view of teaching that includes the teacher's heart and energy as an authentic subject of conversation poses a profound challenge to the profession. Simply put, we can't dictate heart, we can't legislate genuine caring, and we can't hand out a teacher's manual that scripts vitality. But even if we can't inject teachers with passion or jolt their hearts with electroshocks of enthusiasm, the good news is that most teachers come to the profession with ample supplies of idealism, passion, and commitment. If we learn to protect this essential resource and support teachers who want to reclaim and sustain their vocational integrity, we're making progress.

I vividly remember walking out the door after my first day as a teacher at Sheepshead Bay High School in Brooklyn. I was twenty-one years old, and as I walked down the street, passing children playing ball, high schoolers waiting for the bus, and seniors lugging groceries home, I felt so worthy and important. I was a teacher, and this was important work—important in the manner that philosopher Robert Nozick describes as an elemental human need to "count in the world and make a difference to it."[9] It was electrifying, and I'll not soon forget the raw jolt of earnestness and responsibility that came with the realization that I had my own classroom and that 180 young people would look to me for direction, support, and guidance.

My idealism matches what we know of most teachers. In survey after survey of teachers, we find that people come to teaching to make a significant contribution to society and to experience the satisfaction of helping people grow and develop. A recent survey of new teachers conducted by the public policy organization Public Agenda found that when teachers were asked to rate the most important attributes of teaching for them, "their responses indicate an idealistic personnel corps looking do work out of love more than money."[10] Other studies of teachers confirm this finding: teachers are called to the profession because they believe that they can play a thoughtful, caring, and influential role in the lives of young people.

Most teachers feel drawn to the classroom for reasons of the heart. We heed the call to teach for reasons of ideals and virtue: we desire to connect with children, convey our passion for a subject, or hope to inspire a love for learning and goodness. Bill Ayers calls teaching "world-changing work" and then goes on to say:

> People are called to teaching because they love children and youth, or because they love being with them, watching them open up and grow and become more able, more competent, more powerful in the world. They may love what happens to themselves when they are with children, the ways in which they become their best selves. Or they become teachers because they love the world or some piece of the world enough that they want to show that love to others. In either case, people teach as an act of construction and reconstruction and as a gift of oneself to others. I teach in the hope of making the world a better place.[11]

Ayers's words evoke the best hopes and aspirations of almost every teacher I have ever known. Teachers choose teaching for reasons of the heart. They see their work as a form of public service that has vital social value. The wellspring of motivation and energy for many of our teachers is their belief that teaching is more than a job and more than merely doing routine work—that

teaching is a vocation to which they were summoned because they
have something worthy and important to contribute to the world.

This earnest passion to make a difference, this zeal to contribute, this desire to share the richness of learning with students
is what animates our teaching—yet the demands of teaching are
intense.

WHAT UNDERMINES THE ENERGY
AND VITALITY OF OUR TEACHERS?

As I listen to my parents, my colleagues, and other teachers whom
I have come to know in my research, I am moved by the honesty,
poignancy, and profundity in their voices. Their reflections on
their teaching lives reveal a powerful ambivalence with their
choice of profession. On the one hand, they celebrate the power
and promise of their work: teachers believe in the enduring possibilities of teaching. On the other hand, they lament the demands
and impositions that deplete their vitality and resent the lack of
honor accorded teachers in our culture. A sampling of voices from
teachers that I've spoken to or worked with over the years evokes
the current crisis in the profession:

> I am at a decision-making point. I truly enjoy teaching, but I
> feel buffeted by the public assault on teachers; the strain of
> dealing with especially needy students; the day-in, day-out
> structure of teaching; and my own personal development
> issues. At times I feel drained, uninspired, and just plain
> tired. I've considered leaving teaching and in fact have taken
> classes in preparation for a change in career.

> I want to love this job, and there are times that I do. But I'm
> getting jaded, and I'm losing my vim and vigor fast. I came to
> teaching to be there for students, but every memo and missive
> that comes through my mailbox tells me to prep for the test or

remind students about how important their scores are. Important for whom? Important for the institution, maybe. I came to teach students, but that's feeling harder and harder to do.

As these voices indicate, there's something awry in our schools that's exacting an emotional, physical, and spiritual toll on teachers. In fact, there is a growing body of evidence that suggests the teaching profession is in peril. Teachers are leaving in droves. Those that leave cite the difficult working conditions, the excessive demands on a teacher's time, the cumulative toll of working for an institution that fails to honor the commitment of teachers, and the frustration of working for a society that refuses to respect and fairly compensate the profession. As noted earlier, at least half of all new teachers leave the profession by the time they reach their fifth year of teaching. Others slog on, feeling demoralized and sapped of the energy and idealism that sparked their original choice of profession.

The depletion of the teacher's heart and energy has dire consequences for education. As we explored in the prior section, the real triumphs in education are won in the connections among students, subject matter, and an alive and present teacher. We need teachers who can connect in the face-to-face, voice-to-voice, and heart-to-heart interactions of the classroom. Yet the evidence suggests that teachers are struggling to maintain the psychic and emotional energy essential to their work. Why? What forces have brought on this situation?

We Feel Underappreciated

Although teaching can yield enduring rewards that come from working with students, many teachers report feeling frustrated, disappointed, and underappreciated. Teachers believe in the elemental worth of their work. They believe that what they do is vital to families, children, and communities, but they also believe that society doesn't reward them in ways commensurate with the importance of their work.

As one of my colleagues said, "I believe in what I do. I know that my work with kids is valuable. I teach them to write; I help them clarify their goals; I help them figure out who they want to be and how to get there. What can be more important than this kind of contribution? I chose this work knowing I wouldn't get rich, but there's a difference between being rich and being comfortable. I'm struggling to just get by. Sometimes I'm furious and sad."

The annual salary survey conducted by the American Federation of Teachers (AFT) affirms this point.[12] The teachers' annual salary, adjusted by the cost-of-living index, is at its lowest point in forty years, and of bitter irony to many teachers who have listened to all sorts of rhetoric regarding the precipitous shortage of teachers is that the average annual salary increase in 2000 was among the lowest in forty years. As one teacher said, "The hypocrites! They wring their hands about the teacher shortage, and yet they pay us less real money than ever. What does this say about the regard for teachers? This society measures respect in money; how can I feel appreciated? I feel abused. They're taking advantage of me and my colleagues."

The bottom line, as AFT president Sandra Feldman puts it, is this: "Low salaries are preventing quality people from both entering and staying in the profession."[13] The average teacher salary (which turns out to be for someone with about sixteen years of experience) is $40,574, according to the AFT report. This compares to average figures of $68,294 for engineers, $66,782 for computer systems analysts, and $49,247 for accountants. For many teachers, the low salaries are not as tough to swallow in the early stages of their career, but when faced with mortgage costs, college tuition, and other expenses later in life, the frustrations of compensation intensify, particularly when they compare their salaries against those professions that require a similar level of education but pay significantly more.[14]

Aside from the frustration and resentment many teachers feel about the low salaries, teachers also feel that their work is underappreciated in other ways. Many teachers work in subpar facilities and have to spend their own out-of-pocket money for supplies. Lack of necessities such as phones, computers, and up-to-date textbooks also are seen as symptoms of society's disrespect for the profession. As a friend said after the town had just voted down a bond issue to renovate the school, "What do the people in this community want? They expect us to care for their children, but they won't pay for it. It's dispiriting, it's demeaning, and it's abhorrent. Do they expect an extra effort from me now? Do they expect me to head off to work all smiles and eager?"

We Feel Undermined

We act with integrity when the source of our actions flow from our deepest beliefs and principles. When our actions align with what we care about and emanate from the source of our moral commitments, we act with integrity. When we are compelled to act in ways contrary to our principles, our sense of integrity is deformed and diminished. Many of the present reforms and mandates in education have proved to be incommensurate with the belief system of many teachers.

There are a multitude of examples. Some school districts have become so narrowly focused on test scores and test preparation that teachers have been forced to jettison successful curriculum units of long standing because they don't explicitly connect to the exam. In a Massachusetts district close to where I live, the superintendent has put together teams of administrators to trawl through schools in search of teachers not adhering to the test prep curriculum.

A good friend who teaches in a community that he describes as being "obsessed with standardized test scores" laments how the fixation with scores and rankings has insidiously infected the way he, his colleagues, and his administrators have come to view their students:

> I've always believed that my mission as a teacher has been to take a child from where he or she is at and to cajole, support, and inspire growth. It has been important to understand a child's ability and skill level so that I can orchestrate learning experiences that nudge them ahead. But in the current climate of test mania, I find myself looking at children and wondering how they'll impact the average score of my class. I sometimes find myself doing calculations where my students are not learners but assets and liabilities toward the class average on a standardized exam.

These situations are deeply felt by teachers. Teachers believe in the moral imperative of teaching. When they are forced to be complicit in work that they believe undermines their beliefs and principles, the toll is substantial.

The current preoccupation with standards and high-stakes exams has intensified our feeling that our integrity is being undermined by forces outside our control. Teachers experience the testing mania in a range of ways that debilitate their morale and spirit. When you speak with teachers about what testing is doing to their sense of self and to their practice, the tales are chilling. Some teachers see the tests as transparent forms of surveillance that will allow technocrats to track, rank, and evaluate their performance. Others resent the focus on narrow cognitive skills. Others feel the press to teach to the test limits their ability to be creative and spontaneous in the classroom. A sampling of responses by teachers illustrates the pressure that teachers feel to teach to the test and focus their curriculum on limited testable objectives:

- In Virginia, a teacher described in the *Washington Post* by parents and colleagues as "superb" quits, saying, "Every day you go to work and everything is geared to getting these test scores up, how we raise those test scores. The exams dominated conversation in the math department office, in staff meetings, in professional development seminars.... It was SOL [Standards of Learning] this, SOL that.... It was not about 'How are you doing today?' or 'Let's learn something exciting.' . . . It was just not a healthy environment."[15]

- In New York City, the strains of administering the high-stakes state tests has driven off veteran fourth-grade teachers. They describe the pressure as oppressive and the single-minded focus on the exams as destructive for children. In a *New York Times* article, a fourth-grade teacher is quoted as saying, "The whole school is looking at how our kids are going to do, so the pressure is enormous. The test-prep books have basically become our curriculum." The pressure the teachers talk about has to do with multiple factors. The fourth-grade scores affect whether principals stay in their schools and whether they receive merit bonuses. One teacher leaving his fourth-grade position said, "I need to not feel that intense pressure that if kids don't improve, our school will be closed down. I need a break so I can recover my strength."[16]

- In Tennessee, teachers are both punished and rewarded on the basis of students' achievement on the standardized exams. One teacher says, "All this rewards business is reinforcing one of the greatest things that's wrong with our society: greed.... I try to teach well because it's the right thing to do. I've got a young kid's mind in my hands.... I don't give a hoot if somebody is going to pay me $3,600. ... That money isn't going to make the school better.... You can't deal with [schools] as a business and have

Introduction

rewards and sanctions and stuff like that. . . . They forget the personal side that's attached—that you want these students to learn and that you care about them."[17]

We Feel Overwhelmed

All indicators suggest that teaching conditions have deteriorated over the past few years. There is too much to do, too little time, and too few resources.

In an article titled "Teacher Time (or Rather, the Lack of It)," Marty Schollenberger Swaim, a teacher, and her husband, Stephen Swaim, an economist, analyze the workload problem teachers face and conclude that teachers are caught in a pulverizing time bind that forces them to choose between preserving their energy and adequately preparing for class and reviewing student work. They conclude that the average high school teacher with 125 students would need to spend seventy hours per week on teaching if he or she wanted to spend fifteen minutes planning for each class and thirteen minutes per week on reviewing the work of each student. When you combine the time required for that kind of commitment with the other average responsibilities of a teacher, the hours quickly pile up.[18]

The level of intensity that teaching requires wears people out or forces them to make debilitating compromises on the way they approach the job. Marty Swain captures this dilemma well:

> Teaching is wonderful, fascinating, and . . . never dull; [it is] one of those professions in which you can really say, "I change lives." At the same time, although I love teaching, I could leave it tomorrow. The personal price that I have to pay to work as a teacher is very high. I have to work far more than 40 hours per week because, like other teachers in America, almost all of my official work time is committed to the

classroom instruction of students. As a result, most of the necessary planning, preparation, and grading must be regularly done at night or on weekends. And just as important, I have little or no time for individual students.[19]

The welter of things to do takes its toll on teachers' energy and vitality. It leaves them fatigued and frustrated. As Stephen Swaim says, "Sometimes I get depressed about the consequences for my personal life; I could not travel to Pittsburgh to see my mother-in-law when she was ill. We had fewer people over for dinner [once my wife started teaching], and we did fewer things with our children because one day of each weekend was always obligated to school."[20]

The fear of becoming ground down by teaching weighs deeply on the hearts of new teachers in particular. As one of my former students said after finishing her first year of teaching, "I don't think people have any idea of how hard teachers work. I don't have time to date, work out, hang out, or play. And all my nonteacher friends tell me that once I get some experience, the workload will abate. But I'm not so sure. I see all the more experienced teachers as busy as I am, but in a different way. They may have planning and preparation down, but they get roped in to this committee and that project. Besides, the teachers whom I aspire to be like seem to always be planning something new and novel."

When the pace and quantity of work become so demanding, the quality of our work is diminished, the tenor of our relationships is eroded, the ability to innovate is deflated, and our capacity to be present and connected with our students is undermined.

We Feel Isolated

Prior to my first teaching job, I worked briefly at a publishing company. I worked in a cubicle in a small city of cubicles. When I started, I had a stream of visitors who came by to show me a trick, offer some advice, and check in on how I was doing. With the support and counsel of my colleagues and supervisors, I quickly learned the ropes. My job was to file, do a little background research, and keep the expense accounts.

When I started teaching, I was there a full semester before I had a sit-down chat about teaching and lesson planning with any of my colleagues. While this says something about the induction process, it also says something about our habits of privatism and the organizational ethic of isolationism that pervades most school cultures. Susan Rosenholtz notes that the individualistic culture of teaching results in isolation among colleagues that resembles commuters waiting briefly in a train station. Each commuter is headed toward the same destination but is standing alone, ensconced in his or her own thoughts, newspapers, and private space.[21]

The isolation teachers feel depletes their heart and energy. We know that people thrive in communities that include mutual praise, collaborative problem solving, shared values, and respectful relationships. These practices help people function at their best, but the structure of the school day and teachers' schedules deter genuine collaborative effort.

As I mentioned, my father and I calculated that he had taught approximately thirty thousand classes. That's an astonishing number, but it's true: 180 school days a year, five classes a day, for thirty-three years. As we talked, I asked him about the specific classes that left a durable, enduring imprint. He had no shortage of stories, but what became oddly apparent was that every class episode that he described had a common strand: every memorable class and activity he reflected on was one where he had been observed by another adult.

When I asked him why, he paused and said, "Every day, you work by yourself and it's just you and your students. There's nobody's there to witness your work. You do your thing without recognition, appreciation, or witness. I guess having somebody there to recognize my work made it feel more important."

There's an irony to teaching: we ply our craft in densely crowded rooms, but teaching can be psychologically lonely for teachers. Ms. M., a world history teacher from Soldotna High School in Alaska, captures this odd tension with powerful eloquence:

> I love it [teaching]. It's stimulating. It's rewarding.
>
> But teaching as a whole is very, very, very lonely. You're in a classroom alone with a lot of kids, but you don't have much contact with adults. There's rarely an adult that really understands what you're doing. Other teachers rarely come into my classroom, and I don't have time to go to theirs. We're too busy. In other jobs, people see what you do, and they understand. But in teaching, you can have everybody do really well on a test [and] nobody knows about it. Or you had a great discussion of the difference between the Romans and Greeks, and you were just absolutely ecstatic. But nobody ever knows about that.
>
> It's a very lonely profession. You're in there every day doing it and having a wonderful, time, but [there's] not much recog-nition. Except that you know you're doing a good job.[22]

These feelings of isolation, of toiling behind closed doors, can leave teachers feeling insecure and unsure about their impact. As my dad and Ms. M. note, we do our work without witness, without support, without constructive critique, and without reinforcement. The cost of this isolation exacts its toll and often gives teachers a distorted view of their own efficacy and of their sense of themselves as adults. These distortions become amplified because of the fragile, uncertain rewards that teachers derive from their work.

We Feel Vulnerable

Summoned to teaching by my inner conviction that my work was to make a contribution to the lives of my students, I quickly realized that figuring out success and failure was a baffling experience. I could quiz my students on whether they knew the plot to *The*

Great Gatsby. I could have them write essays and be able to discern whether they were mustering evidentiary warrant for their arguments, but that feedback didn't get at my true hopes for myself as a teacher. What counts as success? Was it teaching them to write, engaging them in a conversation about police brutality, or getting some of my truant students to come to English class five days in a row?

Although I'm not sure what should count as triumph and what should count as failure, I do know that I was hungry to believe that I was making a difference in the lives of my students. Like most teachers, according to Dan Lortie's study of teachers,[23] I pursued the psychic rewards of exerting moral influence, evoking a love of learning in students, and creating opportunities for students to encounter new experiences that alter their consciousness—lofty goals, but too elusive to ever count or quantify with any certainty. Not knowing whether we've achieved success leaves us feeling vulnerable. In an essay titled "The Uncertainties of Teaching," Phil Jackson captures the elusive nature of our goals:

> Teachers sometimes have a hard time proving their worth, even to themselves. Why this should be so is easy enough to understand. It derives in large measure from the fact that teaching, unlike masonry or brain surgery or even garbage collecting, has no visible product, no concrete physical object to make or repair or call its own. Consequently, unlike workers in the forenamed and many other occupations, teachers suffer a distinct disadvantage. When their work is finished they have nothing tangible to show off as a fruit of their labor; no sturdy brick wall, no tumor-free brain, no smoothly purring engine, not even a clean back alley to point to with pride as evidence of a job well done.[24]

There's a lot of faith, hope, and optimism in teaching, and when we lose it, our spirit wavers and deflates. Russell Clarke, an English administrator, describes the experience well: "You have to believe, in this business, that you are making things better and moving things on. If that particular spark is not there—if something happens that makes you think things are going the opposite way—it can be a very destroying occupation."[25]

The uncertainty of truly knowing whether we've improved the lot of our students leaves us with questions that worm their way into our psyche. As a veteran teacher told me one day early in my career, "What makes this job really tough is that you don't make enough money to rationalize doing it for the money. What we do get is priceless. Those moments of realizing that we've shaped a world or inspired a young person. Too bad those moments don't come more often or come in ways that we can discern their presence." In the face of constantly pumping out energy and heart, the lack of feedback leaves many teachers bowed.

The factors inventoried here diminish the dignity, honor, morale, and energy of the people to whom we assign the responsibility of tending and educating our young. Who can blame teachers for saying, "Maybe, just maybe, I would do this again, but I'm not thrilled with the idea that my son or daughter would do this"? The blunt reality facing the American public and the educational system is that we have an alarming exodus from the profession at a time when the demand for teachers is spiraling upward. Demographic analysts forecast a need for two million new teachers in the next decade. This need will be due to increases in student enrollment, the graying and anticipated retirement of significant numbers of veteran teachers, and the high rate of attrition among young teachers.

The upshot for policymakers and educational leaders is that we must find ways to recruit promising teachers and then provide conditions that allow them to develop and flourish in their professional roles. We won't attract, sustain, retain, and prepare teachers who respect and care for the hearts, souls, and minds of children unless we provide conditions where our teachers feel respected, cared for, stimulated, and appreciated.

WHAT CAN BE DONE?

What can be done for teachers so they can go forth and do their best and most inspiring work? The essays that make up the core of this book describe teachers working to reclaim their commitment to teaching, to education, to colleagues, and to students. The stories they tell are not inspirational triumphs or tales of mystical reclamation of the spirit. Nor do the essays offer a recipe of get-inspired-quick ideas or easy-to-follow techniques that will illuminate the path to more rewarding and productive teaching while ameliorating the suffering we sometimes endure as teachers.

What this book does do is share, in the words of teachers, their efforts to reclaim and sustain their hearts so that when they are present in the classroom, they can serve their students faithfully, cultivate their own well-being, work toward a common purpose with their colleagues, and despite the many obstacles they face, work to bring, as Parker J. Palmer writes, "more light and life into the world."[26] In their effort to keep heart, rejuvenate their spirit, and resist the deforming force of stagnant, uninspiring environments and despairing loneliness, these teachers have documented three approaches.

The essays in Part One, "Turning Inward: Sustaining Our Own Hearts," describe teachers who turn inward to find the strength to reclaim and sustain the original source and passion that called them to teaching. The essays in this part document teachers fighting back against what Daniel P. Liston calls the "enveloping darkness"[27] by pursuing self-discovery and the process of discerning an answer to the questions, Who am I? Why do I teach? And to what extent is there integrity between what I believe and what I do in the classroom?

In the essays in Part Two, "Reaching Out: Forging Relationships That Sustain Our Hearts," teachers tell of resisting the tendency to fall into the cellular, isolating patterns that are endemic to many teachers' lives. Rather than be driven into working alone, these teachers describe their efforts to weave connections with one another, with administrators, with students, and with parents. These stories describe teachers who have found ways to deepen their participation in the lives of their schools, students, and colleagues. They find power, sustenance, and strength in joining with others.

The essays in Part Three, "Making Change: Reforms That Honor the Teacher's Heart," shares stories of teachers and educational leaders who have shifted their efforts away from viewing themselves and their colleagues as deformed and deficient and in need of fixing. Instead, they look toward their institutions and ask, How do we reconstitute the practices of our organization to better support the whole person? The stories document educators who have engaged their institutions and the powers that hold sway in the service of change. The narratives describe a diverse range of initiatives to create institutions sympathetic to the overarching and operative principle that the human heart is the source of good teaching.

Part Four introduces a detailed description of the Courage to Teach (CTT) program founded by Parker J. Palmer. The fundamental mission of the program is to support the personal and professional renewal of public school teachers and administrators. The CTT program uses an approach called "teacher formation," and the logic of the approach is based on the following premise: "We become teachers for reasons of the heart. But many of us lose heart as time goes by. How can we take heart, alone and together, so we can give heart to our students and our world, which is what good teachers do?" The single chapter in this part describes the theory and methods used by the program to advance its goal of restoring the heart and hope of America's teachers.

As this book moves to press, our country is still reeling in sorrow and confusion in the aftermath of the tragedy of September 11, 2001. We feel vulnerable and insecure. We feel frightened and fragile. Beset by often conflicting emotions, the adults I know press ahead with their daily routines. As lawyers, accountants, truck drivers, and cashiers return to work, they huddle with colleagues and friends talking through their fears, anxieties, and bewilderment.

As difficult as this is for the grown-ups, our children experience the uncertainty of our times with even more intensity. They return to schools often racked with emotion and confused about how to respond. Waiting for them, as they are every day, are the teachers—men and women who are devoted to helping children grow, learn, and become contributing members of our civic community.

In times of despair and complexity, we all need caring, committed people in our lives to help us feel connected and to guide our thinking so that we can engage with complicated events in careful ways. The overwhelming number of teachers I know desire to fulfill that role in the lives of our children. This is not easy work. It demands intelligence, courage, resiliency, flexibility, and passion. The stories in this volume honor teachers who work, often against punishing odds, to keep heart so they can give heart to their students.

NOTES

1. National Commission on Teaching and America's Future. "What Matters Most: Teaching for America's Future." (Report.) New York: National Commission on Teaching and America's Future, Sept. 1996, p. 10.
2. American Council on Education. "To Touch the Future: Transforming the Way Teachers Are Taught. An Action Agenda for College and University Professors." 1999, p. 5. [http://www.acenet.edu/resources/presnet/]
3. Shulman, L. S. "Autonomy and Obligation." In L. S. Shulman and G. Sykes (eds.), *Handbook of Teaching and Policy.* New York: Longman, 1983, p. 504.

4. Hochschild, A. R. *The Managed Heart: Commercialization of Human Feeling.* Berkeley: University of California Press, 1983.

5. Palmer, P. J. *The Courage to Teach: Exploring the Inner Landscape of a Teacher's Life.* San Francisco: Jossey-Bass, 1998, p. 10.

6. Palmer (1998), p. 11.

7. Palmer (1998), p. 11.

8. Fox, M. "Like Fireworks, Not Mud: The Role of Passion in the Development of Literacy." *Reading and Writing Quarterly,* 1996, *12,* 251–264.

9. Nozick, R. *Examined Life.* New York: Touchstone, 1989, p. 170.

10. Farkas, S., Johnson, J., and Foleno, T. *A Sense of Calling: Who Teaches and Why.* New York City: Public Agenda, 2000, p. 10.

11. Ayers, W. *To Teach: The Journey of a Teacher.* New York: Teachers College Press, 1993, p. 8.

12. Nelson, F. H., Drown, R., and Gould, J. C. *Survey and Analysis of Teacher Salary Trends, 2000.* Washington, D.C.: American Federation of Teachers, 2001.

13. Gursky, D. "The Teacher Shortage: How Bad Is It? What's Being Done About It?" *American Teacher,* Dec. 2000–Jan. 2001. [http://www.aft.org/publications/american_teacher/dec00_jan01/supply.html]. Aug. 20, 2001.

14. Johnson, S. *Teachers at Work: Achieving Success in Our Schools.* New York: Basic Books, 1990.

15. Seymour, L. "SOL Tests Create New Dropouts." *Washington Post,* July 17, 2001, p. A1.

16. Goodnough, A. "High Stakes of Fourth-Grade Tests Are Driving Off Veteran Teachers." *New York Times,* June 14, 2001, p. A1.

17. Kannapel, P. J., and others. "Teacher Responses to Reward and Sanctions: Effects of and Reactions to Kentucky's High-Stakes Accountability Program." In B. L. Whitford and K. Jones (eds.), *Accountability, Assessment, and Teacher Commitment: Lessons from Kentucky's Reform Effort.* Albany: State University of New York Press, 2000.

18. Swaim, M. S., and Swaim, S. C. "Teacher Time (or Rather, the Lack of It)." *American Educator,* 1999, *23*(3), 1–6.

[http://www.aft.org/publications/american_educator/fall99/s waim.pdf]

19. Swaim and Swaim (1999), pp. 1–2.
20. Swaim and Swaim (1999), p. 2.
21. Rosenholtz, S. *Teachers' Workplace: The Social Organization of Schools.* New York: Teachers College Press, 1989.
22. Marquis, D. M., and Sachs, R. *I Am a Teacher: A Tribute to America's Teachers.* New York: Simon and Schuster, 1990, p. 59.
23. Lortie, D. C. *Schoolteacher: A Sociological Study.* Chicago: University of Chicago Press, 1975.
24. Jackson, P. W. "The Uncertainties of Teaching." In *The Practice of Teaching.* New York: Teachers College Press, 1986, p. 55.
25. Haigh, G. "To Be Handled with Care." *Times Educational Supplement,* Feb. 10, 1995, pp. 3–4.
26. Palmer (1998), p. 7.
27. Liston, D. P. "Love and Despair in Teaching." *Educational Theory,* 2000, *50,* 81–102.

STORIES OF
The Courage
to Teach

Part One

Turning Inward
Sustaining Our Own Hearts

Carpooling home one day a few years ago with a fellow English teacher, we heard an interview on National Public Radio with a poet who was describing her work habits. The poet, whose name I don't recall, spoke about her work as "drinking in the stillness and receiving the pulse of the land." She described sitting quietly while words and images wove themselves into slow coherence.

Playfully, my colleague asked in an NPR-esque voice, "Well, Sam, what words characterize your work habits?"

In the spirit of two men who spent their day exhorting students to bang words and language together, we reeled off a list that aptly characterized our days. As English teachers, we tried to spark interest, raise questions, provoke insight, generate momentum, facilitate conversations, introduce new material, review for upcoming exams, establish a schema for understanding and assessing the progress of our students. As teachers of adolescents, we counseled, listened, humored, disciplined, and tried to be present in their complicated lives as best we could. We also attended meetings, called parents, photocopied materials, and marked papers.

If the poets' words were languorous, gentle, and contoured, ours were charged, careening, and jagged. The poet described her work as contemplative. We described our work as a crazy quilt of roles and tasks. If the poet strolls forth taking the world in, the teacher bustles about trying to create those high-octane connections between students, subject matter, and teacher.

The gusting and squalling conditions of the teaching life often leave us so absorbed in merely maintaining our footing on the heeling deck that it's hard to find the will and the space to turn inward. Teachers everywhere are under pressure to provide action and results: we must orchestrate class, serve our students, cover the curriculum, prepare our students to clamber over the hurdles of high-stakes tests, meet with our colleagues, and contribute to reform agendas. A principal with twenty years' experience explained the consequences of this pace:

> I'm absolutely convinced that the amount of stress and complexity that teachers confront every day does not allow them to be in a healthy way. . . . Teachers need time for themselves. They don't get that. Teachers need reflection time. They don't get that. If people aren't at a comfortable place with who they are, then they don't do a good job in the classroom.
>
> The relentless giving, doing, and acting demanded by teaching derail opportunities for teachers to slow down, take time, and listen deeply to themselves. The cost of this is not just harried and fatigued teachers, but teachers whose inner vitality gets blown out.[1]

In reflecting on her life as a poet, May Sarton writes, "I, in my normal life, am alone all the time. I work alone. Therefore, when someone comes for tea and it's the only person I see all day, that is precious too, because solitude without society would be meager and would, in the end, make for a dwindling of personality, perhaps. You can't eat yourself all day and all night. There has to be something in that brings life-food from the outside."[2]

The message for teachers is the mirror message: *We, in our normal teaching life, are mostly with and for others.* We work in crowded classrooms, amid throngs of students, in an environment that demands total emotional and cognitive presence as we make upward of eight thousand decisions in the course of a day. The pace of our work is feverish and becoming more accelerated and fragmented. A small play on Sarton's words tolls loudly here: *Society and action without solitude would be meager and in the end make for a dwindling personality, perhaps. You can't eat with others and for others all day and all night. There has to be something that brings life-food from the inside.*

Teachers need nourishment from the *inside.* In my experience as a teacher, administrator, and researcher, I have heard teachers give voice to their visceral need to speak and be heard regarding questions of vocation and purpose. When we're deprived of the opportunity to talk, think, and muse about the deeper meanings in our work, it's easy to lose sight of what called us to teaching. The questions at the center of Part One are the meaty questions that come when teachers turn inward: What is my way as a teacher? How can I sustain my ideals in this work? What are the consistent sources that give me energy? How can I cleave away the excess to leave myself focused on the truly important? And as Parker Palmer likes to call it, the close-to-the-bone question: Who is the self that teaches?

One elementary teacher explained to me what happened when she took time to turn inward and reflect on her life as a teacher: "It was life-altering to . . . step outside the frenetic pace of your life. To sit down beside the road and be contemplative. It gives you time to consider how to be in this world and how to be with your students. It offers an opportunity to kindle or rekindle the sense of mystery and wonder about life and the precious lives of each student."

Turning inward has nothing to do with meeting the standards, improving teaching, and staunching the dire attrition rate of teachers—but as you'll learn in the stories in Part One, it also has everything to do with it.

—S.M.I.

NOTES

1. Intrator, S. M., and Scribner, M. *An Evaluation of the Courage to Teach Program.* Kalamazoo, Mich.: Fetzer Institute, 1998, p. 18.
2. Schade, E. R. (ed.). *From May Sarton's Well: Writings of May Sarton.* Watsonville, Calif.: Papier-Mache Press, 1994, p. 34.

The daily challenges of the classroom can grind teachers down, leaving our initial ideals and hopes for teaching smoldering and distant embers. Amy Symons, a high school teacher from the San Francisco Bay Area, feels overrun by late, unmotivated students and bureaucratic incursions that deplete her spirit and erode her morale. Though exhausted and close to her wit's end, Symons reframes her disillusionment and resentment and speaks to her students from the heart. While successful on this day, Symons, like so many of us, wonders where to get the strength to continue to work in an environment that often leaves her with feelings of "frustration, heartbreak, and anger."

—S.M.I.

Speaking from the Heart

Amy Symons

My enthusiasm for the lesson plan I've been conceiving of since the summer dissipates as I sling on my backpack and slog my way through bodies in the lunchtime crush. I sign in to school and sigh. I knew I hadn't left enough time to get to my second-floor classroom before the bell rang. Despite the fact that I am six or more inches taller than most students, which affords me a good view of how to maneuver between yelling girls, strutting young men, cowering frightened freshman, I still feel squashed and disrespected as an adult and as a teacher at this school.

I finally find my way through the last hallway to my shared room, where my colleague is conducting a student meeting. Although my fellow teacher tries to protect my preparation time in our classroom, an increasing number of students spend time here for legitimate but annoying reasons all the same. The first bell rings, and about a third of my class trickles in on time. I deliver my daily mantra to write down the homework assignment in their study planners as I take roll. *Is there any point to filling out the attendance sheet? So many of these absent students will turn out to be tardy.* I stand and begin to explain the homework. The phone rings. Two more students arrive, laughing and seemingly oblivious to the fact that they are now in class. On the phone, I talk to an anxious mother who works downstairs, checking to see if her daughter's in class. I tell her no.

"Have you seen her? Do you know where she is?"

"No, sorry, she's not here." *Why is she so surprised at her daughter's absence? She's started to skip more and more of her classes. Why doesn't this mother call either before or after class? She knows I'm teaching.*

I return to the chalkboard to continue explaining the homework and notice how jumpy and unfocused the students are. I tell them I need their attention. As soon as I start speaking, I'm interrupted. I stop and wait. "Focus," I exhort, with a smile. Stretching my arms wide, I slowly point my index finger into the other palm. "Focus!" I start again, and now other students from the other side of the room begin to talk. I shush them and the phone rings again. This time I'm greeted with a rush of demands and breathless questions.

"Amy, this is Georgia Kahn, the special ed teacher. Is Shaquila Dimond there? How is she today? And you know I need to know what your homework is every day, and you haven't given it to me yet. What exactly *are* you doing in class? You need to let me know ahead of time because these students legally have a modified program and you need to remember that when you grade them this marking period."

"Yes. Georgia, hi." *Even though I've told her not to, this woman always calls in the middle of class expecting to have a full conversation. Why?*

"When can you do this? We need to meet. You *must* remember about these students!"

Take a deep breath. Breathe deeply. I listen to my students raise their voices and spin off into more lunchtime behavior.

"Georgia, I'd love to talk to you about this, but I'm in the middle of class. I'll put the homework in your box. OK? 'Bye."

"Great, great, but—"

I hang up. I sigh and return to the easel where the ideas the class generated yesterday are listed. As I begin to speak, after calling for attention again, three more girls walk in. The class's attention shifts away from me to them as they sign in the tardy book. The girls continue their conversation, making no effort to modify their voices or behavior.

"Girls! Why are you late?"

Silence.

"When you come in late, it affects me—I lose my train of thought; it affects everyone else here; and most important of all, it affects you. Come in, be quiet, and sit down."

They shuffle to their seats. One waits a moment and then starts talking to her tablemate as I ask for the class's attention for what feels like the fiftieth time. *That does it! What should I do? Cry? I sure feel like it. Yell more? Not a great solution. Be honest about how hard this is for me?* I notice the special education aide—an adult—has just arrived, fifteen minutes late. I lower my voice and start speaking quietly. The side conversations fade away after the first sentence or so.

"Do you guys know why I'm here? Why I stand up here every day? (*Pause.*) I do this . . ." (*I can't believe I'm doing this*) "out of *love*."

Guffaws. Twitters from both sides of the room.

"I do this out of love—for you. I feel like you deserve more out of school and out of your lives than you may have received in the past."

Their cynicism radiates.

"I do this out of love—for education. I love what education can do for you and where it can take you. Most of you say you want to go to college. I want to help you achieve your goal."

I'm getting more eye contact, especially from the girls.

"I do this out of love, because I love teaching," *Is this true?*
I'm not so sure anymore.

"I love what I do—I love reading and hanging out with you guys and helping you learn."

Everybody's quiet.

"But I don't love how much time of *your* education we're wasting and how long it takes for us to get on track. This is your life, your trajectory toward college, and I want to help you. But *you've* got to help, too.

"So let's try this again. *Please,* if you're not ready to listen now, fifteen minutes into class, please let me know. You can leave class with my permission. But we've got to move on so we can wrap up this idea we've been working on for several days. Are you ready?"

Wait.

"OK . . ."

I begin my spiel on health, prompting the students with questions about how mental, physical, and social health are interrelated. For the next span of time, they're participating and engaged. As I check in with different groups, I wonder if there's a correlation between my approach today and their engagement; I want to believe there is.

Speaking from my heart is one of the reasons why I teach. I like speaking truthfully and working alongside students to make sense of our world, our literature, our lives. I am not a great authoritarian; I wonder if my shortcomings in that area will keep me from feeling successful and confident in this school setting, where the teachers who bark seem to have few to no management problems. Yet when I yell, my voice breaks, and I feel like my students see my sham for what it is: not me.

I took the risk of being myself that day, and the room felt different—maybe not only for me but for them, too. I was aware of the strength it took for me to reframe feelings of frustration, heartbreak, anger, and resentment and give them a positive spin, forming them into a "teacher speech" that wouldn't further alienate the kids. I wonder how they perceive me. I'm beginning to realize how skeptical they are of me—a white, young, new teacher with untraditional curricula who attempts, and frequently fails, to push them to think and conceive of English in different ways. I don't hand out worksheets; I don't assign book reports; I don't yet give vocabulary lists. I'm new to them and therefore a new teacher. That's a hard role for me to swallow again, as this is the fourth school I've been new at.

I started the year with excitement, confidence, and lots of ideas. But I find that the encounters I have in my classroom often feel like battles, and I'm the one who ends up with the most bruises and lost lifeblood. I am proud of myself for taking the risk of speaking from my heart that day, but I feel so misunderstood and disrespected that I only want to further protect myself and barricade that self who desires to teach.

Since 1994, Amy Symons has taught English and humanities courses in a broad array of school contexts. She began her career teaching seventh-grade language arts and social studies at the Keys School in Palo Alto, California, and then proceeded to teach at the St. Paul's Episcopal School and the Oakland Technical High School in Oakland, California, before coming to her present position at Hayward High School in Hayward, California. She writes that she feels most alive in her teaching "when there's a feeling in the room that we've come upon something that is *real*, something that transcends the classroom and is about life. I love discovering new analogies or ways to translate information that kids get and can really ingest."

There comes a time when we find ourselves in the crosshairs of a parent's wrath or on the receiving end of a student's fury. No matter how confident we are in ourselves as teachers, these moments unsettle us and bow our spirit. High school English teacher Jim Burke describes receiving an angry letter from a student. While the letter bites deep, he does not turn away but works hard to hear the student's voice as an invitation to be the teacher he feels called to be.

—S.M.I.

This Is Where Teaching Gets Real

Jim Burke

Teaching is so public, so personal, so dangerous. You walk in each day, to each class, to begin that unit, that lesson, that activity as if for the first time because you have never taught that lesson to that class or this kid.

You can, of course, stand on the hill looking back over the years of teaching that brought you to this moment. You can recall the long, proud tradition of which you are now a part and to which you feel a serious obligation. You can reflect until your eyes themselves resemble two burnished mirrors and your hands are filled with all you could ever know. You might even, as I have, become more public by writing about what you do, how you do it, offering to both teachers and the public your own insights into the complexity of learning. You might even, as I did tonight, speak on behalf of a former student at his Eagle Scout ceremony in a church filled with many of the students you taught and their parents, most of whom come up to you afterward to thank you for your teaching.

None of this, however, will prepare you for the messages such as the e-mail I found waiting for me after the ceremony.

Dear Jim,

I have decided to call u Jim b/c i do not feel inferior to you, in fact if anything you are inferior to me. Anyways, since I am leaving Burlingame High School next year to attend a school with better english teachers than you since you just plain suck at teaching, i would like to tell you that the one year i had you for a teacher was the worst experience in my time at school. You have no idea how to teach. instead you ramble on about how your new book is coming out. Too bad your book sucks and proabably nobody bought your book because your techniques were pulled out of your ass. From students i talked to that had you this year and last also have made remarks about your poor preformance of the year and at times you are aloof during class. I agree with that but also think that you are an arrogant bastard who needs to give up teaching. I feel sorry for your kids because they will grow up with a father who holds expectations way to high to meet.

I wish you the worst luck in all that you fail in. Enjoy the rest of your life.

Sarcastically,

The student you screwd over and tried to keep out of sophomore honors english.

I could dismiss this letter, which contains just enough information to tell me who probably wrote it. I could ignore it, write it off, and turn my ear toward the songs of praise my former students and parents offered only hours before. But are we in this only for the people who like us, who take whatever we offer—however brilliant or banal the assignment is—and make us look good? Is the measure of our success the obvious success of our students as measured by their scores, grades, awards, or the testimonials we receive?

This is where courage comes in, for it would be so much more comfortable to hit the delete key and simply erase the e-mail and all its anger. But this kid is extending to me an invitation, one I need to take if I am to be the teacher I want to be. This is where teaching gets real.

I don't need to play the martyr to this boy's misplaced anger. I am that boy, or was, when I was his age. It is the greatest irony that I grew up to become the teacher of such students as I was.

The poet William Stafford wrote a poem called "Vocation," which ends with a line I keep with me at all times:

> Now both of my parents, the long line through the plain,
> the meadowlarks, the sky, the world's whole dream
> remain, and I hear him say while I stand between the two,
> helpless, both of them part of me:
> Your job is to find what the world is trying to be.[1]

This kid does not know who or what he is trying to be yet. And one of my many jobs was—and is—to figure out what kind of teacher each student needs me to be for him.

It's July now, midway through the summer I need so I can return in September and be the teacher to others that I was not to that disgruntled young man.

It will take courage. My own adolescent eyes will be watching me, wanting to know what I am doing today to help me find my way to what I want to be tomorrow. I will need to be my own teacher. This does not let me off easy but makes me do the work I must—to be the teacher I am and always try to be.

NOTE

1. Stafford, W. *The Way It Is: New and Selected Poems.* St. Paul, Minn.: Graywolf Press, 1998, pp. 102–103.

Turning Inward

Jim Burke is a full-time high school English teacher, the moderator of a dynamic on-line discussion list called CATENET (California Teachers of English Network), the author of seven impressive books on teaching, and the designer of an award-winning Web site on teaching (www.englishcompanion.com). Two of his most popular books are *The English Teacher's Companion: A Complete Guide to Classroom, Curriculum, and the Profession* (Boynton-Cook, 1999) and *I Hear America Reading: Why We Read What We Read* (Heinemann, 1999). His latest book is *Illuminating Texts: How to Teach Students to Read the World* (Heinemann, 2001). He began teaching special education students in Tunisia while he was in the Peace Corp. Upon his return, he taught English in Northern California, first at Castro Valley High School and now at Burlingame High School. He has won several awards for his outstanding work with children in the classroom and other awards for his service and scholarship to the profession, including the Intellectual Freedom Award presented by the National Council of Teachers of English in 1999, and in 2001 he was given the prestigious Hall of Fame award by the California Reading Association. In his classroom, he feels most alive "when working with kids who want to succeed but do not know that they can or do not know how. I feel like I am helping them gain access to another self and choices they did not think were theirs."

M any of us become teachers for reasons of the heart, called to the classroom by a desire to serve society and connect with children. Our belief in the importance of our mission often fuels expectations that society will value our work and contribute the resources necessary for us to be successful with children. The reality is often the opposite, and many of us lose heart and hope. We become bitter and disillusioned and feel victimized by the system. Thirty-year veteran John Rockne begins his career enthralled by teaching, but his initial enthusiasm is ground down, and he experiences a fallow period that lasts for decades. Rockne shares how, through stories and imagination, he is able to forgive his and the school system's flawed realities and become genuinely present and engaged in the search for "expressions of earnest sincerity from students."

—S.M.I.

Teaching Had Become an Ordinary Job

John Rockne

The source of my calling sprang up in my college years, the late sixties. During this time of turmoil, I had no idea what I wanted to do with my life. But quite by chance, I got a part-time job working with young students as a tutor five days a week. The interaction with these kids affected me quickly and profoundly. On Wednesdays, I shot baskets with Mark and then helped him do penmanship. He was a fourth-grade boy who had broken both arms. After they mended, he had forgotten how to write. Helping him remember writing was satisfying. Unknown and forgotten parts of my nature were called out spontaneously in this human exchange. I changed my major to education and soon found myself in a fifth-grade classroom.

My connection to teaching was personally fulfilling. I felt I had found the work I was born to do. Daily student interaction was a continual spring that fed my intellect, intuition, and emotions. I remember a young girl at lunch asking me shyly if I would please "open" her banana. Things like that just charmed me. My enthusiasm and energy for the work was automatic; I didn't think about it.

I did, however, think the problems of overcrowded classes, inadequate supplies, parental neglect, and low teacher pay were about to be solved. I fondly remember one of my first experiences as a member of a book adoption committee. When the salespeople made their presentations, I actually believed the one that absolutely guaranteed that "within three years" of using his company's new series, the majority of my kids would be reading at grade level. I also believed the legislature was finally going to "fully fund" basic education. The current problems of the educational system were just temporary aberrations. There was good and bad, and good was about to win.

Over time some of the grim realities of the educational system finally wore through my simple views. I remember suddenly realizing one day that none of the big problems would ever go away. These were permanent conditions. The day when even half of the class would be at "grade level" would never come. The respect and resources I expected from society would not be arriving next year. These discouraging truths entered my inner life, and I began to dread going to school. I could not remember the compelling allure that had once excited me.

In short, my feelings were hurt. I felt I was the victim of a devious sort of manipulation for which I was in no way responsible. Innocence and beauty made way for rage and resentment. Rather than go deeper into my work, I sought to involve myself less. I moved to junior high in hopes of making teaching a more clearly defined task, a strict exchange of time for money. I wanted work I could just show up for, like a job in a factory. I put teaching into a tidy compartment and managed it strategically. I planned appropriately and executed my responsibilities adequately. But I was not inspired to enthusiasm by teaching, nor were my students showing many signs of being enthusiastically inspired by my instruction.

I promised myself that as soon as my class sizes decreased and my pay increased, I would again put my heart into the work.

I busied myself with an active private life clearly separated from my work life. I found part-time jobs to make more money and investigated other career choices. A sense of wonder from work was no longer experienced or expected. *Teaching had become an ordinary job.*

Even in my sorry state, some moments in the classroom penetrated my heart. For example, Anna was a plain, poor, unpopular girl who wrote lengthy fantasy stories in my ninth-grade communication arts class. When she wrote, it was as if her ear could hear the song of creation, and she was dancing to it. Her writing was hard to follow, but she worked with dedication. The quality of her devotion touched me. This girl reminded me of the saying that even if we don't control our own fate, we do have the power to choose how it will be experienced. I wanted to give her writing, her earnest gesture of exchange with the world, some kind of personal response. But I did not know how to be present for her. I could not find the connections to my feelings and intuitions because my whole self was not showing up for work.

I reluctantly acknowledged I could not find my whole self. I had lost my true way. Part of me whispered, Be lost for a while. Just stop what you are doing and become aware of where you really are. So I consciously spent time just being in the midst of my students rather than being over them or ignoring them as I corrected papers at my desk. I found a few students like Anna, sincerely trying to become educated. But most kids were in a state of unconcerned boredom while others smoldered with a brooding anger ready to flare up if I disturbed them. "We'll behave pretty well if you don't make us work very hard" was the controlling agreement in my classroom. Had I become my own worst nightmare, the hardened veteran teacher recycling canned lessons grimly enduring until retirement? I felt foolish and embarrassed by the mediocre state of affairs in my classroom.

Feeling like the fool became my turning point. Either I would find a way to feel good about what I was doing, or I would leave this work. I spent too much time teaching for it not to furnish me with satisfaction. Then the image of the Wizard of Oz appeared in my mind. This solemnly self-righteous part of myself undergoing self-inflicted agony was the magnificent Oz. But my heart, the little fat man behind the curtain, was saying, Get over yourself, you pretentious fool. This is just junior high! I started laughing at my own self-importance.

The reason I was shut down at work was because I had simply been pouting about how unfairly the system was treating me. It seemed so trite, so commonplace, so childish. Seeing myself as childish was refreshing. It made it easier to forgive myself for being so simple. The way I approached work began to change. Laughter and forgiveness began to drain away the pool of resentment that blocked the connections to my emotions and intuitions.

Applying a literature perspective, I asked myself if pouting about a clunky system should be the main sticking point of my personal struggle. The answer was no. If I wished to play the hero in my own life story, I needed better antagonists—such as the students right in front of me. That is where my fate needed to be worked out.

Placing my own self in a story felt corny, but I was optimistic that these sentiments could truly be my guides. To feel important enough to have a destiny was something I had given up long before. Being a hero just wasn't something I could take seriously. But revisiting my notions about flawed heroes locked in epic struggles seemed the path my emotions and intuitions wished to take. I found that these ideas had seasoned and matured with time and new layers and textures in my own character were now exposed.

My sense of humor continued to find new pockets of self-importance to laugh away. I began to feel more kinship with others as I realized that my struggle was not really so unique. A willingness to risk appeared that was quite freeing. After all, if I tried new ways of teaching and they flopped, I would be no worse off than I already was. I asked myself, What do I really want from work? The answer was simple: I wanted more expressions of earnest sincerity from students, since that is what pierced my heart in the first place.

I recalled an inscription over the door of a chapel I had been to years earlier. It read, *"Abyssus invocat abyssum."* Deep calls out to deep. Anna's call to me had reawakened my own personal sense of destiny. Simple truths hit me. For example, the reason I wasn't finding much genuine fulfillment from teaching was that I was not looking for it. For teaching to work, I needed to need it. It won't give me what I don't ask for. Could teaching save my life? That question kept me in continual suspense. It even now describes how I am when I am at my best.

Posing deep questions to my students elevated my struggle. My revised lesson plan objectives were for learners to "do compelling, meaningful, and sincere things." I am glad my supervisor didn't check those plans. The projects entailed making pictures (which was new for me), writing, and then presenting work that described the students' hopes and fears. It was messy and bewildering at first; many students "didn't get it" or thought it was "stupid" or "none of my business." It took more time than I expected, and I felt vulnerable and ridiculous. But there were a few students who took the assignments as serious invitations to express themselves. These students became the source of guidance for the rest of us.

One student, Darren, pictured the mystery of himself as a net cast into the sea. In his net were elements symbolizing important things he was catching, such as his friends, a basketball, and some CDs. Other elements had passed through, such as an old girlfriend and some cigarettes. In the deeper water ahead of the net were things such as a car, a job, and some blank faces of the important people he had yet to meet. He explained his picture, and students asked many questions in the ensuing discussion, which ended with comments like "Is that all you have to do?" or "I've got an idea like that." Darren had inspired us.

That was in 1992, and things have been getting better ever since. Now in my introduction to a new class, with a robust enthusiasm and a straight face, I tell kids that they are stuck in the predicament of being a teenager. They are the main characters in their own life stories, and their choices are creating their destinies. With their whole lives in front of them, they do have epic dimension. If they use skill and imagination to read, write, talk, and listen, they can begin to unravel the baffling puzzle of their lives. To succeed in this adventure, they need to be brave and bold and look to each other for inspiration. I end by explaining that I, their teacher, am so old that I can't remember being a teen, so my ability to help them is limited.

To illustrate how I find a satisfying path through the confounding plight of being a public school teacher, I offer a story about another old man, much wiser than I. In act 5 of Shakespeare's *King Lear,* Lear and his daughter Cordelia are being led off to prison. She wishes to escape, but Lear says:

> No, no, no, let's away to prison.
> So we'll live,
> And pray, and sing, and tell old tales, and laugh
> At gilded butterflies. . . .
> And take upon's the mystery of things.

Prison, song, butterflies, and mystery are images that describe my current inner landscape. Prison can be the blemished public education setting where I live and work as well as the resentment and blame it arouses in me. Committing my wholeness to this prison without reservation is a paradoxical task. I would not usually seek out the restriction and restraint of the rigid time management of a school day. I would rather experience freedom and awe like a sunrise on a mountaintop. Consequently, to bring my whole heart, mind, and imagination into the classroom demands that I tolerate the tension of these opposites. Going "away to prison" means accepting and forgiving the system I work in as well as my own failings and limitations. This forgiveness was the breakthrough to my feelings. To commit to the imperfect is not easy. The collective attitude that happiness is all about having perfect things still holds sway in me, and this tension causes suffering. But choosing what to suffer about changes the experience. One becomes less of a victim.

For the next image, Lear continues with "So we'll live and pray, and sing." Helen Luke interprets this as "the expression of joy in the harmony of the chaos."[1] Chaos is an apt description for at least some of my day in a junior high. Finding harmony in that chaos presents another paradox. Going even further to find joy begins to test the limits of holding the tension of the world of opposites. But I do believe there is joy and harmony if only I can hear the song.

The reference to butterflies can represent my students. A butterfly is a momentary being coming from a caterpillar. Junior high students are undergoing a metamorphosis not unlike this. They can soar like butterflies and behave like worms all in the space of a single hour. Taken further, the butterfly image can represent the "fragile yet omnipotent beauty of the present moment," as Luke later states.[2] A lot of human energy is contained in a classroom, and the company of thirty youngsters sometimes puts an "omnipotent" edge on the present. By saying, doing, and being in ways that find their origin in my heart rather than intellect, I take upon myself "the mystery of things."

The lens of paradox and story has opened my eyes to the wonder and mystery of life. I now go into the class relishing the tensions and the polarities, seeing in them the opportunities for creativity. The challenges no longer defeat or limit me but call forth my best. Teaching is no longer an ordinary job.

NOTES

1. Luke, H. M. *Old Age.* New York: Parabola, 1987, p. 28.
2. Luke (1987), p. 28.

In 1973, John Rockne began teaching third and fourth grade in the Bethel School District in Spanaway, Washington. Since 1982, he has been teaching communication arts and social studies at Bethel Junior High School. He has served the children and parents of the Bethel School District for twenty-eight years. He describes that he feels most alive in his teaching when "students' comments, behavior, or work surprises me. The most lively and invigorating exchanges happen in the moments when I have to improvise."

Good teachers long accustomed to doing their work with passion and energy can sometimes experience stretches in their careers when they find themselves disconnected from their students, detached from their colleagues, and disenchanted by their work. These lulls can be deeply unsettling, particularly for those who have long believed that teaching was their life's vocation. Sixteen-year veteran Leslie Young, freshly honored as District Teacher of the Year, describes her own terrifying loss of her sense of self as a teacher. She shares how developing an inward focus, slowing down the pace and level of commitments in her life, and focusing attention on her own learning help her revitalize her commitment to teaching and refind the "grooves in which to place [her] pedagogical wheels."

—S.M.I.

An Experiment with Truth
One Teacher's Path

Leslie Young

When you yearn for things that you cannot name and you grieve not knowing the course, be certain that you are growing as all things that grow, and rising towards your higher self.

KAHLIL GIBRAN

My shoes hit the pavement in a steady clapping rhythm, as though through my daily walk I was trying to remind myself that I was still alive. I was at the height of my teaching career: I had been named District Teacher of the Year the previous spring, followed by a prestigious state award for innovative curriculum projects, and I was well on the way to preparing my National Board Certification for Professional Teaching Standards. Yet every morning I woke up praying that the inner anguish I felt would dissipate, only to find the anxiety of emptiness growing by the minute. The meaning of life had slowly been seeping out of me for the past four months, and nothing I did seemed to bring it back. I stood in front of my thirty fifth-graders every day, going through the motions.

I was beginning to recognize that the reasons why I had gone into teaching in the first place had vanished. Although the recognition I had received was based on my dedication to think and teach "outside the box," the new rigorous state standards required my district to create a uniform course of study for our students, and expression of creativity in teachers and students was no longer a desirable commodity. Many of my other honored colleagues had moved on to more administrative roles, abandoning the work for which they were recognized in the first place. And I was about to enroll in a graduate school program for which I had no passion but felt I should go because it would "look good on my résumé." As Parker J. Palmer wrote in *The Courage to Teach*, I was "disconnected from the inner teacher,"[1] and I was about to have my own "experiment with truth." I didn't know where it would take me, and I was terrified.

> Do not wish to be anything but what you are, and try to be that perfectly.
>
> UNKNOWN

Teaching had been an unpredictable accident. I decided to follow a lifelong passion to live in France. Working at a regular job was out of the question, yet teaching English to the "natives" was in high demand in this provincial town. Suddenly, I found myself at the beginning of an eight-year overseas adventure. In facing the French students daily—children and adults in various educational settings—I found what Palmer calls the "undivided self": every thread of my own life experience was honored, and with this golden net I was able to hold my students, my subject, and myself in a glorious exchange. The hours were long and the pay was modest, but the work demanded constant creativity. The love I found personally and professionally liberated me in unforeseen ways. I lived and breathed my work; I taught not from pedagogical theory but from my gut, "from the inside out." The real teacher had arrived.

He who has a why to live can bear with almost any how.
FRIEDRICH NIETZSCHE

I returned to the United States with the desire to continue to teach embedded in me. I received my teaching credential and found myself teaching elementary school children—mainly Hispanic immigrants or their sons and daughters. Again, I discovered my passion. I was teaching what I had lived: my students' frustrations with a foreign language and culture. Whereas many of my colleagues found these students "too low" or "unmotivated," I found them captivating. Their parents handed me their precious children with the implicit plea to educate them, to guide them toward a life that they, the parents, knew they could never achieve for themselves. I was a contributor to the true mission of public education. My students were determined to succeed in their adopted homeland, and I was to be the bridge. Our classroom sparkled with new projects, and I was tacitly given carte blanche by my principal to try out new ideas behind closed doors. Yes, there were some students who strayed from what I felt most of the time to be a perfectly synchronized dance. There were even those who could not keep up. Yet I was fortunate to be able to maintain this spirited existence for eight years, all the while making sure to steer clear of those who only saw teaching as a "job" and not a vocation.

Who we are as individuals reflects who we are as teachers.
PARKER J. PALMER

Those were the joys of the beginning, but after eight years in France and eight in the United States, I cracked. "You've lost your balance," one set of colleagues would advise me. "You're probably just experiencing teacher burnout," another set would chime in. I was terrified that I had lost the teacher inside. Without knowing who I was anymore, I could no longer find the grooves in which to place my pedagogical wheels.

I decided to take a break, far away from all I had constructed. I withdrew my application for graduate school and instead enrolled in acting classes. I threw all my education-related books in the closet and read only what I felt like reading. I turned down district opportunities to serve on committees or present workshops and instead enrolled in an exercise program. I stopped running on the "career treadmill" with my blinders on and took a leisurely walk, enjoying the people and places I discovered on the way.

In order to teach, I realized, I had to become a learner again, but this time in a totally new arena. It took a while; but with breathing space and the permission from loved ones to do what I felt like doing, the world began to move from black and white back to subtle color. Slowly, my teaching took on a new dimension as well. As my life outside the classroom expanded, so did the one inside. The students seemed to be more motivated, and so was I. I was able to take up my crusade of "creative insubordination" with new knowledge and flair.

The moral of the story? To be a better teacher, don't be afraid to find yourself, even at the most inopportune of moments. As the sole constant in life is change, so it is in teaching. If teaching means to touch lives and at its best change lives for the better, so must you do so for yourself. Only if you learn what gives you true joy will you be able to help your students find what gives them joy.

NOTE

1. Palmer, P. J. *The Courage to Teach: Exploring the Inner Landscape of a Teacher's Life.* San Francisco: Jossey-Bass, 1998.

Leslie Young began her work in education as a curriculum specialist in Vichy, France, where she developed a model program for the French Ministry of Education on English in the primary schools. In 1992, she began teaching at the Patrick Henry Elementary School in Anaheim, California. In 1999, she received her National Board for Professional Teaching Standards Certification. Aside from her classroom responsibilities, she also serves in a number of teacher leadership positions, including mentor teacher, a Beginning Teacher Support and Assessment provider for the Anaheim City School District, and instructor for the Orange County and Los Angeles departments of education. She is the author of *The Storytelling Handbook for Primary Teachers* (Penguin Books, 1991) and a recipient of the Golden Bell award for *The Immigrant Project* (California School Boards Association, 1998). She has also received a nomination for the Outstanding Educator Award by the Anaheim Chamber of Commerce and in 1998 was the Teacher of the Year in the Anaheim City School District. She says she feels most alive teaching "when I am discovering along with my students."

Many teachers are drawn to the profession by their belief that through teaching they can do great things. This heroic vision is a source of inspiration, but it can also become a source of great frustration when a teacher's efforts do not yield the triumphs pursued. Initially, Mary Alice Scott comes to teaching, like so many of us, to move mountains and transform the world. Frustrated by real impediments and overwhelming realities, she leaves the classroom. Years later, while teaching in a different context, she discovers that teaching is less about doing "great things" and more about "doing small things with great love."

—S.M.I.

Doing Small Things with Great Love

Mary Alice Scott

My high school yearbook sold advertisements each year to parents of graduating seniors to print inspirational quotes and congratulatory messages for their children. My mom bought one. She put a picture of me as a little kid, looking silly, with spaghetti on my head or something and a little note that said "congratulations"—pretty typical. But at the bottom was this quote from Mother Teresa: "We can never do great things, only small things with great love." I don't think I ever told my mom how much that affected me. I'd gone through high school determined to do great things, just because they were great. It never occurred to me to do things out of love.

I did have a sense of responsibility to make change in the world, but that came more out of my guilt in my own life situation—upper-middle-class, intellectual, athletic—than out of a love for the world or even my own community. I flew off to college and enrolled myself in as many social activist groups as I could find and decided that I was an atheist. I honestly don't know what connection that had with anything. I just decided it one day, literally. I remember the day I decided. I was sitting in my room, not feeling particularly depressed or happy, not stressed or relaxed, just kind of sitting. I looked out the window and didn't see anything—I mean, I saw the sun and the sky and people sitting outside, playing Frisbee, but I didn't really *see* anything. And so I thought that if I couldn't see anything, then there must be no God. It was a completely unemotional decision.

Of course, looking back now, I think that decision was what put me in a place to find grace. I didn't expect anything. I didn't know at the time what I was being prepared for. I just felt frustrated with my life in general and couldn't quite put my finger on the cause.

In college, I enrolled in the secondary education program, deciding that I would change the world through teaching. Somehow, instead of working in a high school history class, I ended up teaching writing to a small group of fourth graders. That was OK with me. I just wanted to teach.

I walked into the school on the first day and was introduced to my students—Kevia, Cheyenne, Demarcus, and Shawn. Kevia immediately attached herself to me, dragging me into the room in which we would be working together for three hours a week for about four months. My task was to work with these four students on writing exercises so that they could pass the end-of-year writing test and move on to the fifth grade. I pulled out the first writing assignment given to me by the teaching assistant in my education class.

"Start by inciting their imagination. Writing should be fun, not a chore."

I agreed with that. I'd written in a journal since I was nine and loved every minute of it.

"Ask the students to think about a time in their lives when they were the happiest. Have them write about the scene in which they find themselves. You might start by exploring what the scene of a story is."

Great! I could do that. I began by talking with them about what a scene is. It was going well. They got it. Then I asked them to think about a time in their lives when they were the happiest. They screwed up their faces, doodled on their paper, asked each other, and came up with nothing.

"My mom's in jail right now, but it's not right. She shouldn't be there. That doesn't make me happy," one student said.

"Yeah, my dad's girlfriend is pregnant, and my mom's mad, and all she does is cry."

"I don't want to write."

"Yeah, me neither."

What was I supposed to do with this?

"OK, let's write instead about hard times in our lives. Can you describe that scene?"

What was I thinking? I just didn't know what to do. I was so shocked by the responses I got that my brain just wasn't working. Shawn began writing. Thank goodness. The others saw him, picked up their pencils, and bent their heads over the papers, working slowly, methodically forming each letter. I relaxed. I thought that Shawn must have picked up on my inability to connect with them and was trying to help me out.

About ten minutes later, Shawn showed me his work. I couldn't read it. It wasn't that it was messy. In fact, the letters were very neatly formed; they just weren't letters from the alphabet I knew. He didn't know how to write. The other kids passed in their papers. All the same. Every once in a while on each paper there were a few letters I recognized, but in general, they were pictograms and forms masquerading as letters.

I had a sneaking suspicion that these kids couldn't read, much less write. I pulled out a book that I had brought and opened it to the first page. The kids gathered around me, looking up, waiting for me to start reading. I handed the book to Demarcus, who immediately started running around the room, asking me what different things were, and needling Shawn until he got angry and started fighting back. The two girls started pulling things off the craft shelves and asking if they could do art. It was suddenly chaos. It wasn't a sneaking suspicion anymore. They couldn't read. How was I supposed to prepare them to pass a writing test in three hours a week for four months?

I have to admit that I gave up at that moment. I gave up on those kids because I just didn't know what to do. The rest of the four months I spent bringing in books and trying to teach them to read. Maybe, just maybe they would get far enough to . . . what? I didn't know. They weren't going to pass the writing test. There wasn't time, and I didn't know how to teach them. I was so far from their experience. I didn't know what it was like to have a mother in jail or one who cries all the time. I didn't know what it was like to sit in a classroom of kids who can read when you can't. I didn't know what it was like to be ignored as these kids had been.

I gave up on teaching. I decided that I wasn't cut out for it. I dropped out of the teacher education program and decided that the thing for me to do was to take my senior year of college in Mexico. I was going to be a student, nothing more. I didn't really know it at the time, but I was ashamed. I blamed my failure in teaching on the program's not having prepared me for the job presented to me, but it wasn't the program's fault. I blamed myself for not thinking of something immediately that would engage these kids, but I couldn't expect myself to be prepared for that.

In Mexico, I studied the first semester and took the second semester off from school to do some work in a village in the southern part of the country. I could talk for hours about the things I learned from the women in that village, but what stays with me is Angela.

Angela was small for her age and had a terrible case of scabies. The parasite had moved into her face and was making her miserable. Her mother tried to treat it with medicine she got from one of the nurse volunteers who came to the village on the weekends, but she didn't understand how to use it. Rather than putting the cream on once, waiting five days, and putting it on again, she put the cream on her daughter's face every day for an entire week. The chemicals burned the child's face and left her with gaping sores that wouldn't heal.

Angela's mother sent her to live with me and the director of the program in which I was working. I wound up taking care of her most of the time. At first it was kind of charming. We'd walk around the city together, and I got to practice my Spanish and just play a lot of the time. Then she started complaining a lot and stealing money from me, and people would stop me every five minutes to ask what was wrong with her and she would cry. Every night I treated her face with chamomile tea because everything else was too strong for her face to handle. She would lie down on the bed and close her eyes while I washed the burns with cold tea and gauze. I know it hurt her. But I also knew that nothing else would heal her.

One day, as I was washing her face, I was just overcome by a sense of gratitude that I had been put in a place where I had the opportunity to wash this little girl's face. I didn't understand where it came from. I felt so completely fulfilled doing that. I just forgot myself. I forgot myself for a minute, and God slipped in. I had never in my life felt so honest about anything I had done. I knew then that I wanted for my life to be one in which I was real, where I could just forget myself, where I could feel so completely connected with God through touching the burns on a little girl's face.

In that moment, I became a teacher. What was missing in me when I was working with those fourth graders was a sense that this world is bigger than me. I was selfish, and I didn't know that I was. I thought I was going into teaching to help the world, but really, I was going into teaching to help myself. I thought that if I could inspire children to want to learn, I would be able to inspire myself as well. It didn't work that way.

How could I possibly have imagined that the quote my mom included in my graduation advertisement would come back to me in this way? "We can never do great things, only small things with great love." My mom and Mother Teresa were right. Only when we have cared so deeply that we forget ourselves can we understand how incredibly insignificant we are and at the same time how beautifully essential.

I am working now as the program director for the Self Knowledge Symposium, an organization that seeks to help young people find answers to questions like "Who am I?" Although I do not teach in a classroom, I hope that my work with young people inspires them to be open to finding answers in unlikely places, to accepting the possibility that there is more to this world than meets the eye, and that in order to learn who we truly are, we have to forget ourselves, doing not great things but small things with great love.

Since 1997, Mary Alice Scott has worked with students of all levels in a broad array of programs. She has taught leadership classes for middle school and high school–aged youth in a program called Youth Voice Radio, and presently she is the director of the Self Knowledge Symposium, an organization connected with Duke University and the University of North Carolina–Chapel Hill. The mission of the organization is to invite youth to come together to pursue with passion and commitment a fuller understanding of who we are and what we believe. In her work, she feels most alive "when the level of authenticity in a room is markedly higher than in everyday life, when the class becomes a community willing to support and challenge its members to really go into asking important questions about their lives."

Many of us come to the profession filled with hope and enthused by ideals, but often we find we've lost our heart and passion for teaching. When we lose something that once held deep meaning for us, we can slide into a state of despair. Daniel P. Liston describes the anguish of realizing that he had lost his connection to students and his subject. Drained and bitter, Liston embarks on an inner journey that rejuvenates his love for teaching. He describes undertaking "despair work" to reaffirm his love and commitment for his teaching, his students, and his subject matter.

—S.M.I.

Despair and Love in Teaching

Daniel P. Liston

Some years back, I woke up to realize that I was no longer interested in going to the library, browsing the shelves, and checking out new titles. What used to be one of my favorite journeys, a delight and so much a part of my professional identity, now seemed dry and uninviting. For fifteen years, I had been engaged with the education of future and experienced teachers and with inquiry into the social and political contexts of teaching.

But after a while, I discovered I had lost interest. I no longer cared about the scholarly developments in "reflective teacher education" and found the political literature wanting. "Reflection" had become a technical educational slogan, one that didn't seem to resemble the original orientation. Critical commentary on schooling had taken a nihilistic turn, with

This work is drawn from Daniel P. Liston, *Love and Despair in Teaching: Feeling and Thinking in Educational Settings* (New York: Routledge, forthcoming).

authors composing extreme positions that didn't connect to teachers' lives. I was still interested in teaching teachers and in pursuing topics related to teacher reflection and issues of educational justice, but I needed to find another way in. I was lost. I needed, but did not know it at the time, to reclaim my love of teaching.

Around that time, I also began to see my institution, and many other higher educational institutions, as bordering on being unresponsive to students' needs and inattentive to their desires. At my institution, students found few open doors or attentive ears. When they did find an opening and some attention, they poured out their souls. I became drained from taking on too many student concerns and bitter about the institutional arrangements. My love of learning and teaching were sorely tested and found lacking, and I fell into a big, dark, deep, seemingly unfathomable hole. It took what Joanna Macy identifies as "despair work"[1] and Iris Murdoch's understanding of love[2] to pull me out of despair's hold.

It took a year to see that my loves had been squashed and to find ways out. And I was fortunate. I work in a privileged environment. I'm a professor at a Level 1 research institution. No matter how dismal my work conditions, my work setting is relatively easy compared to the teaching situations of many others. I have multiple resources at my fingertips, the student-teacher ratio is low, and when I did crash, there were people around who helped break my fall. Others are not so lucky.

I was lucky in more ways than one. Some twenty-five years ago, I had the good fortune of being mentored by Robert Ubbelohde. While I was an undergraduate at Earlham College, Robert had arrived from the University of Wisconsin with a newly minted doctorate in hand, intellectually alive and fresh, soft-spoken, outgoing, and engaged in philosophical and practical pursuits. He introduced me to the work of Iris Murdoch (among others), especially her then newly published *Sovereignty of Good*.[3] He enabled me to see the beauty, power, and dilemmas of a teacher in love with investigating the worlds in which we live. When I did fall into despair, I had available Murdoch's notions of contemplation and the good, a history of beloved and significant teachers who had put me in touch with the grace of great things,[4] and loving family support. It was during that time that I came to rely on and understand further the notions of love and their relation to teaching and learning. It was during this time that I faced one of the paradoxes of teaching, one to which Parker Palmer alludes in his *Courage to Teach*[5]: to resuscitate scorned love, one needs to embrace love.

I don't suppose that all those who lose their loves while teaching can have them resuscitated through despair work and embracing a larger love. But it appears that others have experienced similar terrain. One of Palmer's key understandings in *The Courage to Teach* is the recognition that as teachers, we need to attend to our inner lives. That work sanctioned and authorized the journey I was about to take, a journey that emphasized the intellectual, emotional, and spiritual components of teaching. It was a journey that gave me crucial sustenance and enabled me to resuscitate my love of learning and teaching. There were two "stops" along the way: first, I needed to deal with my feelings of despair, and then I had to affirm, once more, my love.

DESPAIR IN TEACHING

I don't think I'm alone in experiencing despair. It seems to come with the turf of teaching. But first, it might be helpful to distinguish this despair from disillusionment. Both are experienced in teaching, but they are not synonymous. In teaching, as in many of life's other ventures, we frequently encounter unfulfilled expectations, dashed hopes, and an altered, grimmer sense of reality. Many new teachers face this disillusionment. Such disillusionment feels disheartening and can be demoralizing, but as I understand the phenomenon, it neither strikes to the core of the person or endeavor nor undercuts an enduring sense of hope as despair does. Disillusionment bespeaks the possibility of a "reasonable" re-adjustment to a difficult situation. Despair entails a sense of doomed foreclosure, a circumstance that requires some sort of radical personal or contextual transformation.

As I understand it, despair arises from a numbness, an emptiness, and brings with it feelings of pain and anguish. For teachers, it is an emptiness that seems to have as one of its sources a sense of betrayal around and a rejection of our love of learning and teaching. Despair in teaching is a sense that one can no longer be the teacher who loves his subject, the worlds it opens, and his students. When the subject no longer enchants, it is difficult to invite students to engage in those other worlds. The invitation to share in the allure seems empty, and the attentive approach to students seems pointless. It is a sense that one cannot be the teacher one desires to be.

Some of this is captured by Chai, a Chinese emigrant in John Derbyshire's novel *Seeing Calvin Coolidge in a Dream*, when he recalls a former teacher's gifts and stories. Chai talks about his beloved teacher, Ouyang, who practiced an "art . . . so pure as to be transparent, but I see now that he was in fact an extraordinarily gifted teacher who took his work very seriously."[6] Ouyang told his students the following fable, one in which a crooked doctor would take money from people and give them ineffective medicine. Sometimes the medicine was poisonous and the patient died.

> In the natural course of things the doctor himself left this world at last and found himself standing in judgment before Lord Yan-Wang, the emperor of hell. It is difficult to imagine any crimes worse than yours, said Lord Yan-Wang. When people were suffering and helpless they placed their trust in you and paid you with silver and gold. You repaid them with poison and death. Eighteenth level! (In our old Taoist religion there were eighteen levels in hell, the deepest levels for the worst sinners.)

STORIES OF THE COURAGE TO TEACH

Well, there was the poor doctor—though of course we should not feel *very* much compassion for him—down on the eighteenth level, resting up between tortures, crying out in remorse for his evil life, when he heard a knocking from below. Then very faintly he heard a voice coming up from beneath the floor of his dungeon: *Who are you? What crime did you commit to be immured so deep in hell?* The doctor was astonished. He had never heard that there were more than eighteen levels in hell; yet here, apparently, was a nineteenth level! Placing his mouth close to the floor he called down: I was a false doctor! But what great crime did you commit that you have been banished to a level so deep it has never been known to men? Came the answer: False Teacher.[7]

Teachers in despair feel like they're in hell. For the teacher who knows the power, beauty, and wonder of being touched by the grace of great things, who has been given that gift by another teacher, who has experienced what it means to attend lovingly to students and then have it taken away, the sense is devastating. The guiding direction, the integrity, the identity of a teacher vanishes. If one continues to teach, one becomes a false teacher, one acts in bad faith, one sits in despair.

While teaching at the university, I had fallen into despair. I no longer felt the power and allure of my beloved subjects. I had lost touch with the transformative power of education and with the power of teaching others about education. I grew wary and skeptical. I still approached my students with respect, but I began to fear that I might say something caustic or derisive, either in class or on one of my students' papers. I became frustrated, angry, and paradoxically, numb and empty. I slowly realized that my faith and intrigue in what I had to offer my students, my own love of education, had diminished. I felt like I had little to offer them.

Gradually I came to understand that I had to engage in what Joanna Macy calls "despair work." She writes:

Despair cannot be banished by injections of optimism or sermons on positive thinking. Like grief, it must be acknowledged and worked through. This means it must be named and validated as a healthy, normal human response to the situation we find ourselves in. Faced and experienced, its power can be used, as the frozen defenses of the psyche thaw and new energies are released. Something analogous to grief work is in order. "Despair work" is different from grief work in that its aim is not acceptance of loss—indeed, the "loss" has not yet occurred and is hardly to be "accepted." But it is similar in the dynamics unleashed by the willingness to acknowledge, feel, and express inner pain.[8]

"Despair work" in teaching is needed. We need to approach it as a normal and healthy response to our teaching situations. I needed—teachers need—to understand the contours of this kind of despair, recognize that it is assiduously avoided by members of our culture, understand that its expression is not morbid, and feel and articulate the pain and discomfort associated with it.

When I have talked with practicing teachers who describe themselves as "burned out" or on the precipice of burning out, they frequently express feelings of emptiness, loneliness, frustration, and anger. They look at me as a teacher educator and ask, "Why didn't someone at the university tell me what I was getting into? Why didn't someone warn me?" They seem to be saying that if only someone had told them about the pain, the suffering, maybe they could have avoided it. In my classes at the university, I have had teachers walk in unsure if they are still teachers. They have left their classroom and come into mine, feeling devastated, tending their wounds, and wondering what to do. For each of these teachers, it is helpful to recognize the pain and discomfort, to honor the struggle, and to find avenues to discuss those feelings. Sometimes we're successful; other times we're not. Slowly I've come to believe that we need to contemplate one of the key sources of our despair,

STORIES OF THE COURAGE TO TEACH

our scorned love of learning and teaching, and confront one of the paradoxes of teaching: to resuscitate scorned love, one needs to embrace love.

Affirming Love in Teaching

How do we resuscitate scorned love, and why would we want to embrace a love that has caused such pain? This isn't simple terrain, but I think there are some ways to walk through it. I am suggesting that there are at least three kinds of love involved in the narrative of despair: a romantic love of learning and teaching; an attentive, loving orientation toward students; and a transformative, enlarged love. Good teaching entails a kind of romantic love of the learning enterprise. It is motivated by and infuses others with a love of inquiry. This love is a yearning for and reaching beyond oneself to engage other (natural and social) worlds. To infuse others with this love of learning, we have to attend to our students. We do this so that we can connect them with the material we have found so alluring. An attentive love looks clearly and with determination for the good in our students so that we can see their desires and the ways we can put them in touch with the grace of great things. Teaching in and with these loves is a vulnerable undertaking, one that leaves the teacher open to pain and rejection. When a teacher's love of learning or attentiveness toward students has been scorned, he may find himself in despair. This despair afflicts the teacher's soul.

We come to a larger love when we experience pain and suffering. In parenting, I have come to a larger love when my children face life's obstacles and enormities and I realize they must do it "on their own." In teaching, we come to a larger love when we see our students' lives disfigured by the forces of greed and selfishness and domination, when we've become worn down by the weeks, months, and years of struggling against these and other forces. We also come to this larger love when, as teachers, we experience our own scorned love, a love that may have been disfigured in the past, distorted by powers greater than you or I. When confronted with our students' pain and our own scorned love of learning and teaching, we experience pain and suffering. In these situations, I have relied on a larger love to see me through those difficult times and help me stand the pain and suffering.

This larger love seems to be one way to come to terms with teaching's despair, to inform the quiet heroism that teaching must become. If guided by an enlarged love, teaching can become an ongoing struggle that nourishes our students' souls and our own. Through exploring and understanding our teaching despair, along with our love of learning in teaching and its loss, we may come to see more clearly the possibilities in a larger love. An enlarged love entails a diminished sense of self (ego) in the teaching enterprise, an attentive gaze outward toward the other, and an accompanying search for the good. With this larger love, I have refocused my attention so as to see more clearly the muddles and the opportunities, the headaches and the delights before me. I have had to look for and underscore the good, the beauty, and the grace that lies within the situation while recognizing the inescapable struggle and pain that also exists. And I have had to work at getting beyond my own selfish concerns, my "ego noise," so that I could discern the terrain more clearly. These are the contours of a larger love.

This larger love holds us in the pain, in the paradox, so that we can see it through and see through it. It is during these times, at least in teaching, when we recall the grace and power of our earlier loves. A teacher in despair, whose love of learning has been lost or scorned, may come to understand how to embrace love again. If we do, we come to transform the terms of our love of learning and our love for students. We become reacquainted with the grace, wonder, and beauty of both the lure of learning and attentive love. If we learn to suffer the opposites, during those times of hardship and suffering, we also learn the grace that attends enduring and living with the pain. In this way, a teacher comes to understand the world as a place of connection and pain, one that can be tilted toward goodness and love. The teacher comes to understand that the material world is not all that exists; a spiritual realm is also reality.

Not all teachers come to a spiritual place. Parker Palmer did; others have, and so did I. This is difficult and uncomfortable material for me (and perhaps many others) to explore. In many ways and for many years, I have shied away from things spiritual. I have attempted to embrace a sense of beauty (and horror) of the worlds around us. I have approached these worlds with awe and wonder. I have tried to approach other individuals with a sense of respect. But to call this spiritual, to designate these experiences as within the realm of, or partaking in, the spirit, has taken some time for me to consider and accept. Others need not accept the spiritual tenets proposed here. One can, perhaps, embrace a larger love without embracing the spiritual. I'm not quite sure. It seems, however, that when we step into this larger love, we are placed in front of a window that opens up to the spirit.

Much of what I've talked about focuses on an inward journey. If we are to teach with some integrity and wholeness, those interior spaces have to be explored. But I have overlooked much in my account. There is a world of power, structures, and institutional forces that contort and distort our loves and contribute to our despair. And not only do these forces foster our despair, but they also cloud our understanding of our lives and work. In an era of narrow educational accountability and standardization, an awareness of teaching's despair, love, and spirit tends to get lost. As a teacher and teacher educator, I struggle against that.

As a teacher educator, I recall that the teachers who taught me the most loved their subjects and cared for their students. Mr. Keener, my demanding high school social studies teacher, showed us how history illuminated our worlds. He made us sit up straight in class and take notes, and we understood these demands as marks of his respect for us. Mr. Fleenor, my geometry teacher, lured us into the world of geometry by helping us think logically, clearly, and elegantly. When we entered his room, we knew we would work at this together. Miss Dutro, my biology teacher, could look at a roadside weed and show us its ecological niche. She turned weeds into fascinating subjects, and she also believed we were fascinating.

All three of these teachers taught with a love of learning and attention to the students they taught. Their invitation to learn amounted to more than classroom order and an offering of facts, skills, and concepts to master. It was based on their love of learning and yearning to connect students with their beloved subject matter. What would they do in this era of narrow accountability? I don't know, but I do know that they have passed on to me an honored and valuable legacy.

NOTES

1. Macy, J. *World as Lover, World as Self.* Berkeley, Calif.: Parallax Press, 1991.
2. Murdoch, I. *The Sovereignty of Good.* New York: Schocken, 1971.
3. Murdoch (1971).
4. Parker Palmer draws on this notion to convey the power and wonder entailed in understanding the world, others, and ourselves in educational settings. See Palmer, P. J. *The Courage to Teach: Exploring the Inner Landscape of a Teacher's Life.* San Francisco: Jossey-Bass, 1998.
5. Palmer (1998).
6. Derbyshire, J. *Seeing Calvin Coolidge in a Dream.* New York: St. Martin's/Griffin, 1996, p. 85.
7. Derbyshire (1996), p. 85.
8. Macy (1991), p. 16.

Presently a professor of education at the University of Colorado at Boulder, Daniel P. Liston began teaching prereading and math at the Children's School in Richmond, Indiana, in 1976. Two years later, he moved to the Rosa Parks Middle School in Baltimore, Maryland. In 1982, he began his career in higher education and has taught at the University of Wisconsin at Madison and at Washington University in St. Louis. Aside from teaching, he codirects the Roaring Fork Teacher Education Project and is a research fellow at the Center for Educational Research, Analysis and Innovation at the University of Wisconsin–Milwaukee. He has received several awards for outstanding teaching, including being named as a finalist for the Presidential Teachers Scholar Award, and he received the Teacher Recognition Award at the University of Colorado, the most significant student-generated award for excellence in teaching on the campus. Liston has published many articles on teaching, and his latest book, *Love and Despair in Teaching: Feeling and Thinking in Educational Settings* (Routledge, forthcoming), focuses on the role of deeply personal feelings and beliefs in our teaching. Earlier works include *Capitalist Schools* (Routledge, 1987), *Teacher Education and the Social Conditions of Schooling* (with Ken Zeichner; Routledge, 1991), and *Curriculum in Conflict* (with Landon Beyer; Teachers College Press, 1996). Liston says he feels "most alive in my teaching when our classroom conversation takes on a life of its own; when we listen, think, laugh, and cry, and we are changed."

Many career teachers struggle for decades to make their peace with their chosen profession. Underpaid and overworked, many teachers are acutely aware of how little status they are accorded in our culture. As a result of the perceived indignities, some teachers abandon the profession, others plod on resentful and angry, and some come to discover the value, meaning, and dignity of their work. Rosetta Marantz Cohen chronicles how her husband moves from resisting to resenting to coming to terms with and then embracing his profession. Through this journey, Sam Scheer is able to finally see "teaching as a whole way of being in the world," and with this realization comes energy, heart, and peace.

—S.M.I.

Sam Scheer
Coming to Terms with a Lifetime of Teaching

Rosetta Marantz Cohen

Located two exits up from Hartford, Connecticut, on Interstate 91, Windsor High School is in many ways a quintessential American public school—large and ethnically diverse, vibrant and chaotic. A visitor senses immediately the power and complexity of such a school: a pulsing rap beat blares from a car in the parking lot; Latin music rises out of a classroom; an ad for the Black Gospel Choir hangs above the cafeteria door next to a poster for the Gay and Lesbian Alliance. What an interesting and challenging place to teach, one thinks, walking down the hallway to Sam Scheer's classroom. What a perfect place for Sam to have found his niche.

In room 202, Sam Scheer, twenty-year veteran, sits in a circle with his sixteen Advanced Placement English students. They are discussing the narrative voice in *Pride and Prejudice* as the sound of jackhammers rises up from the parking lot—the remnants of a renovation project begun months earlier.

"I want to remind you," Sam says, "that the narrators we have seen in twentieth-century novels are not always trustworthy. In *The Great Gatsby,* for example, the narrator is himself morally implicated in the action of the novel." Sam speaks in beautiful prose sentences, elliptically constructed, effortlessly fluent. "In *Portrait of the Artist,* the narrator is immature at the start. We're conditioned to root for the narrator, to take his word for things, but in those modern novels we saw that it isn't always right to do so. . . ."

Students are writing down his words, nodding. "But what about in the nineteenth century?" Sam asks. "What is your impression of the narrator's voice in a nineteenth-century novel like *Pride and Prejudice?*" There is a lag of silence as students make the sleepy transition from passive listening to participation. Sam waits it out.

"She seems trustworthy to me," offers a boy to Sam's right. "She seems objective."

"Why?" Sam presses. "How do you know she's trustworthy?" Gradually, with the grudging help of all sixteen students, Sam begins to extract the evidence: The narrator's voice is the "golden mean," he says, the harmonious balance against which all other characters are measured. Students look, in turn, at every major character in the book, comparing the characters' voices to the elegant vernacular of the narrator. "Find it in the text," Sam says, again and again. When a student gives a rushed or unsupported answer, Sam hesitates: "I must respectfully disagree," he says—his language always perfectly attuned to the cocky, fragile sensibilities of bright adolescents. By the end of the forty-five-minute period, he has built a seamless argument, alluding along the way to Mozart and Aristotle.

"And wouldn't you know it," he says, "as the hero and heroine come together at the end of the book, whose language do they start to emulate?"

"The narrator," a girl whispers under her breath. "The golden mean," says another. "And the Mozart-like harmony of the narrator's voice becomes the voice of the couple," says Sam. Everyone is scribbling away. Then the bell rings.

Slightly ragged from the work of Austen, Sam encounters class number two, a senior English standard-level class for college-bound students. After the all-white A.P. class, the diversity of this group is striking. Now there are only six Anglo faces in a group of twenty-eight. The sleepy compliance of the A.P. students has been replaced with a distracted energy; some students come in dancing; one gives Sam a high five as he enters. "Yo, Mr. Scheer!" says a boy in a giant black parka.

"OK, listen up," Sam says. "I've got some good news for you." The shuffling and talking continue, settling into a light patter. "We're reading *The Joy Luck Club*," he says. Though they have been working on the book for three weeks, Sam tells me he must remind them each day. "Every day we start from scratch," he says.

"This book is divided into four sections, and you guys have already read three with me. I know you've had some difficulty with it, and that's cool. But we're at a really great part now, and I'm going to read it out loud to you, and then I'm going to explain it to you." He begins to read, and the class falls silent.

"This is Suyuan Woo's story of exile," he says, "and of the giving up of her two babies." His voice is lilting and dramatic; the story unfolds in a dreamy, easy way: the mother grows sick, struggles to carry her children, leaves them with a note at the side of the road. . . . Sam interrupts his reading every few minutes to root the listeners on: "Now listen to this," he says, and "You're going to like this; hang in there with me. . . ." They do. The end is poignant, emotional. Many in the class seem genuinely moved.

"Now I know that some of you are the children of immigrants," he says. "I wonder if this story seems true to you; I wonder, does it remind you of stories you've heard at home?"

One after another, the students tell their own family stories. Someone's mother treats her like she was still a child in China, affording her none of the freedoms enjoyed by other American children. Someone's cousin was shot at the Mexican border. Someone else speaks about how different life was in Jamaica. When the bell rings, only a few students stand up to leave.

"That was a good one," Sam says afterward. "I really enjoyed that."

After so many years in the field, after teaching in five schools, after being riffed and underpaid and taken for granted, Sam has come to truly love the work he does. At the same time, he has become a passionate champion of the profession—a "master" teacher in the truest sense of the word. His transformation is as much a surprise to him, I think, as it is to me, his wife, who has watched the American educational system buffet him about year after year, undermine his morale, and test his mettle. It is not easy for anyone to continue to love work that is so demanding and unglamorous. But evenings, at the dinner table, it is clear that Sam has moved into a new relationship with the profession. The old ambivalence seems to have vanished. Sam speaks about his students now, and his colleagues too, with genuine affection, interest, and pleasure.

What has brought about this recommitment to a problematic profession? I think that a number of converging factors have influenced his transformation. The first one may simply have to do with Sam's age and the changes that affect many teachers after years in the field. There is a vast psychological literature that seeks to explain such transformations. Erikson[1] and Levinson,[2] for example, describe a predictable period of equanimity that besets many men of Sam's age—a quieting of ambition, an impulse to help others. Super and Hall,[3] writing specifically on career development, describe a similar stage, after age forty-five, when many teachers examine their life choices and make critical final decisions about careers. This midlife moment is perceived as the last point at which the profession can be abandoned—a crisis that, once weathered, can lead to a sense of recommitment. Finally, Francis Fuller,[4] in her seminal work on "stages of teacher concern," offers what seems like a neat description of Sam's current state: having navigated the early, tumultuous years, Fuller would identify Sam as a mature veteran, possessing the characteristics that mark that passage: an interest in student concerns and needs, an interest in the philosophy of the profession, and a marked loss of interest in popularity.

Like so many teachers, Sam began his professional life in another field altogether. A child of the counterculture, he spent his twenties as a musician, living a kind of itinerant life—without schedule or boss—touring as the opening act for various 1970s folk groups. This artistic life was followed by an intense period of graduate study, at Oxford, where he earned a master's degree in philosophy, writing on the late poetry of Wallace Stevens. Neither one of these life stages in any way foreshadowed his future career.

Sam, in fact, stumbled into teaching in a rather grudging way. Home from graduate school and deeply in debt, he came to teaching as a way station on the real, as-yet-undecided path to his life's work. He started off in private schools, teaching guitar and English, with (I glean from the stories he has told me) a somewhat laid-back attitude about his job. This stage I would call "ambivalence and detachment." Every once in a while, Sam would become engaged by the mind of a student—usually a very bright one—and would work hard to find ways to stimulate the student's curiosity about literature. But mostly he taught on automatic pilot, using the classroom as a forum for talking to himself about books and ideas.

"In college and graduate school," Sam says, "I fell prey to a misguided form of 'bardolotry'—of hero worship for the great writers. I was so enamored of certain texts—it was a kind of religion for me—that it kept me aloof from the kids I taught. I thought [about my students], Either you get it or you don't; either you see it or you don't; and if you don't, I'm not going to put too much effort into you. . . . I don't want you to think I wasn't a competent and responsible teacher. I was. But my heart was with the text, not the student. I thought, the kids were there for the literature, not that the literature was there for the kids."

In the past few years, however, Sam says he sees his work in very different terms. "I now see reading," he says, "as a political act, as a way to help kids become advocates for themselves and know themselves. You can do it with the classics; you don't need to teach watered-down stuff; you just need to go at the literature in a different way. I used to teach writing as if every kid should become a literary critic. Now I teach it as a tool, as a way to redress grievances. I say, 'You have a gripe with a colleague or a corporation? Lay out your reasons; argue it logically.'" Sam says that he is now a pragmatist. "In the past," he says, "I had a kind of old-fashioned idealism that couldn't hold up against the realities of the classroom. I see now that you can be pragmatic; you can teach to where the kids are without debasing the material, without compromising your integrity. In fact, there is more integrity in doing it this way."

Changes in the economy and in the culture at large may also help explain Sam's recommitment. Sam began his teaching career in the late 1970s, at a time when the work of the teacher seemed less "cool." Graduates of good colleges in those days went immediately to law school or else to Wall Street, where hostile takeovers and the beginnings of a boom market were making millionaires out of the most pedestrian intellects. In the early 1980s, living in New York City, Sam would walk each morning to his battered Honda Civic past scores of young men in Armani suits, hailing cabs to their bank jobs. At night, he would curse the stubborn part of him that insisted on a life of literature. Having grown up in a lower-middle-class household, Sam suffered greatly from his decision to live in what he called "dignified poverty." It colored his view of teaching for many years. It created a nagging sense of dissatisfaction.

By the late 1980s, however, states like Connecticut had passed laws that dramatically increased teachers' salaries. Though teachers were still not high-paid professionals, their salaries were respectable. Moving to the country, to a working-class, academic community in western Massachusetts, also helped blunt the sense of being a have-not. Now, living on two teachers' salaries, he says he felt suddenly "upper-middle-class"—a dramatic change in lifestyle and mind-set. "I owned a home; I had a wife and child. I was far away from the tantalizing alternatives that had distracted me in New York. It was easier to feel good about teaching in Northampton," Sam says. "The cushion of financial security was very liberating for me. It allowed me to see my work for what it was—as useful and meaningful."

Sam could also assess his choice to teach in light of the growing professional dissatisfactions he saw among his friends. "All around me, in the last few years, friends were reassessing their careers, feeling spiritually bereft, looking for ways to volunteer their time to make a difference. That's not a problem for a teacher. You help a kid reimagine his or her possibilities and you've made a difference. You get a kid to connect with poetry, and you've changed that person for life."

When I ask Sam to describe his relationship to the profession today, he says that he is now at peace with his choice. "Teaching is a whole way of being in the world," he says. "It's self-creation and service. It's artistic and altruistic. When I started out in this field, I saw teaching as a short-term job. I resisted *being* a teacher, in the fullest sense of the word. Now I see it as my life's work."

NOTES

1. Erikson, E. *The Life Cycle Completed.* New York: Norton, 1985.
2. Levinson, B. *The Seasons of a Man's Life.* New York: Knopf, 1978.
3. Super, D. C., and Hall, D. T. "Career Development: Exploration and Planning." *Annual Review of Psychology,* 1978, *29,* 333–372.
4. Fuller, F. F. "Concerns of Teachers: A Developmental Characterization. *American Educational Research Journal,* 1969, *6,* 207–266.

Rosetta Marantz Cohen began her teaching career in 1980 as a high school English teacher at the Calhoun School in New York City. In 1988, she joined the faculty at Trinity University in San Antonio, Texas. She presently teaches in the Department of Education and Child Study at Smith College in Northampton, Massachusetts. The recipient of many research fellowships and grants, she writes about the life of the teacher in American society. She is the author, with Sam Scheer, of *The Work of Teachers in America: A Social History Through Stories* (Erlbaum, 1997) and *A Lifetime of Teaching: Portraits of Five Veteran High School Teachers* (Teachers College Press, 1991). "I feel most alive in my teaching," she writes, "when I am teaching material I love in a school that values teaching."

There are many moments when teaching feels too hard and painful—days when we walk out of class distraught by how lifeless or hostile our students appeared, weeks when our efforts to connect with students feel clumsy and mechanical, occasions when the institutional forces seem too contradictory to continue. That teaching is hard and exacting is not news. But what keeps teachers going? What keeps their hearts energized despite myriad obstacles? Researcher Sonia Nieto and thirty-year Boston high school teacher Stephen Gordon came together as part of an inquiry group of veteran urban teachers to explore how teachers keep heart despite the challenges they face in their work.

—S.M.I.

Adult Conversations About Unasked Questions
Teaching for Educational Justice

Sonia Nieto and Stephen Gordon

What are the truths that teachers believe about what they do, and how are these truths evident in their practice? What does it mean to teach with integrity, especially among culturally and linguistically diverse students in impoverished urban schools? And what inspires the most devoted teachers to continue in spite of the challenges they face on a daily basis?

These questions have become especially compelling for both of us, although for slightly different reasons. Sonia has been working with prospective and practicing teachers for over twenty years, and she finds this work more significant yet more challenging than ever before, especially given the public's diminishing support for education. Steve, after working for more than thirty years in the Boston Public Schools, is as devoted as he has ever been to his students, colleagues, and the profession of teaching but ever more impatient with the absence of student success and teacher respect. For both of us, conditions both in and out of school—inequitably financed schools, a crumbling infrastructure, overcrowded classrooms, mandated quick-fix nostrums, a climate of blaming, and hopelessness and despair—have made our work more difficult. But we also know that in spite of disintegrating support for urban schools and the growing numbers of disengaged students and despairing teachers, some teachers refuse to give up, sustaining a fierce belief in their students and in the work they do. What it is that keeps some teachers dedicated and enthusiastic in spite of the many challenges they face? What makes the difference?

THE INQUIRY GROUP: "WHAT KEEPS TEACHERS GOING IN SPITE OF EVERYTHING?"

Sonia decided that the best way to find out was to listen to and talk with teachers as they struggled with hard questions related to teaching in urban schools today. She wanted to hear from superior teachers who continue to teach in spite of the numerous individual, institutional, and social obstacles that get in the way of their work. Her research design was simple and straightforward: She just wanted to talk with teachers. She convened an inquiry group of eight veteran teachers to share and discuss what it was that kept them in teaching.[1]

The inquiry group met monthly throughout the 1999–2000 school year, culminating with an all-day meeting in May 2000 at a retreat center outside Boston. All of those who took part in the group are highly respected teachers. They are passionate about teaching, and they think of themselves as intellectuals and professionals. They also unabashedly love their students and hold high expectations of them. Most are veteran teachers, although two had been in the system for less than ten years. They teach a variety of subjects, including algebra, English, African American history, and language arts in Cape Verdean Crioulo or Spanish. Some have mentored new teachers into the profession, and a few have been involved in professional development activities in the district and beyond.

They participated together in a number of activities, including writing in response to specific assignments related to their work. They also talked about the books they read together and about the challenges of daily classroom life, and they occasionally exchanged e-mail with one another. The meetings were what Steve Gordon, the most veteran teacher of the group, described as "adult conversations about unasked questions."

LESSONS FROM THE INQUIRY GROUP

Collaborations between teachers and professors are often based on unequal and unrealistic expectations. Professors are expected to hold most of the theoretical knowledge, and teachers are expected to be experts in terms of practical knowledge. We have come to understand, however, that in the best cases, teachers' practice is based on theorizing about actual classroom experiences and professors' theoretical knowledge is based on work in real settings. Through our collaboration in the inquiry group, we have become convinced that teachers and university professors have a great deal to teach and learn from one another. The inquiry group helped us put into words what it means to teach with integrity and hope, particularly in urban public schools today. It also helped us understand that teaching can be thought of as "doing educational justice," particularly when it is done in the kinds of schools that have largely been abandoned by the public.

Teaching from Deeply Held Values

bell hooks describes the classroom as "a location of possibility,"[2] and this sentiment cogently captures the fact that it is in their classrooms that teachers enact their most deeply held values. The inquiry group confirmed for us what we had already suspected: teachers' beliefs are deeply embedded in their classroom practices. Teachers do not—indeed, they cannot—leave their values at the door when they enter their classrooms. As much as they might want to hide or avoid them, their values and beliefs slip in the door with them. As Ambrizeth Lima, a member of the inquiry group, explained, "Even in our indifference, we take a position." If this is true, then the best that teachers can do is confront these values candidly to understand how they help or hinder the teachers' work with their students.

How teachers' values make their way into their classroom practice became clearer to us as we continued to meet. One of the first activities was writing "teaching autobiographies." In these narratives, the teachers described how and why they came to teaching as a career. Several of them addressed their sociocultural and sociopolitical realities as the fundamental reason they became teachers. That is, their own identities were often the guiding forces in steering them toward teaching. For some, it was their growing realization as young adults that literacy and education had been systematically withheld from their people and from other culturally and politically dominated communities; for others, it was political work in antiracism or antiapartheid work or in community organizing for educational equity.

Affirming Identity

Because the inquiry group teachers understood the significance of identity in their own lives, they worked hard at affirming their students' identities. They rejected the notion that culture, race, or language is responsible for school failure. Instead, they believed that affirming students' identities could support their learning. Rather than exclude students' social and cultural identities from the curriculum and instruction, the inquiry group teachers used many opportunities to encourage students to explore their backgrounds, language, and communities. This was evident in the curriculum they developed, the books they used, and the other activities in which they engaged students. At the same time, the teachers recognized that it was both necessary and positive for students to grow beyond their own limited experiences, and so these teachers focused their curricula on ways to get students to engage with realities different from their own. Consequently, rap could exist alongside Shakespeare as exemplars of language, discourse, and culture: understanding one should help a student understand the other.

For instance, Steve would ask students to share and discuss the lyrics of hip-hop recordings, believing that developing student literacy includes their expressing and examining how the words in rap songs capture their views of American society. Steve has used rap in class for students to see lyrics as poetry and to direct students' attention to the form and function of language and to their ability to interpret author intent—in this case, the rapper's. He describes how he did this in one of his classrooms: "I taught minicourses called Poetry Through Music where students were required to copy lyrics, including rap; distribute them to the class; play the song; and then discuss the meaning and structure of the lyric." Through this course, he learned a great deal about hip-hop, especially about the politically focused group Public Enemy. "I continued to ask students to bring in hip-hop that expressed views on social issues, for I believe that developing students' literacy includes their analyzing to what extent and in what ways the words they hear in rap accurately express and describe their view of American society—Freire's 'reading the world.'" In another assignment, he had students pick one of Shakespeare's soliloquies, discuss the meaning and import of the character's words, and then translate the soliloquy into conversational English or a rap lyric.

Believing In and Loving Our Students

Another deeply held value shared by all the teachers in the group was what Steve called "a fundamental belief in the lives and minds of students." This was foremost among all their reasons for remaining in teaching, and it was the one response everyone agreed on. What did this mean in terms of their practice? For one, it meant that they refused to accept excuses for students' lack of effort or achievement. They stubbornly insisted that their students were capable and smart, in spite of the labels the students may have inherited after years in the school system. The teachers focused not on personal failings on the part of the students but rather on *conditions in the school* that could help explain these problems. These teachers also knew that personal connections with their students were crucial to learning, and they worked hard at building relationships with their students. Though these connections are important, they are not always easy. At one point, Steve Gordon shared with us an entry from his journal that illustrated the uncertainty, dread, and indecision that even veteran teachers can face as they struggle with how to make their classes relevant and make these important connections with their students.

My story begins Sunday afternoon, February 28, at vacation's end. I have just finished *Fist Stick Knife Gun*,[3] Chapters 17–25. With the exception of Chapters 22 and 24, the chapters are about what Geoffrey Canada did to help the kids of Harlem. What do I want my students to do? As I think this, fear comes over me. What is its cause? What is it about teaching these ninth graders that generates such uncertainty and dread? Why do I feel that it is so hard, that coming up with what is worthwhile is so hard, that being with them for one hour is so hard? What causes this anxiety? Yes, it is a challenge. Yes, I believe in doing it. In fact, it is my chosen profession, my decision to do this with students or teachers. But why is it so hard, so indefinite, so fraught with anxiety as I try to decide what to do, thinking that Tashia or Crystal or Thomas or . . . will not approve of my decisions, my work?

I think of June and Seth and Denise, my colleagues, as if I am supposed to be able to do something that will affirm that I am a good teacher, appreciated by my students because I have come up with something that will empower them, that facilitates their learning, that gives them the choice to learn. . . . I am trapped by my own psyche and soul, which strive to do the right thing, yet I do not want to work so alone, so hard, and so emotionally in order to do the right thing.

I want some certainty, some peace, a feeling that I cannot have. Do I just live through the anxiety of being a responsible adult who will have to fight for what he believes in, who will have to demand that students do *x, y,* and *z,* even as I search for the ways to involve them, engage them, on their own so that the class is theirs, so that literacy grows out of activities that are valued by them and consonant with my deepest values and beliefs?

Doing Educational Justice

Throughout our meetings, it became clear that this particular group of teachers thought of teaching both as intellectual work and in terms of social justice. For them, teaching was not simply mastering technical skills, or "tricks of the trade." That is, while they conceived of their learning as ongoing and necessary in order to improve their craft, they also thought of their professional growth as necessary in the struggle against the injustices faced by youngsters who attend schools that do not live up to the promise of educational equality. This idea was most powerfully expressed one day as we were discussing the profession's growing obsession with "best practices." Steve Gordon responded, "Rather than 'best practices,' we should have 'loving practices.' " This admonition was one that we referred to throughout the remainder of our meetings.

Having read and studied Paulo Freire's letters to "those who dare teach,"[4] Sonia asked the inquiry group teachers to write a letter they would give to a new teacher. Steve took this assignment as a way to think about his own commitment to the profession and to express the inescapable but necessary dilemmas that accompany being a teacher. He expressed his ideas about what it means to "do educational justice" with and for students in urban schools. This is, in part, what he wrote:

LETTER TO A NEW TEACHER
Dear Colleague,

You have made your decision. Against the advice of relatives and friends who may have counseled you against this career path, you have decided to teach. Reasons beyond starting salary and perceived prestige have called you to become a teacher, fully aware of how little gratitude and respect teachers receive in our free enterprise society, which values wealth over justice.

You have concluded that being an adult responsible for the education of children is your calling. Why is that? What do you hope to give and receive as a teacher? When you see yourself in a classroom working with other people's children, what do you see yourself doing and saying that is so necessary to you—and them? Why do you want to teach? Why this school? Why these particular children? I suggest you write the answers to these questions now; examine and discuss them with those who care about your happiness. I hope that your answers motivate and sustain you in your day-to-day struggle to make a difference in the lives of your students. I hope the answers give you the courage and self-knowledge to endure and succeed—and to find allies in your work.

I welcome you into my chosen profession. Beginning on your first day of teaching and perhaps never leaving, anxiety and self-doubt may be your constant shadow. They have been for me. In my worst moments, I have felt isolated and ineffective, even abandoned by colleagues and administrators. I see and feel the realities of my students, their wants and needs, and I think I have failed them, that I have not done the right thing, not done enough. And I have become angry, ascribing my students' failure to racial and economic injustice.

I have learned to accept, even welcome, this dread, guilt, and anger. These emotions I believe have kept me honest, a spur to understanding what I must do and a shield against facile, mindless so-called solutions that repeatedly surface in a culture that refuses to recognize complexity and confront injustice. Rather than give you advice, let me share with you how I have attempted to sustain my commitment to my students, colleagues, and students after thirty years of teaching high school in Boston.

I have learned to acknowledge and express the anger that arises from the wide discrepancy between my goals for my students and their current achievements. I ascribe this disparity to the failure of our system to do educational justice for my students. I have seen students whose power and will to learn seem to have atrophied, students who do not possess the motivation and self-discipline necessary to excel, students who seem conditioned to compliance or resistance. I interpret these student attitudes and behaviors as the result of low expectations, misguided pedagogy, and spurious systemwide "solutions"—including the current standards and high-stakes testing movements. Nevertheless, I continue to hold my students personally responsible for their performance.

No matter how emotionally seductive and satisfying, I have consciously sought to avoid generalizations and accusations that might mitigate my disappointment at the expense of my students—their language, their parents, their race and culture. I acknowledge my frustration and do not repress my anger. By expressing my anger, I am forced to examine my students' learning needs and my teaching practices. By so doing, I am affirming hope and the willingness to take responsibility for my students' success.

I try to express my hopes and disappointments to my students, telling them what I expect and want from them. I believe that my expressed expectations will help teach them to

73

take more responsibility for their own education so that they will not merely comply or resist. I frequently ask them to evaluate the educational validity of what and how I am teaching. They must participate in their own education: a respectful fit between their individual cognitive and linguistic development and the school's academic requirements must be found. I have not yet succeeded in creating such a classroom community that counteracts years of negative school culture, but I will continue trying. This has been hard for me because I do not yet know how to engender sufficient student self-discipline and self-determination. Maybe you can help me. I have much more to learn.

To survive and grow, I had to find colleagues who share my angers, hopes, beliefs, and assumptions about students and teaching. When I have discussed my teaching with these caring colleagues, I work to specify exactly what troubles me; I fight the fear that having problems means I am doing something wrong. By example, I seek to help my colleagues become more professionally vulnerable, to name the individual classroom realities that inhibit their success and threaten their self-image as competent professionals. I avoid solving colleagues' problems by giving them advice; instead, through questioning, I work to find a way for them to reveal exactly what is troubling and why. Sharing difficult truths and emotions has been necessary for my personal and professional development. Fortunately, I have been a member of several teacher-research and inquiry groups that have supported this honesty, helping me examine and improve my teaching.

But these truths and emotions have been necessary but not sufficient to endure. I have learned to turn what troubles me about my students or my classroom into a researchable question. This may be difficult at first, for I have had to cultivate an inquiry stance about my teaching practice. I have

STORIES OF THE COURAGE TO TEACH

learned to do research about my troubling questions, finding and reading what fellow teachers and researchers have discovered. For example, as an English teacher, I joined the National Council of Teachers of English and the International Reading Association. I read their professional journals. I want to create an intellectual community in my school wherein teachers share and discuss articles and books. I have become a teacher because I believe in intellectual development. I must take care of my own.

I am happy that I found a profession that combines my belief in social justice with my zeal for intellectual excellence. My career choice has meant much anxiety, anger, and disappointment. But it has also produced profound joy. I have spent my working life committed to a just cause: the education of Boston high school students. Welcome to our noble teaching profession and our enduring cause.

With hope and faith,

Stephen Gordon

To "do educational justice" is no simple matter. It means teaching with hope and integrity, moving beyond bureaucratic fixes to educational problems to considering why the educational problems exist in the first place. Most of all, it means having the highest respect for our profession, for the work we do, and for the students with whom we work.

Through the inquiry group, we learned that teachers' identities, beliefs, and values influence their work with students; that a belief in and love for students is a paramount requirement of teaching; and that teaching is both intellectual activity and social justice work. It is our belief that both teacher education programs and school professional development efforts can benefit from these lessons. It would mean changing as well as engaging in the in-depth study of both the subject matter and the subjects—the students—they will teach.

NOTES

1. Sonia Nieto first approached Ceronne Daly, who at the time was the high school restructuring coordinator for the Boston Public Schools, and shared her idea of forming a yearlong relationship with a group of teachers. Daly enthusiastically helped recruit a small group of high school teachers, and in the spring of 1999, Sonia initiated the What Keeps Teachers Going in Spite of Everything? inquiry group. Twelve teachers showed up for the first meeting, and eight remained with the project for its duration: Judith Baker, Claudia Bell, Ceronne Daly, Sonie Felix, Karen Gelzinis, Stephen Gordon, Ambrizeth Lima, and Junia Yearwood.
2. hooks, b. *Teaching to Transgress: Education as the Practice of Freedom.* New York: Routledge, 1994, p. 207.
3. Canada, G. *Fist Stick Knife Gun: A Personal History of Violence in America.* Boston: Beacon Press, 1995.
4. Freire, P. *Teachers as Cultural Workers: Letters to Those Who Dare Teach.* Boulder, Colo.: Westview Press, 1998.

Sonia Nieto is professor of education at the University of Massachusetts, Amherst. She has been a teacher for thirty-five years, teaching students at all levels from elementary grades through graduate school. Her research focuses on multicultural education, the education of Latinos, immigrants, and other culturally and linguistically diverse students, and Puerto Rican children's literature. Her books include *Affirming Diversity: The Sociopolitical Context of Multicultural Education* (3rd ed., Addison-Wesley, 2000), *The Light in Their Eyes: Creating Multicultural Learning Communities* (Teachers College Press, 1999), and *Puerto Rican Students in U.S. Schools* (Erlbaum, 2000). She has received many awards for her advocacy and activism, including the 1989 Human and Civil Rights Award from the Massachusetts Teachers Association. She feels most alive in her teaching when she can see "the 'light in their eyes.' I wrote a book by this name, and that title still captures my sense of that moment when teaching is most exciting and fulfilling. Whether it's with young people (whom I taught for the first several years of my career) or with university students and teachers (whom I've taught since 1980), there is something quite magical when that light goes on."

For the past thirty-six years, Stephen Gordon has taught a broad range of students at the high school, college, and graduate levels. Since 1974, he has taught at Snowden International High School in Copley Square in Boston. He is presently the school's literary specialist and facilitator of teaching inquiry groups on student literacy and learning development. A strong believer in the power of teacher research as a vehicle for professional growth and development, Steve joined the Boston Writing Project and the Urban Sites Writing Network of the National Writing Project. In 1998, Steve was honored as a recipient of the Golden Apple award. Steve feels energized as a teacher when "students find the truest words for their experiences and understandings, expressing how they see the world and what they understand or do not understand; when they speak about their learning and my teaching, convinced that they must participate in their education and help me become a better teacher; when they struggle to understand authors and peers whose words and ideas may make their world more explicable; and when in passionate speech and writing, they claim and proclaim their respect and identity as adolescents who have power over their lives."

Part Two

Reaching Out

Forging Relationships That Sustain Our Hearts

I t is one of those days when I slouch around muttering the refrain from the old *Wide World of Sports* promo: "the agony of defeat." My sophomores hadn't read, my juniors hadn't done their essays, and every question I asked was met with the special bland, lifeless silence that can exist in a classroom occupied by a teacher and adolescents. To top it off, my car stalled at every red light, and my briefcase bulged with papers to read.

I drop my car off at the shop and explain to the mechanic that the car starts fine but as it idles it begins to stall. The mechanic, a young twenty-something fellow about the same age as I, listens carefully to me and then pops the hood. After a few minutes of tinkering, he stands up and looks down at the car with a furrowed brow. Almost immediately, an older man in a well-worn blue work shirt comes over from the other bay and asks, "What's going on, kid?" The younger mechanic fills in the older man, who leans over the car. He asks, "Did you check the exhaust level?" The young man tells him, "I did." After another few minutes of probing, a third mechanic comes over.

By this time, I've sat down in a chair and pulled out a set of papers on *To Kill a Mockingbird* that need to be marked. The first paper up is Tommy's essay. One of my 158 students, Tommy comes to school only sporadically. In the top margin of his essay he has inked an elaborate rendering that resembles a cross between an acid-rock album cover and subway graffiti. The caption reads, "Boo Radley as Scout would dream him." It's a creepy image but one that conveys literary insight. I'm impressed. His essay, though, sags my English teacher shoulders: one long paragraph, shifting tenses, and little coherence. I sit there thinking, Here's a kid who comes to school one out of every three days, I think he's smoking dope regularly, I glean from things he's said in class that his family situation is pretty bleak, and his basic writing skills are desperately weak. Tommy's not unique: out of my 158 students, 30 of them have similar profiles.

I look up to hear the older mechanic say to the younger one, "Good idea about the vent. If you pull it off and test it and then put it back, you'll get it running." It's a poignant moment for me. I'm frustrated and upset about what to do for Tommy. How do I help him make better decisions? How do I support his obvious artistic talent? How do I help improve his abysmal writing skills? Here I sit, watching three mechanics put their head and talents together about the stuttering idle on my jalopy, and I've got these kids back at school teetering in their lives and I have nobody to talk to, work with, or confide in about what's going on.

The young mechanic starts my car, and it hums. The older guy pats him on the back, and he lights up, obviously proud of his accomplishment. I couldn't help thinking that if it took three mechanics sharing their insight and expertise to fix my crummy car, how was I ever going to help Tommy? What I would give to be able to sit down and problem-solve with a wise and experienced colleague about how to prepare for tomorrow's class or to have the luxury to stop in the middle of my teaching and have an experienced and gentle expert offer me feedback and guidance.

How I yearn for a moment of calm when I could sit down with Tommy and some of my other students and have a heart-to-heart with them.

Teachers rarely come together to probe and prod a problem of practice or perform their work in the presence of colleagues. I'd been teaching for two years before anybody ever came into my room to watch me who wasn't a supervisor evaluating me. My supervisor was a smart, experienced, savvy assistant principal—but every time she walked into the classroom, I was gripped by an anxiety akin to stage fright. Teaching in her presence felt like driving on the interstate next to a police cruiser. In short, watching those mechanics reach out to each other in an effort to fix my car shone headlights on some dramatic shortcomings in my life as a teacher.

I drive away from the garage muttering, "It doesn't need to be this way. How can teaching be less lonely, less private, less disconnected?"

The essays in Part Two are by teachers who resist the forces that would have them work in isolated and disconnected ways. These teachers recount their efforts to reclaim a sense of wholeness and unity in their work by reaching out and reconnecting to themselves, their students, their colleagues, and the subjects they teach. Rather than retreat in fear or circle their wagons, these teachers face the challenges of teaching by listening to their inner dialogue and then reaching out and connecting more fully.

Reaching out to forge connections is not an easy venture: students resist us, the organization fragments our time and energy, the norms of the teaching culture value privacy and individuality, and many of the accepted methods and assessment procedures of teaching promote distance rather than connection between subject matter and student.

Despite the imposing odds, these teachers find ways to navigate through the shoals of resistance and the cultural commands that suggest they go to their classroom, close the door, and have at it. Undaunted, these teachers describe their efforts to clarify their own sense of self so that they can work with integrity by themselves and with others.

Facing a context and a culture where collegial interactions are sparse, these teachers reached out and found colleagues with whom they could make common cause. Facing students who are weary and chronically angry with teachers who have long under-valued their voices, these teachers persisted until they could build meaningful, life-affirming relationships between themselves and their students. Facing expectations to treat their subject matter as if it were objective data only needing to be transmitted from them—the expert sages—to receptive students, these teachers generated opportunities for students to engage in an honest and intimate interchange with the knowledge to be learned. Facing a culture that condones the closing of the classroom door and prac-tice in the insular cells that are the norm in our schools, these teachers swung their doors open and invited colleagues in to wit-ness their craft and join them in pursuit of better understanding and teaching.

We defy our fear when we resist the instinct to flee or put obstacles between us, our colleagues, our administrators, our par-ents, and the others we serve. We act with courage when we reach out. To reach out means to stretch toward those who need us. To reach out means to invite others to join us. It is an act of hospitality. It is, in our schools today, an act of defiance and courage.

—S.M.I.

We, students and teachers, struggle with formidable and eternal questions of meaning: Who am I? Where am I going? What's important to me? Teaching, for many, involves finding ways to weave these questions into the subjects we teach. Robert Kunzman, a high school English teacher and administrator, describes his search to bring deeper meaning to his classroom interactions through a project he calls "The Meaning of Life Assignment." Though there are some risks, he discovers that joining his students in this project has benefits beyond his classroom walls.

—S.M.I.

The Meaning of Life Assignment

Robert Kunzman

Two days before my first year of high school teaching began, I stapled construction paper letters above the blackboard in my room to spell out I MAKE A DIFFERENCE. Those words were there for each student to read daily, as an affirmation that they matter in this world and that they mattered to me. It also served to remind me during that first year that my efforts mattered as well. But as the year unfolded, I wondered if I were making the kind of difference in my students' lives that I had hoped to make when I entered teaching. I wanted to create a classroom experience in which students could be challenged but also cared for, in which we could engage in that demanding but rewarding endeavor of learning that enveloped our whole selves.

The early years of my teaching career saw me struggling to balance an attitude that conveyed demanding expectations with an intimacy that nurtured this sense of community and connection with my students. While I still negotiate that challenge of drawing my students and myself into the learning experience in authentic ways, those first years were especially tough. The initial narrow age gap and my beginning insecurities as a teacher impelled me toward a strictness and distance that obscured my message of valuing the experiences and perspectives of my students and hindered my efforts to engage authentically with them.

As I gained confidence in my role, I increasingly sought ways to cultivate deeper connections between students' lives and our time together in the classroom. By my third year, I had become relatively comfortable in my explorations of literature and writing with my students, and the relationships I developed in the classroom were pleasant and gratifying. In junior-senior English that year, we had spent seven months exploring themes of personal identity and meaning, analyzing the literary and philosophical contributions of dozens of authors. Through our intensive study of Ralph Ellison's *Invisible Man,* for example, we had wrestled with questions of race and personal identity. Samul Beckett's *Waiting for Godot* had confronted us with the challenge of meaninglessness. We debated issues of social convention and individuality as illustrated in Jane Austen's *Pride and Prejudice.* Students were willing and engaged participants in the discussions and explorations, but only to the extent that fans in the bleachers chime in to lend support or debate with one another the strategies and events of the game. We weren't climbing down to throw ourselves into the fray.

This difference became clearest to me in our study of *King Lear,* long my favorite Shakespearean play (beware the teacher who yearns for his students to share his tastes!). I had hoped that the conflicts between parents and children and the struggle for power would provide rich material for engagement. When a broken Lear is reunited with his faithful daughter Cordelia, he beseeches her, "Pray you now, forget, and forgive. I am old and foolish," and through her tears she insists she has "no cause" for anger against him. This moment of piercing honesty between them never fails to move me, but again, while my students willingly mused on the themes I suggested, a sense of authentic connection was missing.

With all these works, we had stood at the edge of this vast expanse of meaning, perhaps even wandered around a bit on the fringes, but it was not really our own in the way that signaled deep engagement and lasting value for our lives. I searched for ways to ask, How do these stories, these insights, *move* you? What insights into personal identity and meaning resonate with you? We spend so much time in the classroom—how does any of it connect with what matters most to you? I needed a way to bring our conversations to this place of intimacy and authenticity for all of us. What emerged—the Meaning of Life Assignment, as I grandly titled it—was simple enough on its surface.

> The question is surely as old as the subject: What is the meaning of life?
>
> Your assignment, your challenge, is to answer that question as best you can. We've read and discussed different viewpoints on the issue, and your personal insights, beliefs, and experiences certainly provide your own perspectives.

I handed students a single sheet of paper with these words and a few more and told them that they could use whatever media and format they felt best suited their responses and that they would share their "answers" with the class in some sort of presentation.

Their reactions varied but struck me as promising. Some students were incredulous—and appreciative—that a major project was being devoted to this question. A few, of course, wanted to know how I could possibly grade such an assignment. The most common response, however, was a combination of "This looks really hard" and "I can't wait to get started." I remember one girl returning to the next class in exasperation—the assignment had taken hold of her, and she complained of having done no work for her other classes. I wasn't sure what exactly to expect when presentations began in two weeks, but I grew hopeful that students were starting to move away from the fringes and strike out on their own paths. I wondered whether they would be able to communicate those journeys to the class and if their peers would truly listen.

I won't forget Jenny's presentation on the first day. A sweet, quiet young woman who rarely spoke in large group discussions, she began her presentation in a soft, halting voice. "It's kind of ironic that the one day I'm supposed to talk about the meaning of life, I watched someone die," she said. "This year, I've been volunteering some mornings at a hospice before coming to school." Her eyes began to fill with tears. "Today, I sat with a man as he died." With those words, our class entered a space we had never experienced together, and my worries about respectful listening vanished. We had been given the gift of hearing a student reflect on this awesome event, to consider connections between our learning that year and the learning in our lives.

Stan was the class clown, borderline immature, and often one to throw together an assignment at the last moment. His scheduled spot on the first day had me worried that he might set a low standard of effort for the assignment. But he showed up that day with his father and presented a heartfelt—and obviously memorized— dramatic dialogue that ended with his testimony to the value of family and a surprising embrace of his father. He chose to take a tremendous emotional risk in front of his classmates, and they responded with a loud and long ovation when he finished.

Other presentations that day weren't quite so dramatic but still revealed deep engagement and contributed to the emergence of this authentic space Jenny and Stan had initiated. I videotaped many of the presentations from that first year, and recently I sat down and scanned through them. Musical and dramatic performances, sculptures and videos, poems and paintings—all accompanied by the creators' commentaries and reflections. Some explained their sense of personal meaning by describing the course of their life thus far. Others shared philosophies based on accumulating rich experiences or pursuing religion or knowing different kinds of people. One young man presented a study of the flowers on his farm as an example of slowing down, stepping back, and taking in the world around him. Another student thoughtfully and honestly explained that wrestling with the question was the best part for her; trying to present an "answer" felt as though it devalued the question. Although the core question generated a range of deeply personal responses, there was also room for students to approach the topic on a more abstract level. Personal revelations and autobiographical disclosure, though welcome, were not required. One student, for instance, presented a rich portrait of the major world religions and how various believers tended to answer questions of purpose and meaning. Although I believed our classroom had developed a strongly supportive atmosphere, not all students may have felt that safety, and some may have been skeptical of their peers' capacity to truly understand their particular perspective.

I am still struck by the focus and gravity that students brought to their projects, their stirring wisdom, and the earnest and genuine questions that their peers offered after they finished. This assignment gave me a chance to listen to my students in a new way, very different from when I had led discussions on the literature. Here I had no list of points to make, no metaphors to unpack, no literary themes for them to identify. I was there to listen and appreciate and, quite frankly, be exhilarated by my students' sharing.

But my listening also turned into a fuller conversation in a way I had not expected and brought the notion of reaching out to connect with students to an unfamiliar and uncertain depth. The presentation schedule was scattered over the course of a few weeks, and at the end of that first day, as students were packing up, Bonnie asked, "Hey, Mr. Kunzman, are you going to do a project, too?" Over those first three years, I had begun to find ways to bring myself authentically into the classroom and the lives of my students while still maintaining an appropriate professional and pedagogical distance. But Bonnie's invitation, enthusiastically echoed by her classmates, presented itself as a whole new level of challenge—and opportunity. The questions I had desired my students to answer were now before me as well: How do these stories, these insights, move me? What resonates within me? How does our time in the classroom connect with what matters most to me?

I've always been in favor of teachers doing assignments along with their students. I don't do it enough, usually because of limitations on my time, but the experience of vulnerability that often accompanies the presentation of my work to students helps me keep in better tune with their perspective. But this was a whole new level of openness and risk—not only sharing parts of myself that mattered most deeply but knowing that in some ways I would have to navigate vital professional boundaries of self-disclosure and expression of personal beliefs. How could I be authentic while remaining ethically mindful of my fiduciary role? Would my "position of power" in the classroom create an unfair dynamic if I presented my perspectives on the meaning in life, particularly during the questions and conversations afterward? How could I avoid diminishing or alienating students who might think differently about these deeply personal and often sensitive issues? Could I show that I care passionately about these questions, that I believe they're important to ask and wrestle with? Could I allow myself vulnerability and yet preserve my role as teacher, a distinction on which I believe students depend?

Since Bonnie's class met on alternating days, I had two nights to stew over my decision. After considerable hesitation, I told my students I'd make an attempt and began working on my own project in the evenings. I gathered a series of quotes and literary passages that illustrated my perspectives on life and then composed my own reflections and reactions to those passages. I focused on issues of family (the birth of children and the death of loved ones), faith (the struggle to believe in the midst of tribulation), and values (how I wanted to live my life). The day of my presentation, I was nervous. My thoughts were probably not much different from those of my students when they presented: Will the others appreciate what I have to share? Will my efforts toward authenticity be honored? And just as our growing sense of community provided a space for students to listen to one another, they also listened to me, talked with me, considered with me.

Through all these presentations and conversations, we had participated together in something deeply meaningful, something of great value in and of itself, and something that enriched the remainder of our year together. I was reminded in a powerful way of the worlds my students inhabited. Author Frederick Buechner writes of the difficult "in-between" existence that adolescents endure: "Being not quite a child and not quite a grown-up either is hard work, and they look it. Living in two worlds at once is no picnic."[1]

I'm sure we didn't solve those problems, but our time together may have helped draw connections between those challenges of adolescence and the dilemmas that we all confront as we strive to cultivate lives of meaning and purpose. The experience also provided immediate benefits for our remaining months together, with a deeper level of trust and respect that buoyed our subsequent learning. And I found that my sharing hadn't compromised what was important in my role as teacher; instead, that vital balance between professional distance and connection that had seemed so daunting just a few years earlier seemed easier to maintain.

The value of reaching out and connecting with my students extended beyond my classroom walls. A few colleagues heard about the assignment from my students and learned that I had presented my own project. One of them asked to see it, and I gave it to her to take home and read. She called me that very night: "I couldn't wait until tomorrow to tell you how deeply touched I was by your writing, your honesty about these issues." We talked for a while about the project and how it had played out in my class, including the various contributions students had made and what it had meant for our classroom community. Looking back, this conversation helped deepen a pleasant acquaintance into a strong friendship, one that helped sustain me both personally and professionally over the years. My sharing created an understanding between us, a mutual appreciation of purpose, a security in knowing we both cared deeply about making this kind of difference with our students.

Every day in the classroom, for me at least, cannot be one of deep introspection and exhilarating connections with others. There are theorems to prove, verbs to conjugate, dates to memorize, and dangling modifiers to mend. But the moments of authenticity and connection with my students and colleagues fuel the passion that brought me to teaching in the first place. The Meaning of Life Assignment is probably the prime curricular example of my efforts to teach from a place of integrity and authenticity, but I have tried to extend this beyond a single assignment. The opportunity to really listen to my students' voices and lives in a space carved out by questions of profound importance—this has sustained my work, my calling, over the years. The invitation from students to enter that space myself, though I remain mindful of the perils of vulnerability and self-disclosure, has deepened the experience further still.

NOTE

1. Buechner, F. *Whistling in the Dark: A Doubter's Dictionary.* San Francisco: HarperSanFrancisco, 1993, p. 2.

Robert Kunzman began teaching in 1990 and has been a high school teacher, coach, and administrator in Los Angeles and Vermont. He is currently the William R. and Sara Hart Kimball Graduate Fellow at the Stanford School of Education, studying moral and civic education. He also teaches in the Stanford Teacher Education Program (STEP) and was recently awarded its Graduate Student Award for Excellence in Teaching. As a high school teacher, he was recognized by his students as the Key Club teacher of the year. He has a research article forthcoming in the *Journal of Teacher Education* that explores the value of teacher education for experienced teachers, a recently published essay dealing with morally controversial issues in the classroom in the on-line quarterly *FacultyShack.com*, and an essay examining the role of dialogue in public school classsrooms will be published in the *Philosophy of Education Yearbook*. His favorite moments in teaching (and coaching) are "when students invest themselves so deeply in their learning that the joys of growth, discovery, and accomplishment become the sole motivation and satisfaction."

Although their methods differ dramatically, the best teachers I've known share one characteristic: they teach who they are. A strong sense of personal identity infuses their work. Elementary school teacher Kirstin Tonningsen longs to share a dimension of her identity with her students, but she's fearful of possible recriminations. After years of hiding a facet of who she is, the sidestepping begins to deplete her energy and vitality. After reflecting by herself and seeking clarity with colleagues, Tonningsen realizes that for her to continue teaching, she must share herself more openly with her students.

—S.M.I.

Reclaiming Identity
Sharing a Teacher's Truth

Kirstin Tonningsen

This year my students and I focused on asking questions. We asked questions about everything: about the books we read, math problems we solved, the butterflies and moths and frogs in our room, why our spaceship wouldn't stand up, and why some people behave in ways that we wouldn't behave ourselves. First graders are experts at asking questions. Most of these children haven't yet learned the unfortunate lesson most of us acquire, that questioning signals weakness. They do know, though, that when many adults ask questions, there is a "right" answer they're expected to find. Part of our learning requires unlearning this rule, or at least suspending it in our classroom. The more questions they asked, the deeper and more complex their questions became.

There is one set of questions my students always ask that I have, for six years, avoided. Every year, my students ask me about my family. Do I have children? Where do I live? Do I have a mom and dad? When do I see them? How long have I been a grown-up? What kind of car do I drive? Am I married? When will I be?

I love my students. I think it is important to share my life with them, just as they do with me. As a teacher of young children, however, I've never known quite how to answer questions about my family life because I am a lesbian. I live with my partner, Amy, in an adorable 1905 Victorian house. She's a restoration carpenter. We have two cats. Someday we may want a larger family.

Every time I evaded these questions, I felt like I was lying to my kids. Honesty and openness are things I encourage in them, and it felt hypocritical to keep such an important part of my life from them. How can I ask them about their lives when I can't answer their questions about mine?

Tolerance for diversity is something we work on, constantly. The school is fairly homogeneous; the students don't necessarily recognize differences or know how to value them unless we're deliberate about it. What kind of teacher was I, trying to make myself seem like every other adult they knew, hiding my differences? What kind of message was I giving them about the kinds of lives that gay and lesbian people lead by concealing from them that a person they know and trust is a member of that community? If they found out, what message would it give that I hid it? I thought about my brother, who knew he was gay at a very young age. I never had to go through that struggle, but what about kids at our school who do? How could I deprive them of knowing that they're OK, can be accepted, can lead the life they want to lead?

On the other side of the emotional spectrum, I found fear. What will the parents say? Will there be people who say first graders are too young to understand? How will the seventh and eighth graders react? Are people going to accuse me of trying to teach kids to value something their family believes is wrong? Will people think it's selfish to tell my students? Unnecessary? Will I lose the respect I've worked so hard for? Will I lose my job? I tried to rationalize not telling my kids by buying into these fears. Wouldn't I rather be quiet than lose the job I love? I told myself that my home life wasn't relevant to my job. I've known plenty of good teachers who seem to keep their outside lives private. Why couldn't I be one of them?

But I knew, for me, the line between my professional life and my personal life is indistinguishable. I spend between ten and twelve hours a day at school. I'm there on weekends. I take work home. I talk about education all the time. Most of all, my kids, along with my family, are the most important thing in the world to me. My professional life certainly spills into my personal life; why did I think I could keep the personal from the professional? Keeping my "private" life from my students meant lying to them and, really, devaluing my own life and experiences. The separation between personal and professional tore me in half. I wasn't coming to work as a whole person, just a fearful one.

I took this dilemma to my Courage to Teach colleagues as the focus person in a "clearness committee."[1] It took me weeks to reach any "clearness," as I emerged with more questions than answers. Talking to teachers about my dilemma, however, made it less frightening for me. It forced me to realize that this was not something I could ignore. The clearness committee helped me discover that being honest with my students wasn't, as I had feared, selfish. For me, keeping the secret was really the selfish act. I was indulging my fear. I was ignoring all I believed to be good for kids in order to preserve the known, my own status quo.

At our Courage to Teach retreat, I connected with another teacher who helped me understand that I already knew I needed to tell my kids. My question now was *how* to tell them. I told her I didn't know—I could not picture myself doing it. I didn't know the right words to use. She asked me, "Well, do you have to know right now? Is this something you have to do on Monday?" No, I didn't think it was. I'd take my time. I'd wait a month, maybe two. I'd see if an opportunity came up.

The opportunity, it turns out, waited until Tuesday. On Tuesday, I told my students that Amy was coming to visit because she was an architecture student and had just constructed a project for her program that required her to do a small-scale prototype. Seeing her model could help us think about the prototypes we were building of our spacecraft. I asked if they had any questions. Samantha did. "How did you get Amy to live with you?" This time I couldn't lie. I explained the best I could. They listened, and I waited. Finally, Ethan spoke up. "Oh, I get it. She's your family." Yes, Ethan, that's exactly it.

I thought that was the end. I felt relieved. I waited for the parent calls. They never came. On Wednesday morning, I heard the question "When is she coming?" at least thirty times. Every time the door opened, every head turned. Samantha presented me with artwork she'd drawn at home, with a picture of me on one side and on the other a portrait of a girl with long, blonde hair, rosy cheeks, red lipstick, and very blue eye shadow. "That's what I think Amy looks like," Samantha told me. When Amy did come, cardboard chariot and leverage poles in tow, she looked nothing like the picture. Still, Samantha knew her right away. "That's her. That's Amy," I heard her whisper.

I took Amy around and introduced her to the backs of seventeen very silent, very busy heads. It was eerie; we aren't silent all that often. When we are, we've usually decided together we need time for silence. This was different, an unspoken agreement. They were trying, in a way I'd never seen before, to make a good impression.

Amy sat down in front of the room. The children gathered around her. Instead of sitting on the platforms they usually sit on, they sat on the floor as close to her as they could get. One little girl fingered the cuff of Amy's pant leg the whole time. They asked her questions about her project for a full hour.

After she left, I waited for their questions of me. I felt a little nervous about what they'd say. "Can she come back tomorrow?"

98

is what they asked. I wanted to hug them all. I'd never felt closer to my students. I think they all felt closer to me. And I felt whole.

NOTE

1. For more information on the Courage to Teach professional development program, see the essay by Marcy and Rick Jackson (pp. 282–308); on clearness committees.

Kirstin Tonningsen teaches at the Riverdale Grade School in Oregon. Through much of her eight years in the classroom, she has worked with first graders. She has recently taken a new role as the K–8 library media specialist. She has presented several times at national school reform conferences and received an Intel Applying Computers in Education award. She feels most alive in her teaching "when I laugh with my students."

W e've all had students with whom we clash—students who challenge our ability to stay receptive and nurturing. Community college professor Elizabeth Keats Flores challenges us to think about our response to students who test our belief system. She shares a story of her struggle to restrain her impulse to become angry and dismissive of a student whose views violate her own basic principles. Rather than ignore this student or lash out, Flores remains welcoming. While our first impulse is to retreat in fear from students who challenge us or to reach out with a heavy hand and fix what we perceive as wrong, Flores shows that working to gain a deeper, firmer understanding of our students' stories provides us with opportunities to teach, learn, and grow.

—S.M.I.

Of Aliens and Space

Elizabeth Keats Flores

It began on the first day of class. We were writing about our childhood fears, and I called on her. Older than the rest of the eighteen- and nineteen-year-olds, her brown hair hanging over her eyes, Tiffany read, "I was afraid of the colored. We lived in a colored neighborhood, and they were always picking on us. The time they mugged my mother—I wanted to kill every one of them."

At this time I was beginning to delve into Parker J. Palmer's *Courage to Teach,* savoring each new yet strikingly familiar idea. Though his ideas were consistent with my heart and mind, they were not natural to me. For example, in a situation like this, Palmer might suggest sitting quietly, reflecting on his own visceral response to this student's inflammatory words, and then carefully considering what to do next. But not me. I jump in, speak first, and think afterward. The concept of silence and stillness, of patient reflection, goes against my personality, which is hurried, impatient, and quick to react. While I had been spending the early hours of every day in quiet meditation for over twenty years, I was still a strong-willed, opinionated, angry, impatient soul.

So how did I handle this? As usual, I jumped in quickly, not wanting her words to settle into my students' young, white ears. "Yes, I have often had black students talk about the same experience in white neighborhoods," I said quickly, coldly. "Being the outsider can be difficult. So," I asked the class, turning my back, both physically and emotionally, to Tiffany, "why do you think children like to pick on someone who is different?"

While Palmer tells us that good teachers "offer hospitality to the alien other," I knew in my body language, my voice, my words, and my heart that I had dismissed this "alien" as both dangerous and ignorant. Over the years, I have welcomed the gang-banger from L.A., the refugee from the former Yugoslavia, the ex-con right out of prison for armed robbery, the drug addict, even the Satanist. I prided myself on making every one of them feel at home, safe, free to speak and be listened to. Yes, I "offer hospitality to the alien other." Ah, but what about aliens like Tiffany? What about the racist student, the sexist student, the homophobic student? Did I welcome them? Did I listen to their voices? Not at all. Like many other instructors who consider themselves open-minded, the only voices I welcomed were those that did not insult my cherished beliefs.

Forgetting that teaching is about "creating space" for learning, I filled the chilling space that Tiffany had created with my own self-righteous, fearful chatter. Turning my back to her, I did not create space for her to learn; instead, I made an adversary.

I am one of those people who hate prejudice, who fight bigotry, who extol the virtues of acceptance. But I did not accept the prejudiced or love the bigot. In fact, I was not even aware of how inconsistent I was. How can we teach tolerance when we do not practice it? In truth, we cannot. How can we transform our own intolerance when we are not aware of it? Unfortunately, we cannot.

STORIES OF THE COURAGE TO TEACH

During this semester, I was asked to lead a small group of faculty who wanted to explore Palmer's ideas. Using *The Courage to Teach Guide for Reflection and Renewal,* we wrote deeply about our inner lives, inside and outside the classroom. Gingerly at first and then with more confidence, we shared our most horrific moments in the classroom. For a group of teachers, half of whom had been close friends for years, it was difficult for us to avoid fixing one another, giving each other advice. As the facilitator, I was tempted to bring my successes to the group. But instead, I shared Tiffany, my fear, my pain, my impatience, and my anger.

Every Friday morning, Tiffany generously offered me new opportunities for personal growth. When we discussed the plight of immigrants, she wanted them sent back where they came from. When we discussed Gandhi's nonviolent resistance, she said that anyone who did not accept Jesus was doomed to eternal damnation. Her face remained in a permanent scowl, her chin thrust forward, eyes frowning, her voice stung with its contempt of me and everything I stood for. She challenged every word on every page. Her rage was making the class a frightening place for me. I began to dread Fridays.

Her first essay, a memoir, described the most abject poverty in such detail it made me cry. I imagined growing up in the late sixties, white and poor in a black neighborhood seething with righteous anger. Of course it was terrifying. Her dad was gone; her mom was doing the best she could. They had nothing—no friends, nowhere to turn. Her anger was no surprise.

Essay number two was an interview paper. She interviewed a drug addict who had fallen in love with a pretty young girl and then destroyed her life. Alone, the girl was raising their two young children while he sat in jail for another twenty years. She would not consider divorce because the Bible does not allow it. I did not have to ask her who the woman was. She was tearing down my walls and breaking my heart.

Yet I still had no idea what to do with her. Each week, I shared more of my continuing failure with the members of our small faculty group. I told them how angry and ineffectual I felt with this student, how she was feeding the racism of the rest of the class while I felt powerless to stop it, how brilliant her writing was, how contagious her anger was, and how lost I felt.

By then, our group had gotten better at not solving, just listening. I let the feelings out, the fear that I was a lousy teacher, the anxiety that I was only making everything worse for her and the rest of my class. The terror that I just couldn't teach. Over the weeks, as I spoke with my colleagues about Tiffany, I was able to see our conflict more clearly. I was able, through the quiet, attentive, nonthreatening listening of my colleagues, to let myself be who I am. When they did not judge my anger, my impatience, my pain, I was able to forgive myself. A little. In their eyes, I saw the understanding and tolerance I had not been able to give Tiffany. No one gave me solutions to my Tiffany dilemma, but everyone listened me into my own power.

One morning, I sat in my office before class, praying for guidance. I looked up to see Tiffany, smiling and holding out a warm loaf of pumpkin bread. "Here," she said, "I made this for you. I want to apologize. I know how tough I am. I am a very angry woman."

I surprised both of us by laughing out loud. "Me too. I try so hard to be spiritual, to be trusting, and instead I'm always getting angry. We're actually a lot alike, aren't we? No wonder we're having so much trouble." The bread was delicious.

Tiffany and I slowly learned to listen to each other. As much an alien to me as my students from El Salvador or Haiti, she, like them, had much to teach me. I began to genuinely like her. I respected how resilient and courageous she was. Often our combined laughter would spring out in the classroom, not in a ridiculing way, but in a "yes, we sure see things differently, but it's all right" way.

Time for the last paper. We had been studying forms of prejudice, the civil rights movement, and nonviolent resistance. Now I asked my students to research a contemporary issue and consider how Martin Luther King Jr. would feel about what's going on today. I almost looked forward to reading Tiffany's beautiful, powerful writing, but I was still anxious about what she would have to say. Her essay focused on the issue of how minorities are treated differently—better—than whites. The only little black boy in Sunday school had been harassing her son. They got into a fight, and the church authorities were going to meet that night to determine what to do. Tiffany was certain they would decide to kick her son out because they would be afraid of being labeled racist. She was furious and frightened all over again. Despite her years as an active, dedicated member of the congregation, she was sure that they would ask her to leave her spiritual home.

On her paper, I wrote, "Of course, I do not agree with your position, but as usual your writing is powerful and fascinating."

She insisted on meeting me after class. "What do you mean, you don't agree?"

"Tiffany, you know how I feel."

"No, I want you to tell me. Why don't you agree?"

In the years before, I would have eagerly helped her see how wrong she was, hoping to convert her to the "right" way of thinking. But now for the first time in twenty years of teaching, I stopped absolutely still. I said nothing. I breathed deeply. Seeing the anguish in her bright eyes, the exhaustion in her face, I thought, What do I know of her life, her pain, her fear? What do I know at all? Anything I could say would be inappropriate. She needed loving silence, not another self-righteous lecture. She needed safe space.

"I'm so sorry, Tiffany, but I don't want to talk about this. It just wouldn't be right. Your writing is excellent as usual. You're a wonderful writer. I hope everything turns out OK. Please let me know what happens with your son. I really hope he doesn't get kicked out."

On the last day of class, we ate cookies, read our essays, and wrote each other short notes about what we liked about each other.

Later that afternoon, I sat down and read all the sweet, positive notes, dreading Tiffany's. Finally, I opened the folded paper, reading her familiar writing. "I know we clash. But I thank you for the time you've been a part of my life. I've come to understand I am prejudiced. I don't like it, and I want to change."

Two angry aliens had stopped still long enough to listen, to learn, and with prayer and grace, to change—a little.

For sixteen years, Elizabeth Keats Flores has been teaching developmental writing and advanced composition at the College of Lake County in Grayslake, Illinois. In response to the editor's inquiry as to any special honors connected to her teaching, she shared an excerpt of a letter from a former student. She called this form of testimony her greatest honor. Her student wrote, "I have realized how we as students don't just write papers, but when we are lucky we write to our teachers, our professors, purveyors of knowledge and wisdom, triggers of inspiration, instruments perhaps of the great wealth inside us that wouldn't be found, except for the fact that even in the briefest of moments, we feel that we connect and are understood. And that we could become something greater than our daily existence." She feels most alive in her teaching "when my class has formed a safe, warm family where all of us are accepted as we are, where we can be ourselves and so become more than we were. It does not happen in every class, every semester, but when it does, we all know it; my heart leaps for joy and gratitude. And real teaching occurs for every one of us."

As teachers, we aspire to connect in profound and meaningful ways with many students. Yet despite our heartfelt intentions, these moments are few and far between. Mary Rose O'Reilley muses on these moments and observes that while they may be elusive, they do come, often in mystical ways, often through random unpredictable encounters. And perhaps most maddening, when they do come, we may never even discern their presence. Coming to terms with the ineffability and elusiveness of teaching is a way of making peace with the profession. Despite the fleeting and seeming random impact of our work, we must still reach out when we can, however we can, and hope that it makes a difference.

—S.M.I.

You're the One I Expected to Meet

Mary Rose O'Reilley

I don't know much about Sufis, followers of the mystical branch of Islam, and wouldn't know where to find them if I needed to look. But at several significant moments, they have found me. Once, over chips and dip at a suburban party, I met a woman who smiled at me guilelessly (later she would tell me about her Sufi antecedents) and remarked, "You're the one I expected to find." Another time, a man's voice on the phone—a cordial, professorial accent—told me, "My Sufi master has instructed me to meet with you."

Who could resist such compelling summonses? Most of us, I suspect—I hope—who have followed the careers of colorful con men on Friday night TV. How *unwise* it was of me, I'm sure, to meet the professorial stranger on a Saturday afternoon at a neutral coffee bar. Nothing bad happened, though; in fact, nothing at all in the phenomenal world came of these encounters. The suburban woman, in her linen shorts, chatted about day care; the professor and I deconstructed some familiar texts over cappuccino, shook hands, and never met again—which does not diminish the powerful sense of what the Romantics might call *destiny* I felt about both these encounters. Destiny is not always dramatic. The great human endeavors, enacted far from my prairie bungalow, depend on small peripheral actors, grandmas who knit in the frayed ends, weekend carpenters who drive a true nail. I guess Sufis keep track of these cosmic interactions. That is their job in the economy of spirit. It is not mine.

However, Sufis have framed for me the idea that our encounters with other people are contained in some larger scheme of meaning, casual meaning mostly, the cosmic equivalent of getting the oil changed or adjusting the idle. Still, you'd better be there; you'd better show up. Bharati Mukherjee's novel *Jasmine* tells of the adventures of a young woman from India who washes up, confused and bleeding, on the shores of America. Nothing makes sense. She has no idea where to turn. She just follows the signs. "Objects in the mirror are closer than they appear,"[1] she remembers reading on a rearview mirror twisted off a Jeep, and she takes that wisdom to heart. "The incentive," she comes to understand, "is to treat every second of your existence as a possible assignment from God."[2]

"You're the one I expected to meet," I would tell Jacob, if I didn't have more sense. When I became a teacher, I thought I would meet Jacob every day: brilliant, humble, courteous, intellectually hungry, well read and reading, articulate, challenging, and sensitive—well, perhaps a few rough variations on the type. Something for the teacher to do. Students like my grad school friends and co-op mates, at least. But perversely, Jacob didn't show up until my twenty-fifth year of teaching. He was a classics major, and perhaps it was our mutual love of ancient Greek that brought our minds together, though it was poetry he studied with me. He was the kind of student who would come to class with three or four unassigned texts under his arm, who'd bring to the contemplation of a poem by Elizabeth Bishop a poem he'd memorized by Robert Hass. And English wasn't even his major.

Jacob asked me to be his academic adviser, and it was in this context that I saw his true mettle. I was nudging him toward an early-morning Shakespeare class, and he was resisting. "In the morning . . . ," he began shyly.

"You have a job, maybe?" I prodded, thinking he must sleep late.

"In the morning," he went on, as if commencing the most eccentric story ever told, "I study. I work on translation."

Twenty-five years a college teacher, and along comes my first student. The one who knows his business, who reserves his best hours for his *daimon* and the afternoon for us in our chalky tweeds.

A few months later, he came to check out what secondary sources he might use to write about the *Iliad*. "You need only what's in your head," I tell him, "or maybe—" I toss a scratched-up and underlined copy of Simone Weil's essay "The *Iliad,* or the Poem of Force."[3] This being the prairie, I don't say, "This is what you came here to find" or "Objects in the mirror are closer than they appear" or anything fraught with meaning.

In a couple of days, he returns it in a sealed baggie with a note. "I photocopied it. I was afraid I'd damage it somehow. Wait till you read my paper."

Wait. I have an infinite amount of time, incarnations. We may never see each other again. In *Out of the Silent Planet*, C. S. Lewis put these words in the mouth of an alien life-form: "When you and I met, the meeting was over very shortly, it was nothing. Now it is growing something as we remember it. But still we know very little about it. What it will be when I remember it as I lie down to die, what it makes in me all my days till then—that is the real meeting."[4]

The point I am trying to make in this essay is a Platonic one, and it has informed my teaching and my parenting from the beginning. I don't think I got it from Plato, though, but rather from talking to kids, especially bad kids, and before that, hanging out in the treehouse of my own soul: each of us comes into the world with a burning gift or two, a job of work; each of us has a resident angel in place. Paul Lacey has written wisely about this in his essay *Education and the Inner Teacher,*[5] which I always assign my freshmen and which so far none of them has ever understood because I am not the one they expected to meet. Lacey expresses this in terms of the Quaker idea that there is "that of God" in each individual: "Quaker education operates from the conviction that there is always one other in the classroom—the Inward Teacher, who waits to be found in every human being. If we appear to be student-centered, it is because we know that the student has an inner guide to whom he or she can be led. If we appear to be content-centered, it is because we know that another name for the Inward Teacher is the Spirit of Truth."[6]

I became a Quaker myself, effectively, when I looked at the face of my own first newborn. Someone has written about infants, of their look of infinite wisdom that precedes intelligence. They are frightening, these new beings, with that mighty knowing already in place. The mother's job is to guard the light they bring, to let no one put it out, to discern its best nurturance, to nudge and appear never, never to nudge; I believe this is a teacher's job, too.

In school, I was taught to laugh at Wordsworth, the Romantics being then in eclipse against the hard-assed Beats, and that is why, astoundingly, I never heard *Intimations of Immortality* all the way through until a poet read it over the car radio the year I turned fifty:

> Our birth is but a sleep and a forgetting:
> The Soul that rises with us, our life's Star
> > Hath had elsewhere its setting,
> > > And cometh from afar.
> WILLIAM WORDSWORTH, "Ode (There Was a Time),"
> *Intimations of Immortality,* stanza 5

I heard that and took the next exit off the freeway, all in a lather, pulling off the road and yelling, "What? What?"

It's well that I went to marginal schools and didn't read Plato until I was on a post-doc or get serious about Wordsworth until I was into menopause, or I would have suspected that my ideas about the immortal diamond of the soul had been taught into me instead of educated into consciousness by my babies and special-ed students. While we're on the subject of immortal diamonds, let me quote from poet Gerard Manley Hopkins:

> What I do is me
> for that I came.
> GERARD MANLEY HOPKINS, "As Kingfishers Catch Fire,"
>   stanza 1

This we know.

I grew up in the most barren place imaginable for the production of poetry, a Levittown-like suburb. I didn't know why my life's star was destined to rise in that unpropitious place. (I know now.) At school, I would write wild stories set in the thirteenth century or on the Planet Mongo. The nuns would advise in the margin, "Write about what you know." I would think about the sandwich in my lunchbox, liver sausage on Wonder bread with ketchup—my God!

After making it by a series of miracles through graduate school, I have spent my life teaching at a college with rarely a Jacob in it, mostly teaching people I learned in my creative writing seminars to call *bourge WAH*.

I'm the one they did not expect to meet.

Given a different job of work, at some prestigious institution, I might have had students like Jacob at least once a year. I think I would have liked that. But it would not have been *my* work, for which I came. Given a preppier destiny, I would have not been in my office when that singular Jacob came by, but more important, more a matter of life and death, I would have missed Hank.

Hank was the slowest student in a slow class of freshmen I had a few years ago. He was ugly and sullen and smoked a lot of dope. The combination of his first and family names produced a comic interjection that made the other kids titter when I called roll. I can't imagine what his parents were thinking of, since the name clearly compromised Hank's chances to stay out of jail. Just as we don't usually get students like Jacob at my college, we don't usually get students like Hank.

That semester, I taught Peter Shaffer's play *Amadeus,* which is tangentially about Mozart and centrally about the mystery of giftedness. One day, too whipped to lecture, I played a tape of Kathleen Battle singing "L'amero saro costante." Watching the effect on Hank reminded me of the moment when a baby is born, the tiny compressed package flowers outward, the lungs fill, and— Hank wailed. "Why did no one ever give me this before?" Tears were flowing down his cheeks. "This is the most beautiful thing I could even *imagine.*"

Hank flunked out of school, but so be it. He met the ones he needed to meet, and he has the tape along on his journey (at least it disappeared from my cassette player that day). "We met, and the meeting was brief."

In Catholic school, you are always encouraged to do something *great,* but in fact, most of our lives are very small. My daily interactions with students are seldom as dramatic as those with Jacob and Hank. The great thing you do can be a little thing in the world's eyes and in your own, for the true effects of our work are hidden. All surviving teachers know this. We just open a window, play the music. One of Mukherjee's characters put it this way, "The Lord lends us a body, gives us an assignment, and sends us down."[7]

NOTES

1. Mukherjee, B. *Jasmine.* New York: Fawcett Crest, 1989, p. 63.

2. Mukherjee (1989), pp. 53–54.
3. Weil, S. "The *Iliad,* or the Poem of Force." Wallingford, Pa.: Pendle Hill, 1956.
4. Lewis, C. S. *Out of the Silent Planet.* Old Tappan, N.J.: Macmillan, 1952, p. 76.
5. Lacey, P. *Education and the Inner Teacher.* Wallingford, Pa.: Pendle Hill, 1988.
6. Lacey (1988), p. 26.
7. Mukherjee (1989), p. 51.

Mary Rose O'Reilley has taught English at the University of St. Thomas in St. Paul, Minnesota, since 1978. She has written for a wide range of academic, literary, and social-change publications and is the author of *The Peaceable Classroom* (Heinemann Boynton/Cook, 1993), *Radical Presence* (Heinemann Boynton/Cook 1998), and *The Barn at the End of the World: The Apprenticeship of a Quaker-Buddhist Shepherd* (Milkweed, 2000). Her recent awards include a Loft McKnight Award in Creative Prose, a Minnesota State Arts Board Grant, a Bush Artist's Fellowship, a Loft Mentor grant in poetry, a Sears, Roebuck Foundation Award for Campus Leadership and Excellence in Teaching, and a Helen Hole Fellowship for Quaker teachers. She says she "feels most alive in my teaching when conversation, discussion, or argument breaks out in the room—preferably about the subject at hand—that isn't fielded through me; that is, when intellectual energy is sufficient to overcome even midwestern diffidence and students care enough to forget I'm in the room."

The rhythm and pace of the school year, the school day, and the daily schedule can sometimes become numbingly routine and mechanical. The curriculum we've taught many times seems utterly familiar, and the everyday interactions with students, colleagues, and parents feel trivial. The papers pile up, meetings drag on, and we feel smothered. Susan Etheredge, reflecting on more than twenty years of teaching, asks herself, How do I keep myself fresh? How do I sustain my enchantment with teaching? She describes recovering her delight in teaching and maintaining her passion as a teacher through her efforts to forge new and vital relationships with the students that pass through her classroom.

—S.M.I.

Arriving Where I Started
Rediscovering the Newness

Susan Etheredge

I swore I'd never be a teacher. My mother was a first-grade teacher. My father was a teacher and then a principal. My Aunt Bertha was the original one-room schoolhouse teacher, teaching grades one through eight for forty-seven years. I grew up immersed in teachers. Everybody thought I, too, would become a teacher. "It's in your blood," they'd say. In fact, people were so sure that I was going to be a teacher that my high school guidance counselor commented on my college choice, an elite private college in New England, by asking, "Why are you making your parents spend so much to send you to Smith if you're *only* going to be a teacher?"

Although I had great respect for teachers and teaching, I was *not* going to be a teacher like everyone else in my family. Perhaps it was my way of rebelling at age eighteen. Or perhaps it was because of the intense feminist climate of the 1970s. It seemed to me that all the upperclasswomen in my dormitory were preparing for careers in law, medicine, or business. The corporate doors were swinging open for women—and not just swinging open but pulling women in.

There was one senior in my dormitory who was student teaching at an elementary school nearby. At the dining room table, in the bathroom, in the hallway, she talked about her classroom and her children to whomever would listen. She was passionate about her work. Her friends and others in the house would always respond with patronizing comments like "How cute" or "Oh, you're so lucky to not have any really *hard* work to do during your senior year" or "It must be fun to play with little kids all day." I found myself listening to her. In fact, I surprised myself at how intently I listened to her. Her curiosity about children's thinking, her love of children's literature, and the delight she expressed when children mastered a new skill or understanding were contagious. I regularly sought her out for her latest classroom stories. They called to me.

In my sophomore year, I stopped resisting my hometown's notion that I should be a teacher and took two education courses. One course was in child and adolescent growth and development, and the other focused on children's difficulties in learning to read. I loved them. I found them intellectually rigorous and stimulating.

After I returned from my junior year studying in Florence, Italy, I was convinced that I was going to go to graduate school in international relations. But I decided to try student teaching anyway. My parents had insisted that I try it, and *they* were paying the bills. "Get that teaching certificate, just in case" was still a popular mantra for women in the 1970s, despite the feminist climate.

I began my student teaching in a mixed-age classroom of six- and seven-year-olds. It was hard; it was demanding; it was challenging. But it was also invigorating and inviting. I couldn't get enough. This time, the classroom stories that called to me were my own. I was at home in the classroom. "You're a natural," my college supervisor told me one day after she had observed me. Did that mean teaching was "in my blood," as "they" used to say, or did that mean it was the right fit for me?

I started to say aloud, with courage and conviction, "I am going to look for a teaching job when I graduate." My friends would say, "Your parents spent all this money to send you to Smith, and you're going to be a teacher, an *elementary school* teacher?" Where had I heard that before? Or they'd say, "Oh, that's something you can do in your forties, once you've been home with kids for a few years and you don't yet want to go back to the job you had before." What they really meant was the *corporate job* I had before I had kids. (Interesting, that despite the early feminism of the seventies, some still held the expectation that women would leave *even* the corporate job once they had children, not to mention the implicit assumption that you would, of course, have children.)

The resistance was almost too much to bear. I came close to taking that corporate job. In the spring of my senior year, a major American corporation was on campus recruiting seniors for its corporate training program. I was invited to interview, based on some faculty references. I went. I was called back for a second interview, then a third, and finally a large group interview in a nearby city. The offer was seductive: a generous salary, a car, international travel, great opportunities for professional advancement. How could I turn it down? Even my parents told me I'd be crazy not to take it!

I turned it down. I was going to be a teacher. I could not imagine doing anything else. I was tired of resisting. I had begun to fall asleep at night dreaming of my future classroom.

And then it happened: I got my "dream job" teaching third grade in a public school about an hour away from my hometown. That was in 1977. And except for one year at home when my daughter was born, I have been continuously teaching in a variety of settings: first-grade, second-grade, third-grade, fourth-grade, university, and college classrooms ever since. Now I am teaching teachers-to-be in the same institution where I began my journey as a student teacher.

Recently, I came across a talk I had written and given four years ago, when I was just beginning my new faculty position as an assistant professor of education and child study at Smith. In this talk, I was reflecting on how much I felt like a first-year teacher all over again. I wrote, "When folks ask me how I like my new job at Smith, I find myself responding more often than not, 'I feel like a first-year teacher all over again. But I also feel like I've come home again'—a return to my alma mater—a place where I 'grew up.' However, the comfort of familiarity, of this place I call 'home,' is continually challenged by the newness too—the newness I feel every day as I enter a classroom, respond to students' work, and engage in collegial conversations."

Entering a classroom, responding to students' work, engaging in collegial conversations . . . was this not the work I had been doing each day for the last twenty years, either in my elementary classroom or in my college classroom? Why this feeling of "newness"? Was it just because I was starting a new teaching position in a new place? Perhaps that was part of it. But as I contemplate what it is that brings renewal, refreshment, and reconfirmation to me in my work, it is precisely this spirit of "newness" that is inherent in the work of teaching. As I enter my twenty-fourth year of teaching, I find myself seeking and embracing "newness" in conscious as well as subconscious ways. A new school year means new students. New students mean new ideas, new insights, new questions, new energy, and new dreams (theirs as well as mine).

Every semester, I begin again to talk about the "stuff" of teaching with the students in my classes. We talk about what complex and challenging work it is. We talk about children and families, curriculum and instruction, colleagues and professionalism. We talk about the public perception of schools and teachers in the American landscape. These conversations never really end; they're more like explorations, explorations that keep me imagining new ways of looking at familiar landscapes. It is my students who inspire, lead, and sustain my explorations. Explorations which, in the words of ethnographer Harry Wolcott, seek to make the familiar exotic and the exotic familiar. My students inspire me to consider

STORIES OF THE COURAGE TO TEACH

familiar landscapes with new eyes and new ears. Now it is *their* classroom stories that call to me.

STORY ONE: THE NEWNESS OF CREATION

A student in my early childhood foundations and issues class is reflecting on observations she did in a classroom of four-year-olds. She writes in her journal: "To start off, I think that I am regressing back to my preschool days. Every time I observe my four-year-olds, I just want to get down on my hands and knees and build roads with Legos, play with blocks, draw and color with big Crayola markers, and play in the sand. Is this normal?"

I read this entry and am struck by what I see as metaphors for teaching: building, playing, drawing, coloring, sculpting—each one an act of creating as well as the practice of a skill, but executed with passion and commitment.

My student's journal entry is about the unfolding, emergent quality of what it means to teach. Her observations of these four-year-olds immersed in their play beckon her to join in their act of creating. I am not surprised by my student's response. In fact, it feels familiar and authentic to me. I, too, delight in my students' intellectual explorations and creative pursuits. Being witness to my students' creations of new understandings over the course of a semester renews, sustains, and enriches me. Their interpretations and creations inspire me to find new ways of seeing, understanding, and doing in my practice. Teaching is about creating anew. For me, the aesthetic joy I derive from teaching is akin to the joy of creating.

STORY TWO: THE NEWNESS OF RELATIONSHIP

An African proverb states *I learn, therefore I teach*. These words ring true for me in my work, but the reverse feels more apt: *I teach, therefore I learn.* This is illustrated in yet another journal entry of one of my students.

> I spent some time the other day working with Shana and Allie at the play dough table. When I first sat down with them, they had been working on their own without an adult at the table. My presence did not at first seem to affect what each girl was involved in; both the girls continued their play while I picked up my own lump of play dough and inquired about what they were doing. I tried to be consciously aware of what kinds of questions I asked the children as they worked: *What are you going to do next?* instead of *Why don't you (or we) do this?* I noticed, though, that what I did with the play dough sometimes changed what they were doing. But then again, they of course had good ideas that I wanted to try with my play dough, too, hoping that by engaging myself in their ideas, they would see that their ideas were important and valid.
>
> It seems like there is a very fine line between doing enough to keep a child interested in and moving forward with an activity and doing so much that the learning experience becomes artificially imposed on the child from the outside. Perhaps for some teachers, knowing exactly what to say to a child and when to say it comes naturally out of an innate sense, or intuition, but I think that it must also be an acquired skill. That is not to say that those of us who have to learn that balance are in any way less competent than those who act on intuition. I don't know of any innately talented ballerina whose performance didn't improve even more with consistent hard work over time.[1]

Hers is a reflection of teaching that is about responding to the "unscripted" text of students in a skilled, refined, yet still intuitively artful way. To me, her story is also about the reciprocity I have come to value and embrace in the teaching-learning context. The classroom is a place of relationship. Knowledge building is socially constructed activity. A classroom of students engaged in thoughtful reflection, rigorous problem solving, and lively, respectful discourse has become my best teacher. I just need to remember to listen carefully and pay attention. *I teach, therefore I learn.*

STORY THREE: THE NEWNESS OF SHARED WORK AND COMMON PURPOSE

Here one of my students delights in her observation of a three-year-old girl in a preschool classroom.

> One of the options the children had during their free time was to make collages at the round table. The teachers had cut out basic shapes such as circles, triangles, and squares from different-colored pieces of paper. Apparently, this is an activity they have done in the past. This time, however, the teachers added different shapes and colors of cellophane. At meeting time, Ms. H. demonstrated how a piece of cellophane over a blue triangle could change how that triangle looks. Well, I was watching the collage table, and I noticed Marisa pick up a piece of cellophane, look at it intently, and then hold it up to her eyes. Her facial expression changed as she noticed how everything she saw now had an orange tint to it. She excitedly showed Ms. S. (who was at the table), and soon the other children noticed Marisa's excitement and started to look through the cellophane themselves.
>
> However, Marisa enthralled me because she seemed so excited and proud of her discovery. She seemed to delight in trying all the different colors and shapes of the cellophane and peering at the world around her in this different way. She also walked around the classroom, slowly, holding a piece of cellophane to her eyes. It was so exciting and fun to see this

little bit of learning take place. It was fascinating watching Marisa systematically try out all the possibilities and seeing her share her joy with the other children and the teacher.

This is, in essence, what teaching is for me: trying all the different colors and shapes and peering at the world around you in these different ways—trying out all the possibilities and sharing the joy. Sharing the joy of teaching and learning with my students leads us to find common purpose in our work together each semester.

It is a conscious act on my part to share the joy of teaching with my students. I want my classroom to be a place of hopeful, uplifting conversations about teaching and learning. Like Marisa in my student's journal entry, I want students in my classroom to discover new ways of looking and seeing.

Creating, relating, and seeking common purpose *with* my students is a philosophy of life, not a philosophy of pedagogy, that renews, refreshes, and reconfirms my earliest calling to the vocation.

NOTE

1. This reflection was written by a student who returned to college after a three-year hiatus dancing with a national ballet company. It is interesting, therefore, to read her comparison of a teacher to what she knows best—a ballerina.

Susan Etheredge was an elementary school teacher from 1977 to 1987, teaching grades one through four in public and laboratory school settings. In 1993, she joined the education department faculty at Springfield College in Springfield, Massachusetts, where she worked closely with student teachers and teachers in the urban schools. She is currently an assistant professor of education and child study at Smith College in Northampton, Massachusetts. She has received a number of grants to support interdisciplinary collaboration and research in teacher education and development. Her classroom-based research in early childhood and elementary curriculum and instruction has taken her to San Pedro, Belize, and Pistoia, Italy, to work with educators there. She is a coauthor of *Introducing Students to Scientific Inquiry: How Do We Know What We Know?* (Allyn & Bacon, forthcoming). "I feel most alive in my teaching," she says, "when my classroom begins to function as a community of inquiry: when my students are talking to each other, listening to each other, asking questions, and seeking to learn and understand together."

G reat teachers who touched us in profound ways when we were students imprint deeply on how we think about our own teaching. The gift of our mentors is that they awaken in us ideas of how we think about our subject matter and a sense of how we can touch the lives of our students. In this essay, Catalina Rios remembers a mentor who evoked in her a sense of her own gifts. The force of her mentor's influence still lives, awake and robust, in how she seeks connections with her own students and helps them see how they too can make a difference.

—S.M.I.

Feeling, Thinking, and Acting for Change

Catalina Rios

I was eighteen years old and a freshman in college when the letters arrived. The letters were addressed in general to the Latino and African American students at my university. They were hate letters from an anonymous source. Letters that called us niggers and spics and threatened our lives if we did not leave campus. The language in the letters spoke of a powerful and supreme white nation where it was clear there was no room for someone like me: Latina, new, and out of place. I was terrified.

As the on-campus student organizations planned protests and demonstrations to call attention to the letters, I packed my bags and planned to withdraw. I had never experienced this before. The attacks on me had always been more subtle—hard to understand, rational, cold, intellectual—very New England and sophisticated. When Puerto Rico came up in class, which was not often, it was always referred to as "that small island"—a dot on the map, so obscure and distant to most but home to me. Feeling small, and more tragically thinking of myself as insignificant and never as a key player, was reinforced by what was taught in class—peripheral, marginal, small.

Up until these letters, the experiences I had had with racism directed against me, my family, and neighbors were most often institutional and systemic. When attacks were personal, they left me feeling that there had to be some perfectly logical explanation. If I would just take some time to think about it and analyze it, all would become clear. I was encouraged not to take it so personally, to resist my "Latina tendency" to be so dramatic, to think first instead of feel first.

Today we have more words for incidents like these and more words to approach a dialogue on diversity in general. Yet authentic communication and action nevertheless remain rare. Acts of violence, acts of racism, acts of faith, tolerance versus respect—we never quite agree on how to describe them. I know now that the letters incident was a racist hate crime, but twenty years ago I considered it a reminder: know your place. This is not your place; get out!

In fear, I considered first my own immediate physical survival. After a strange day of walking on eggshells around campus and trying to get some reading done, I called a professor I trusted and had developed a good relationship with. Dr. Phillip Hallie listened carefully as I described the recent incidents and my feelings. I told him I was calling to say goodbye and to thank him for teaching me so much in his classes. I was enrolled in his philosophy course on the ethics of good and evil in which he used literature to address the nature of compassion and resistance to evil. The course made a tremendous impact on me, encouraging me to look at my own personal code and the need to develop a moral compass.

After listening to me patiently, Dr. Hallie responded that I could not leave because I had a class to teach. At first, I didn't understand him and asked, *"What?"* "Well," he said, "we will be reading Joseph Conrad's *Heart of Darkness* next, and there's a connection." He went on to explain that literature springs from social circumstance, history, timing, and culture and that at the heart of literature and living was the dilemma of ethical choice. In his mind, fighting racism was about doing the right thing, and by leaving, I would be believing the lies in the letters and giving in to the forces of death. He encouraged me to search my soul and consider facing the challenge, staying at Wesleyan and leading the next class discussion.

Initially, I flat-out refused. He gave me the page numbers of several key passages to read in *Heart of Darkness* and said that he would call back in half an hour. When he called back, I had read the passages carefully, as well as copies of the hate letters that triggered my fear, and I agreed to lead the class in a discussion about the "connections."

Dr. Hallie believed in me when I could not believe in myself. He took time at the right time. He took a chance and released control and power—a power that all educators have either to encourage growth or to discourage and put down. Instead of assuming my inferiority, my weakness, my smallness, he offered me an opportunity to make sense and meaning in a public way.

He taught me that a shared power is a shared vision, a collaborative action that makes goodness happen. He helped me turn the lie around, face it, know it, and thus extinguish it. In 1979, Dr. Hallie wrote the book *Lest Innocent Blood Be Shed,* a masterful study and story of the French town of Le Chambon whose residents saved over five thousand refugees, most of them Jews, from the Nazi death camps.

As a result of this experience and my relationship with Dr. Hallie, I strive in the classroom and in my life to make connections among feeling, thinking, and acting. I aim to create classroom environments where life experiences and family and community stories matter. I guide my students in making connections between their own experiences and perspectives and the content, activities, and challenges we face in our learning. Students also direct their learning by identifying areas, themes, topics, and questions they need to explore.

Instead of being tempted to always ask, "What do you know?" we often ask, "How do you know?" and then we ask, "What now? What next?" In this way, we can have more authentic and open conversations about the stories behind our impressions and conclusions. With regard to honoring human diversity, challenging stereotypes, and confronting and healing racism, having the courage to really listen without judgment is the ultimate leap.

For me, teaching is about making change, seeing connections, and bringing them to life. It is about understanding the distance and journey between intent and impact for myself and for the children and adults I work with. If you have no passions or questions of your own, no need to grow or change, you cannot believe in the human capacity to feel and think. Feeling, thinking, and acting are interconnected.

To be an effective teacher, I must first believe in a child's success. I must expect success, dream it, and believe that it is possible. I have heard many lies since the day the letters arrived and expect to hear many more in the future, but something in me changed when a teacher made room for my story. I am not the same woman as a result. I am not small and insignificant; I matter. Something changed forever when someone believed I could feel, think, and then act for change. Today I believe it too.

Catalina Rios began teaching Spanish in 1990 at the Abington Friends School, where she is also the coordinator of multicultural programs. She also teaches at the Taller Puertorriqueño Community Cultural Arts Center. An accomplished writer and poet, she is presently working on a book of poems. Her poems have been featured in numerous literary publications and featured in Gloria Anzaldua's anthology of literature by women of color, *Haciendo Caras: Making Face, Making Soul,* and in Frances

Negron's *Shouting in a Whisper*. Aside from her teaching and writing, she is also active in numerous educational organizations. She serves as a project leader for the National SEED (Seeking Educational Equity and Diversity) Project and as a presenter at the National Association of Independent Schools Conference. She feels most alive in her teaching when "my students have a real context to work in and are interacting in authentic ways with the topic, materials, and other people—when it 'clicks' and makes sense to them, when they are invested in their own unique and individual ways and are taking new directions that I had not anticipated. And when there is freedom and time to explore, truly addressing a child's question and wonder."

There's little cover for teachers. We're in the open and under scrutiny almost all the time—by our students, our colleagues, our administrators, and our community of parents. Many teachers feel assailed and vulnerable and over time withdraw and disconnect. Lori Fulton, a high school English teacher, describes how the projections and critiques of colleagues undermined her sense of self-worth and led her to begin to doubt her own instincts and beliefs. On the verge of leaving teaching, Fulton found that by turning inward and connecting with others, she began to resist the projections of others and discovered ways to be present as a teacher who is "comfortable in her own skin."

—S.M.I.

Finding the Courage to Be Seventeen in Forty-Four-Year-Old Skin

Lori Fulton

If there is no enemy within,
the enemy outside can do us no harm.

ᴀꜰʀɪᴄᴀɴ ᴘʀᴏᴠᴇʀʙ

I never much liked history until Mrs. Drost came into my life as my junior high school American history teacher. Mrs. Drost wasn't just a teacher; she was more like an adult collaborator—maybe even a conspirator—in her attempt to make history relevant to a bunch of itchy and scratchy Ohio teenagers. Often I felt that she was an overgrown thirteen-year-old instead of a real adult because she could see history through our adolescent perspectives, as if she could wear the same lenses we did to view the world.

She helped me care about what happened during Pickett's charge or how the events in Salem, Massachusetts, during the 1600s related to the McCarthy witch hunts of the 1950s and Nixon in the 1960s. As she encouraged us to make connections with years and facts in our nation's past, she was able to thread

e of commonality, comfort, and safety through herself, all of
rmone-charged students, and the people who helped shape
America. She encouraged us to be ourselves in our exploration of the
curriculum, allowing us to feel safe within our own skins.

Mrs. Drost's ability to create a nurturing climate led to my lifelong love of the narratives found in human history and today influences much about how I try to create an atmosphere in my own
high school English classroom, one that seeks to take students beyond rote learning toward real investment and ownership. I try
never to forget my experiences as an adolescent and this seems to
help me have more courage to be my own true self in the classroom.

Part of the comfort level in class comes from a sense of my
own arrested development. For me, my true inner self is seventeen
years old, just as Mrs. Drost's might have been thirteen. I often get
a glimpse of myself as a still young, dreamy, rebellious, different-
drummer soul, eager to look for new and innovative approaches
to things, somewhat naive, usually seeking out silly fun, willing to
experiment for better results, very empathic, occasionally an embarrassment to the adults around me because of my goofiness, and
continually digging for ways to figuratively flip the bird at those
who only want to look at the world through one narrow peephole.

Although my inner self's *joie de vivre* is important in building personal and academic circles with students, it has often led to
disastrous results with some of my fellow teachers. For if there is
utter ecstasy in being seventeen and willing to go out on a dare, it is
also a bittersweet time; it can be an age raw with the pain and fear
of rejection, replete with the aching need for love and attention,
burdened with an uncomfortable ease to slip into the blame game
as a form of self-protection, and heated with a fervent desire to find
someone whom I value who also values me.

This was particularly apparent during my first few years of
teaching, when my skin was a thin target for what I perceived to
be the slings and arrows that were hurled from all directions, not
only from more experienced teachers but also from within. I'm

sure many new teachers have felt this heightened sense of ultra-sensitivity. Indeed, my soul often sensed many cleavers that wished to divide it—colleagues who, through innuendo or attitude, made it clear that they found my teaching methods questionable, impractical, and not up to their standards because "if kids are having fun in class, they can't be learning."

By my second year of teaching, I was at a crossroads. I was able to see and feel tangible results in academic and relational domains with my students, but I had alienated and often been hurt by some of my more experienced colleagues. For example, I was once referred to as the "fun teacher" by one of my fellow English teachers in a department meeting because my students liked my class so much, and coming from this particular teacher, it certainly wasn't meant as a compliment. Likewise, one of my veteran colleagues actually admitted that he had checked my students' grades to see if I'd given A's to each and every one (needless to say, I hadn't).

In my then seventeen-going-on-forty-something-year-old mind, I just wanted to brush these disapproving peers aside and soap their figurative windows. But that was not the reality of the situation; in truth, I internalized their assessments of me. I second-guessed even what I knew was working in the classroom because, according to the naysayers, these products couldn't possibly have come as a result of my teaching. I constantly pushed their rock of judgment with my nose until I was on the verge of a breakdown. I even began to think that any kid who wasn't deeply connecting with me justified the opinions of these cynical teachers.

Despite the fact that students were asking to be in my classes, parents were delighted that their children were not only learning the curriculum but actually enjoying it, and administrators were pleased with my performance, I found myself less trusting of my own instincts. When former students would call, e-mail, send cards, or randomly drop by my classroom to tell me how well they were doing in their college English classes or how easy it was to write college papers in sociology because of the way I taught them in high school or simply just to hang out with me, you would think I'd have been rolling around like a dog in fresh spring grass. Yet no matter how genuine the accolades, I couldn't accept them. Why? Because all I could hear, all I could focus on, and all I could overanalyze was why a handful of my peers didn't like me, my methods, or my success.

It is difficult to cram into these few pages what Courage to Teach (CTT) both means to me and did for me. One of the most powerful experiences came in a clearness committee[1] during a retreat, when I asked to be a focus person. Simply put, clearness committees give a person the opportunity to unpack his or her issues, whatever they may be, in the safe company of others who listen with double confidentiality in mind and who ask open, nonleading questions. (You can find out all the details of these committees by reading *The Courage to Teach*.) During my time as the focus person, I decided to center on my confusing sense of insecurity:

Why did I feel so inferior in a profession I loved so much?
Why did I let the veterans get to me, or why did I construe their comments as so critical?
Why couldn't I actually enjoy what I truly loved without always second-guessing myself?
Why did I want the approval of my peers, even though I had so long denied this?

Through this, I came to a sense of clarity, realizing that what I had been doing and being in my classroom was what was right for me, although it was not quite a comfortable fit for the colleagues whose approval I was desperately seeking. I began to understand that I had allowed one or two negative voices to completely overwhelm hundreds of affirming ones—as if bad was louder than good. By seeking clarity to find the control knobs to tone down those contrary decibels, I began to trust my inner self. I cannot be anyone except myself, nor can I ever expect anyone to be like me. Indeed, I am not myself when I am trying on someone else's skin, which does not fit, pretending to be someone I cannot recognize when I look in the mirror. Indeed, what I learned is that my seventeen-year-old inner self is just fine, thank you. It is who and what I am; to deny it is to set myself (and those around me, including my students) up for true failure. I can approve of myself, and that's the approval that counts.

I didn't learn to trust and value myself overnight. It has taken me every single moment of the two years of the CTT program to get to the point I'm at now, and I still am working on being comfortable within my own skin. I needed to walk down many fog-obscured paths before I came to the slightest hint of clarity—that perhaps I was doing the right thing. Parker J. Palmer's books, along with our CTT retreats and many hours of inner work, enabled me to see that I had allowed others' perceptions to turn my joyous, seventeen-year-old inner self into my own worst enemy.

I also wrote a great deal in my journal about what was at the core of my insecurity, read other books along the way, and talked with my closest friends and my spouse about my own sensitivity. I also did something I had never done much of before—I sat in silence, listening to the sounds of what my inner self so desperately wanted to say. I came to see that I had denied what was good about me, denied how my own arrested development may give me a special empathy for students that makes me a sort of natural-born teacher.

This realization has been powerful medicine. I now know that I cannot control what others say or do; I can only control my own actions and words. This has helped me feel more confident in my teaching, take compliments more graciously and gratefully, and spread the idea of leading a centered, undivided life as much as possible. I also feel strongly about helping new teachers deal with the same sore spots that I had scratched to the point of rawness for far too long. My relationships with many of my colleagues seem safer now, as if now that I can trust myself, they can trust me as well. I've likewise learned to dismiss the negative people with a nod and a smile instead of beating myself up about what they might think of me.

I still have a long way to go to turn down the negative and play up the positive. But I know now that that power is at my fingertips, and in that power I can be, as Mrs. Drost was all those many years ago, comfortable within my own teaching skin.

NOTE

1. For more information about the Courage to Teach program and clearness committees, see the essay by Marcy and Rick Jackson (pp. 282–308).

Lori Fulton has taught high school English in Michigan at South Haven High School and presently at Mattawan High School. She has been teaching since 1996. Aside from the regular slate of English classes, Lori also teaches yearbook, creative writing, and film appreciation. A presenter at professional conferences, Lori has been involved with developing educational materials for the Rock and Roll Hall of Fame and Museum. She has also participated in the Courage to Teach program sponsored by the Fetzer Institute. Lori feels most alive in her teaching "when I am in community with my students, knee-deep in discussion, where everyone feels safe enough to share what really matters, not what they think others simply want to hear. Through laughter and tears, to reach deep into the hearts and souls of students is what teaching is all about; teaching is relationship building, creating family within the confines of a classroom and a curriculum."

When we stand with high hopes before our students, we're astonishingly vulnerable—vulnerable to the student who dozes in the corner, vulnerable to the students who giggle distractedly through class, vulnerable to the students who reveal through their words, or inattention, or defiance that our approach, our presence, our method doesn't work for them. Rachael Kessler describes these challenges as encounters with the "negative angels" and reveals how these can be among the most instructive episodes in our growth as teachers and people.

—S.M.I.

Adversity as Ally

Rachael Kessler

We must embrace the pain and burn it as fuel for our journey.
KENJI MIYAZAWA

"If you continue to lead this workshop the way you've just led this first hour, it will be completely useless for me."

Sue Ellen's voice comes from the back of the room, high up on the last tier of this choral room.

"I will go back in September," she continues, "and be completely unprepared to bring any of this work into my classroom or present any of this information to my colleagues, which they are expecting me to do."

Her words are like a swift blow to my midsection. After the shock, I take a breath and continuing to look straight at this woman, I respond. "Thank you, that's exactly the guidance I was looking for. Francisco," I say now turning to my colleague, "please move the overhead projector so we can start the lecture."

I was standing in front of forty teachers and counselors in a small Texas town on the first morning of a two-day workshop. I was an hour into the workshop, having plunged into a series of experiential practices designed to help the participants become alert and fully focused. I sensed that most of the group were having fun and were excited about the connections I had been making between social and emotional learning and academic excellence. But last night, Francisco and I decided that we would check in after the first hour to see if the participants needed the more familiar theoretical approach common to the beginning of a training session.

"Yes, I do think you should check with them," Francisco had agreed. "As a matter of fact, I think if even one person feels a need for the theory early on, let's do it."

I appreciated his wisdom. I have often let myself be misled by a more "democratic" reading of the group and discovered later that I have completely lost some people who not only suffer themselves but sometimes disturb the whole group.

So I said to them that morning, "I would like to continue with some more experiential work, but if any of you would like me to present the theoretical framework first, I would be glad to do so."

That's when Sue Ellen spoke, her face in a snarl. She sat with a friend in the top row of this choral room, eight or ten rows behind where the rest of the group was scattered.

Years before, I would have been thrown off balance by feedback given with such a critical and even hostile edge. I would have felt deflated and defensive. My inner critic would have taken this opportunity for a field day—sowing self-doubt and even a feeling of humiliation that could last for days. And to protect myself from my own harshness, I would have struggled with thoughts and feelings of derision for Sue Ellen and her apparently snide companion.

But on this day, I felt gratitude and compassion. I welcomed Sue Ellen's guidance and knew that despite her tone, she was an ally. I continued to be cheerful and focused as I presented, step by step, the rationale for integrating heart and community into the classroom. I knew now that it was time to meet Sue Ellen and other teachers with similar learning styles on their own terms—using research and all the latest concepts in educational reform to build a solid case. I gave them the theory and language to explain how these tools could help teachers meet their academic goals and address the deeper needs of their students to prevent the violence these teachers were all so gravely concerned about in the months following Columbine.

I looked up from time to time and saw Sue Ellen furiously taking notes. Halfway through my lecture, she raised her hand again. "Can you give us copies of those overheads? This is exactly what I need, and those overheads would sure help me with my staff."

"I would be glad to."

During the break, a number of teachers came up to me to apologize for their colleague and assure me that they had found the first hour very useful. "I've been thoroughly enjoying the balance of presentation styles in this workshop," I heard again and again from teachers. One commented: "It's funny, we're talking about social and emotional learning here, and Sue Ellen just doesn't seem to have certain social skills. She's an excellent teacher and really has a good heart, but she just doesn't know how to communicate sometimes without being downright rude."

I assured these teachers that I really did appreciate Sue Ellen's guidance to move us into a more theoretical approach at that time. We went on to have a rich and moving day as the trust built and teachers shared their stories. Tears and laughter were soon welcome, and the sense of community deepened. Toward the end of the second day, one of the teachers raised his hand. "I'm wondering if there's something you're trying to teach us that you're not really talking about. Something you're doing—doing with us. Like when we got started, and Sue Ellen was so harsh in her criticism and you just smiled and thanked her and went on. You really didn't seem ruffled by that—not then and not later either. I thought you might be putting on a show when you thanked her, but then it seemed like you really meant it."

I smiled with surprise and pleasure that someone could name so boldly and clearly what I have been working on for over a decade—what I called the "teaching presence" back in the late eighties, when I began to find words for a deeper level of modeling that I believe is the essence of good teaching.

I really did feel guided when Sue Ellen spoke. Of course, my ego took a slight bruise from the sound of attack in her words and tone. But my body and my heart did not leap into the high-adrenaline reaction I know so well when I actually feel threatened. Instead of feeling "emotionally hijacked,"[1] I felt spiritually guided.

Almost every teacher knows these moments when an unexpected barb or cynical comment comes our way from a student or colleague. Even more threatening can be criticism from one of our superiors—even when the tone is not harsh. What allows us to receive such information in a new way—to have the resiliency that allows us to consider the value in what may be useful guidance? Or to feel compassion for where the critic is coming from, even if the person's point of view is not ultimately useful? I will explore some of the stepping-stones on a journey that led me to respond to those teachers with a kind heart and a mind open to altering my course in response to the need of the moment.

Such rewiring of my system has not come quickly or easily. My capacity to frame adversity as an ally developed slowly over the years of feeling the increasing interplay between my inner work and my outer work. Sometimes the adversity has come in my personal life with lessons for my professional life. Sometimes it is a challenge at work that gives me a pearl of wisdom or stretches me big enough to handle something in my private life. The synergy of growth knows no boundaries between my public and private selves.

My first real awareness that potentially devastating moments could become my teachers came in 1985, when I first began my work in social and emotional learning. I was hired to be the first chair of a brand-new and unique department in a high school— the Department of Human Development. With a husband and three little boys at home, I had taken on my first full-time job since becoming a mother. I was hiring, training, and supervising more than fifteen part-time teachers as well as facilitating six groups of teenagers at three grade levels. We were all on a new journey—integrating heart, spirit, and community into the fabric of school life. My colleagues in other departments were often hostile—jealous and dismayed that resources were being taken from academic and athletic departments for this new initiative. My students ranged from the few who were resistant and cynical about sharing feelings to the many who eagerly flooded the room with deep concerns and yearnings that had been held back for years. I called on all of my strength and resiliency to hold all the pieces together.

I had come originally to the school seeking a part-time position in this exciting new "Mysteries Program" I had heard about. Two weeks later, I was offered leadership of the department, which embraced not only this social and emotional learning curriculum but long-standing programs in ethics and community service as well. The morning after I accepted the position, I said to myself, the only way I can survive in this job is to learn how to meditate.

And so, almost forty, after telling myself for years that I "should" meditate but never even trying, I began a daily practice that serves me still today. Actually, it felt then more like the practice began itself and I simply went along for the ride. What looked like tremendous discipline actually felt like the simple surrender to a refuge and guidance that welcomed me with a firm and gentle hand.

The first two weeks were difficult—boring, tedious, uncomfortable. I was creating my own approach, testing and weaving together practices I read about in a wonderful little book, titled simply *How to Meditate,* that offered a range of meditation techniques from around the world.[2] But after two weeks, something shifted. I entered a realm of calm and clarity, a delicious sensation flooded my mind and body, and my journey to resiliency and perspective had begun.

It happened none too soon. Not only was I challenged at work, but two months into my job, I got some news at home that was devastating. I was overcome with grief. Grief turned to rage when I thought about the timing. How could the universe cut me down at a time in my life when I needed my greatest strength and resiliency for my professional life?

I arrived at school at 7:30 A.M. after a night of tears and less than four hours' sleep. My body was spent, my mind a jumble, my heart broken. How can I possibly teach today? I asked myself as I walked down the stairs from my office to the classroom building. How can I possibly lead a group of sixteen-year-olds this morning without crying and coming apart? I was terrified. I had a firm belief in those days that I could not function without less than eight hours of sleep. I had also built my sense of competency around a mental clarity and emotional control that felt totally inaccessible at this moment.

But when I emerged from that first class, I knew that I had never been a more effective teacher. I was more present, more "in my heart" with these young people than I had ever known how to be. Still able to maintain my own mental and emotional equilibrium, I had a heightened receptivity to the feelings and needs of the class as a group and of its individual members. I was filled with a compassion that without words or explanation seemed to be contagious and set a field for meaningful communication.

As I mounted the stairs to my office, I felt gratitude. My heart had broken, but it had not broken down, had not shattered or been destroyed. My heart had actually been *broken open.* And almost immediately, I was receiving the gifts that come from an open heart.

146

In his poem "The Guest House," Rumi invites us to welcome each feeling that comes to us, "even if they're a crowd of sorrows, who violently sweep your house. . . . Still, treat each guest honorably. He may be clearing you out for some new delight."[3]

I did not know Rumi at that time. But I understood—perhaps for the first time—that a "devastating" challenge was opening me up to grow. And while I knew there would be much more grief, and healing would take its time, I also knew that if I could keep my heart open and my mind clear, this adversity could become an ally, guiding me to essential learning.

I believe that the compassion and resiliency I felt that day in Texas was seeded in the experience of my first year of teaching. "Discovering fearlessness," says Tibetan lama Chogyam Trungpa, "comes from working with the softness of the human heart."[4] In my vulnerability that day, I discovered a new source of courage that altered my inner compass forever. Over the years, I had many opportunities to discover guidance in the most unexpected places and people. Allies and signs, I believe, come in many forms. Experiences of hurt and disappointment, failure, betrayal, and anger often reveal themselves as guidance once I regain perspective.

Regaining "perspective" has been at the heart of my path toward resiliency. Daily meditation practice certainly built a new muscle—the "witness self" that can look at my own feelings and experiences with detachment. Soon my knee-jerk reactions are quieted, and I see new options for both understanding and behavior. As this muscle gets stronger from regular practice, I find myself moving more quickly through irritation to feel calm enough to look for the opportunity or lesson in the experience. Another practice that fosters resiliency is the discipline to look for meaning in my experience and the faith to look for positive meaning in my most challenging moments. "When the universe closes a door, somewhere else it is opening a window." This notion has inspired my imagination in searching for positive meaning or holding myself open for the arrival of a gift when I am feeling thwarted or disappointed.

Adversity, I believe, is not something we resist or merely survive; it can offer us an opportunity to gain something and grow. When I am open to the possibility of these gifts, I am less likely to be rocked off course, even if what I am dealing with is actually just a momentary nuisance. This openness is the foundation of developing the capacity to be fully present as a teacher. A teacher who is fully present can be described as follows:

- Open to perceiving what is happening right now
- Responsive to the needs of this moment
- Flexible enough to shift gears
- Prepared with the repertoire, creativity, and imagination to invent a new approach in the moment
- Humble and honest enough to simply pause and acknowledge if a new approach has not yet arrived

When I am present in these ways, I can change course without feeling rocked and rattled. I can experience criticism or disagreement as the kind of feedback a pilot seeks from the control tower to make adjustments essential to navigating safely and effectively.

A few years back, I coined the term "negative angels" to describe how some of the most irritating people or encounters can awaken us to the need to take a stand for what we want or to choose a new turn in our lives. Sue Ellen was a negative angel, and some of my students have been some of the most instructive negative angels in developing my open heart and mind in my work with people of all ages.

When Sue Ellen's colleague asked me that day what I was trying to teach between the lines, I shared with these teachers the story of Jack, a student whose challenge to me was perhaps the most direct preparation for this moment in Texas.

"I think this kind of class could get sappy and fake," said Jack on the first day of our tenth-grade human development class.

STORIES OF THE COURAGE TO TEACH

"We could all just pretend to be talking about real feelings, and it would all be a joke. Or we could get real and then go too far. I mean, this is school, you know, not therapy, and we could start getting real personal with people's problems, and I think that would be a real mistake."

I listened carefully and watched myself get defensive with every word he spoke. He sat with that posture that said, I know how to throw you off guard, lady; just like I do everywhere I go. I recognized one of those "negative leaders"—the rebel who is determined to gather other students into his mission to use jokes and side-talk and even philosophical debate to disempower teachers. But then, in an instant, I considered another possibility. He was bright and thoughtful and although I disagreed with him, I appreciated the way he spoke honestly about his skepticism. Then I spoke in a way I never had.

"Jack, I really appreciate your honesty. And I think you're right. All those things could happen here if we're not careful. You have an unusual wisdom to be able to see these dangers, and I wonder if you would be willing to take some leadership here in helping our class make sure those things don't happen. And when you see them happening, please let us know."

Jack looked stunned. He was silent for a moment, and I watched his body language change. He straightened up tall in his chair, his shoulders pushed back, and he said, "I could do that. As a matter of fact, I'd be glad to do that—to help in that way."

And he did. In that moment of being honored, Jack decided to become a leader in our class. He was an ally, almost a partner for me that year in making the class a success. And the next spring, Jack decided to run for student body president. Our school had always elected juniors for that position to reign during their senior year. That year, after watching a brilliant and unique campaign, they elected Jack.

The lesson I had learned with Jack has infused all my work since then—with teachers and students alike. When I can genuinely consider and acknowledge my critic as a guide—when I can see in their attack, skepticism, disappointment a needed correction or warning—they can indeed become my ally. And the lesson is never lost on the rest of the group.

I have met adversity in so many forms in my career as a teacher of adolescents and their teachers: the broken air-conditioner on a 90-degree day in a room without windows, the disruption of a class by a fire drill at precisely the worst moment, the class that never comes together because some student has sabotaged trust in an elusively subtle or painfully blatant way, the colleague who has contempt for the way I see things, the boss who whipsaws the faculty with his moods and threats, the graduate student who attacks me for being authoritarian when I assert myself and condescending when I encourage her to make her own choices.

Each one of these incidents has a story—stories that move from calamity to calm, from despair to the restoration of hope, wisdom, and love for all those present in those moments when we, like Rumi, can be "grateful for whoever comes, because each has been sent as a guide from beyond."

NOTES

1. Goleman, D. *Emotional Intelligence.* New York: Bantam Books, 1997.
2. LeShan, L. *How to Meditate: A Guide to Self-Discovery.* New York: Bantam Books, 1974.
3. Rumi. "The Guest House." In C. Barks (ed.), *The Essential Rumi.* New York: HarperCollins, 1995, p. 109.
4. Trungpa, C. *Shambhala: The Sacred Path of the Warrior.* Boston: Shambhala Press, 1984.

As director of the Institute for Social and Emotional Learning (www.mediatorsfoundation.org/isel), Rachael Kessler works with teachers and educational leaders to integrate heart, spirit, and community into curriculum and staff development. The author of *The Soul of Education: Helping Students Find Connection, Compassion, and Character at School* (Association for Supervision and Curriculum Development, 2000) and the coauthor of *Promoting Social and Emotional Learning: Guidelines for Educators* (Association for Supervision and Curriculum Development, 1997), Kessler works with educators to support educational programs that nourish the spiritual development of children. She writes, "I feel most alive in my teaching when I see students awaken to genuine curiosity and compassion for those who are different from them, whom they have dismissed or disrespected in the past. Or when a healing occurs between two students or a student and parent where there has been estrangement. And when I see the joy on my students' faces when they rediscover playfulness and delight."

Part Three

Making Change
Reforms That Honor
the Teacher's Heart

A few years ago, I interviewed a veteran teacher from South Carolina about her work. She struck me as the embodiment of the very best teachers I've known. She spoke of the mystery and complexity of learning and how she struggled to understand the "rivers of her students' minds"; she spoke with affection of her students and the energy they give her; she spoke with concern and respect about her colleagues and said that she learns so much when she has time to talk and work with them; she spoke wryly of the "thrill ride" of teaching—moments of glory and despair; and she talked about the joy of designing creative projects that engross her students in learning.

At the end of the interview, I asked her if she had anything else she wanted to add. She paused and then said, "One more thing. Maybe the most important thing." Then she offered a bit of homespun wisdom that I think quivers at the center of all this: "There's an old saying: 'If Momma ain't happy, ain't nobody happy.' If you get a teacher in the classroom who's not happy, then look out, little children."

In this one remarkable image, I believe she captures the premise of this entire book: we can't teach children well if our teachers aren't well. It's worth lingering on its cold inverse: if our teachers are unwell, our children will suffer.

Several other important principles come up. The "happy" she means is not the simplistic "Don't worry, be happy" jingle of pop music fame. She doesn't mean that we need teachers who derive pleasure from idle amusement and fleeting frivolities. No, this veteran teacher is talking about a weightier sense of happiness, what philosopher Bertrand Russell called "fundamental happiness," happiness that "depends more than anything else upon what may be called a friendly interest in person and things."[1] Russell's conception of being happy has to do with being genuinely vibrant, alive, and whole. I'm reminded of the term *wide-awake*, used by Maxine Greene, Jacques Barzun, and Alfred Schutz to describe a state of full attention and sensitivity to life. Good teachers are wide-awake—tuned in, active, and ready to reach out and be fully present and connected in the world.

As we've read in many of the teachers' stories thus far, our teachers struggle to stay wide-awake and fully alive in their work. The multiple and heightened demands of teaching leave us exhausted and depleted. The tedium of our routines leaves us weighted down by lethargy. The vulnerability that comes from being an object of everyday scrutiny forces us to erect barriers that cut off the possibility of establishing genuine relationships between ourselves, our students, and our colleagues. Although everyday activities in school offer us countless opportunities to live a connected life, we can become teachers who walk through classes, semesters, and years in a semistupor.

If our children need empathic, caring, "wide-awake" adults who can support students' academic, social, and personal development, then we had better attend to how our institutions support and sustain these people. The essays in Part Three engage with this idea by describing a variety of efforts that seek to promote good teaching by devoting resources, employing professional development activities, and encouraging habits of interaction that seek to honor and support the heart and energy of the teachers in the institution.

The essays presented here describe an approach to educational reform that focuses on attending the teacher. The verb *attend* is derived from the Latin *attendere,* meaning "to stretch toward, listen to, and heed." Ironically, the typical approach to attending teachers in educational reform movements has something to do with stretch, but not the humane version of stretch connoted by *attendere.* Instead of stretching toward them in an effort to heed, listen, and understand our teachers, we stretch our teachers. We stretch them thin by asking them to play multiple and often contradictory roles: teacher, counselor, disciplinarian, coach, cheerleader, assessor, parent, school reformer. We pull, tug, and yank them, often violently, in a contorted effort to mold them into practitioners whose techniques are standardized and predictable. And so, given our version of *attend,* they end up stretched on the rack of our expectations, often fraying at the edges.

The essays you will read in Part Three are by and about educators who have focused on a question of major importance: How can educational institutions sustain and deepen the selfhood from which good teaching comes? They recognize that teacher training and even high-quality professional development do not provide opportunities for teachers to attend to the pursuit of their vocational ideals. The programs and approaches described in these stories embrace broad pedagogies but adhere to the following principles.

- *Attend to teachers' outer needs.* Teachers won't be able to sustain their inner passion without believing that their external needs will be met. Along with renewal, revitalization, and resuscitation of the self, teachers must be adequately supported in their external needs, sufficiently compensated, and have the resources on hand essential to their work.

- *Attend to teachers' inner needs.* The source of good teaching is the heart of the teacher. These writers understand that good teaching springs not from the precision of a teacher's technique or from the form of a teacher's method but from a teacher's capacity to be available and present in service of student learning. There is no one best method to renew and grow a teacher's professional heart. What these change efforts have in common is the commitment to creating hospitable spaces that allow teachers to explore their teaching as an embodiment of the connections they make between themselves, their students, their colleagues, and the subjects they teach.

If we are truly serious about improving the quality of our schools, we must focus our efforts on keeping teachers wide-awake and fully alive. These stories describe efforts to renew and sustain our teachers in ways that encourage us to serve students faithfully, nourish our own well-being, connect us in meaningful ways with our colleagues.

—S.M.I.

NOTE

1. Russell, B. *The Conquest of Happiness.* New York: Bantam, 1968, p. 110. (Originally published in 1930)

When we work in an institution that betrays our highest ideals and erodes our integrity, we have choices. We can close our door and subversively practice in a way aligned with our beliefs. But this leaves us open to recriminations and constant reproaches that diminish both our energy and our love for teaching. Or we can adopt the practices and beliefs of the institution, despite our misgivings, and diminish ourselves from the inside out. Texas elementary school teacher Clayton Stromberger describes his struggle to find a way to be the teacher he is meant to be within the often stifling demands and structures of the educational system. His struggle is eased somewhat by discovering compassion for those in the system, forgiveness for the times he is less than he wishes to be, and courage to stand up and speak his truth.

—S.M.I.

So Sweet It Made Me Jingled
Offering My Own Truth
Within the System

Clayton Stromberger

One day, in the midst of another outburst of chaos and squabbling from my class of twenty distractible fourth graders, I stopped my lesson, looked at the kids for a moment, and then slowly and deliberately walked over to the worn-out old green chalkboard and wrote in four-inch capital letters, "WHAT AM I DOING HERE?"

I remember that moment vividly for the silence that immediately settled on the room at the first gesture of this simple action. The kids, suddenly noticing a change in the routine—which was the routine of me trying to charm, cajole, or compel them to sit still and listen long enough for us to get through some basic lesson or discussion or even read-aloud of a story—pricked up their ears and watched what their well-meaning but rather strange teacher was doing. They eagerly called out the words as I wrote them, as if they were trying to solve a puzzle:

"What . . . am . . . I . . . doing . . . *here! What am I doing here!*"

Then came a kind of befuddled pause. "'What are you doing here?' You're teaching."

"Am I really? Or am I just spending my time trying to get you guys to be quiet? What does it mean to *teach,* anyway?"

Had I asked this question of my fifth graders at the same school two years before, during my dive-in-the-deep-end first year of teaching, a spirited half-hour discussion would have followed, with Gweneta weighing in immediately, David raising his hand to say he had "two things," as he always did, and Homero, who hated school and twisted in his seat like a trapped animal—"I'm sufferin' here!" he once hollered out in the middle of class—blurting out something honest and direct. Two other boys might have been carving holes in their desks, and a few other kids might have just been staring blankly into space, daydreaming, but at least a few memorable sparks would have been lit—they were just that kind of group.

But these twenty kids were younger and more restless, full of craving for play and physical freedom, and they were nonplussed by my question. We talked about it briefly, and I once again told them—in what was becoming a too familiar refrain, I'm afraid—that "if I had my own school, things would be different. You'd be here because you wanted to be." Having thus expressed my ideal vision, I was quickly forced to return to reality as the wheels started coming off again—someone started hollering at someone else over a stolen pencil, three kids were up endlessly washing their hands at the sink again. And as I was already on the list of teachers who couldn't "control" their classes, in that moment the only answer seemed to be, once again, some kind of assignment or command, like "OK, that's enough! Get out your math books!" which was inevitably met with groans and sighs and exclamations about math books that had been lost or stolen. We slogged on toward the clanging of the afternoon bell.

But my words stayed on the board all day, and at the end of the year, when I asked the kids to create a mural on big sheets of paper of all the moments and phrases from our nine months to-

160

gether, someone wrote "WHAT AM I DOING HERE?" To be ho can't remember now if it was me or one of the kids, but the was, along with "TAAS ALERT!"—my signal to the class to qui pull out their Texas Assessment of Academic Skills booklets as a particularly prickly administrator was coming our way down the hall; "WHERE, OH WHERE, CAN MY BABY BE?" from our favorite song, the teenage car crash ballad "Last Kiss"; a drawing of a hot-air balloon, which was a frequent and tantalizing morning sight through the windows; and other little highlights I've forgotten.

I tried to find those rolled-up murals the other day, but I think I threw them away last summer, after that year had ground to its awful end. Our school, after years of shoddy leadership and district neglect, was "restructured" that May and staffed with new teachers—a "dream team" designed to raise scores on the TAAS, soon to become TAKS, the Texas Assessment of Knowledge and Skills. I was leaving the Austin, Texas, district. I'd had enough, and those big rolled-up sheets of kraft paper went in the trash along with all the goofy TAAS worksheets I'd been handed by visiting specialists and the terse memos scribbled on "happy face" pads or the surly ones printed on Astrobright red paper. It all went in the dumpster, and I was glad to be rid of the whole mess. I was a man without a country, off to find a school where I could really become a *teacher.*

Like so many other questions I find myself asking lately, the question I put to my fourth graders is both absurdly simple and profoundly puzzling. Life presents us with such riddles, and then we spend the rest of our lives seeking the answers, like a child chasing a butterfly.

I keep thinking these days that if I'm really still, the butterfly will finally alight on my open palm and somehow reveal the answers to my unanswerable questions, the ones that force me deeper and deeper into doubt, like old Zen koans—questions such as "Why teach?"

Easy answers come—"I enjoy sharing something I love with others" or "It's a chance for me to give something back"—but as I reach out for those, off they flit, saying, "Nope, nope! Try again!"

To be a teacher, a real teacher, the kind that kids remember for the rest of their lives, as I remember still the three or four teachers who changed my life, is too hard and too exhausting if you can't stand firmly on the ground of *why*. There are certainly other ways of making a living that are easier on the soul and the pocketbook. So I ask again: Why teach? What is truly worth doing in a classroom? What can I do that actually helps children?

These questions have a fresh urgency for me as I prepare to return to the public school system after a year teaching at a small private high school. Private schools have their own constraints and frustrations, as I found out, but the most pressing one is that they often don't allow a teacher with a family to pay the bills. So I'm headed back into the bureaucratic maze of the Austin Independent School District to teach fourth grade at an elementary on the southeast side of town. As a "new" teacher, I have been asked to end my summer two days early to attend the district's orientation sessions, in which I will sit in a big auditorium and learn about the new Principles of Learning initiative—there are nine or twelve or fifty-seven of these principles, I forget—and about "accountable talk," how teachers are being trained to train kids to talk to visiting administrators about what they're learning and why so that said administrators can be sure that the teachers are really doing their job and not just sitting around wasting taxpayers' money.

Ah, the bitter sarcasm is bubbling up again. Forgive me. You see, I'm already wondering how long I'll hang in there.

But even as I picture myself sitting gloomily in that big hall, fighting the urge to roll my eyes and mutter sarcastic comments about the foolishness of all this committee-created, politically driven silliness—how it kills the very things it seeks to standardize and quantify—there's that butterfly again, flitting overhead. It's bright yellow, and I watch it, and the speaker keeps going on about "academic rigor" and "clear expectations" and "delivery of instruction," but for some reason that I don't understand, some reason more than just needing a job, I stay. And I look up, opening my hand to the receiving air.

A little story from my last year in the trenches still troubles me, like a half-remembered dream. It was late winter, the midpoint of a chaotic and tumbling year of panic over TAAS scores at my school, Blackshear Elementary, a storied old campus on the east side of Austin. We were living your basic, all-too-common public school nightmare: low teacher morale, high turnover, angry and bored kids, a rundown building, and a trash-littered playground. The year before, our principal, whose reign had been a troubled one, had finally been pulled the day after she reduced a fourth-grade teacher to tears on the morning of the all-important TAAS Writing Test. Now our new principal, after much brave talk in August about looking forward to the challenge, was already crumbling under the pressure. We had been designated "low-performing" on the TAAS the year before, and it looked as if we might be headed that way again, and the word from above was, in essence, Get those scores up or we'll *all* lose our jobs!

This meant that my diminutive philosopher, Darnell—who, like Pig-Pen in *Peanuts* always seemed to trail a cloud of playground dust—could no longer stand up in front of the class and read his "Morning Reflections" and tell the class, "Y'all listen to the preacher, now!" because we had to herd all the fourth graders to the cafeteria for an hour and a half of instruction on "TAAS writing," an oxymoron if ever there was one.

I had written this in a journal a few weeks before:

Blackshear has become a cold place. Longtime custodians disappear without a trace or an explanation. Curt memos express official displeasure. New lists of requirements spring up to replace the old ones. Schedules are changed to suit the needs of the administrative team, without even a passing interest in how they affect the delicate ecosystems of each classroom. An implication of blame hangs in the air—for past sins, for the failures to come.

The school's heart has been given over solely to the TAAS, and the test is heartless. Its soil is too shallow to support the roots of dreams. We are starved for beauty here, for the beauty of learning, the joy of it.

On this particular day, after a damp and cloudy morning, the sun had emerged with an entrancing brilliance, casting a whitish-gold light through the long row of scratched-up windows along the back wall of our little shoebox of a fourth-grade classroom. While dutifully checking my students' work on some assignment or other, I looked up to see an eggshell blue sky unfurling like a flag. Without thinking about it for too long, I told the class to grab some paper and a pencil and line up to go outside.

So my students lined up excitedly, this collection of characters who were, in some cases, two grade levels behind where the district said they should be and who were all quite lovely people when you sat and talked with them one-on-one on the playground but who fought like cats and dogs when crammed together in this little room with the erratic air conditioning and the clock that hung precariously from the wall on two wires, caught in midfall.

Out we went, onto a hardscrabble patch of ground near the back far corner of the fence line. The air was moist and cool, and I scanned the terrain for something natural that we could simply *observe,* without having to find its main idea or make it yield its secrets to the problem-solving blueprint. There was a gnarled old oak, a few scraggly little trees, and a small mountain laurel, its purple flowers redolent of grapes. "Spread out without talking," I told the kids. "Find something you can look at that's alive—a tree, a bush, bugs, anything. Watch it and write down what you see. Write down anything you hear or smell or feel." They stood around for a moment, a bit confused, understandably—but gradually they spread out and tried to honor my request. I noticed a few kids hunched over on their knees, writing silently on sheets notebook paper. I'm sure I had to walk a few of my feisty ones "timeout"—the ones who snuck out to the restroom to play six times a day, the three girls who really needed to be at a school that would teach them something real and physically active and meaningful—but that part of the memory has faded.

Matthew, my spirited little commando from New Haven, always ready for a "mission," whether it was to get some books out of my truck or to play a cocky Capulet servant in a scene from *Romeo and Juliet,* wrote:

> The dodropes have water on their little livfs. They feel suft and like a clover. They sparcl in the sun light.
>
> The birds sing like a song. Some of them sing in their nast or they sing ona power line. Birds live different whas then people.

Leon, bright and restless, always proud of finishing his work but loath to spend a second going back over it, wrote:

> The dew drops of a rain. When the tunder of rain come down the trees will sound like this shwish the ground will sound like drip-drop drip-drop and when the big thundering rain is gone then that's when the dew drops come from. Ashl the dew drops come from the shower that comes before the horable thundering rain. The dew drops look like the rain drops but they are tiny.

Margarita, quiet, sweet, a bit lost in my class of twitchers and jumpers, wrote:

> The mountain laurel smeled like a porfum so sweet it made me jingled and I could touch and it felt like my mom's hand's.

After a while, we took a short walk through the neighborhood, stopping in front of some houses to look at flowers or geometric shapes in the architecture or whatever caught our eye. No one shouted or fought. Kaneshia picked a yellow flower and put it in her ear. Then it was time to turn around.

Back in the room, before the bell rang, Margarita came up to me, her round face lit with a smile. "This was a *fun day* today," she said.

"I'm glad you enjoyed it," I told her. And then the bell rang and they all went tearing out of there, and for some reason my heart sank like a stone.

It had been so little, so little: a stroll around a vacant lot where the portables used to be and a half-block walk to smell flowers and see what we could see.

I had gotten into teaching to make a difference, to be the "creative" teacher who, yes, covered the basics but did it in a way that was alive with meaning. My classroom was going to be different, authentic, full of real experiences. I was going to do it all—keep my job while teaching my own way—and the kids were going to have to be *chased* out of the room at 2:45. And now, for the first time all year, a kid had told me something we'd done was fun, and it had been nothing more than an improvised excursion out of desperation. Where had I gone wrong? Why couldn't I give them more?

I've been turning that moment over and over in my mind lately, wondering what its deeper meanings are, what direction it points me. Meanwhile, Margarita and Darnell and so many bright and poetic young people like them are still living out their days in the public schools. Do I have any business being in there with them? Can I function in a system that makes so little sense to me? What will I do half a year from now, in the middle of a required "TAAS writing" lesson, when the blue sky calls through the narrow windows?

I have a basic problem with school. I am bored to tears when I am being taught "a lesson," especially one with an expected outcome.

But when real life appears, I perk up and prick up my ears like fourth graders. At teacher in-service meetings, I find myself wondering when the next break is and where I'm going to go for lunch and then I catch myself and think, I'm just like my kids—and I get mad at them for doing the same thing!

During that last year of teaching, I wrote an article for the local newspaper about my experiences at Blackshear. In it I explained why I thought I had become a teacher. I described how I'd always felt a sense of wonder about the natural world, especially the night sky, and how I'd loved pointing out constellations and planets to the younger kids in my neighborhood. Then I told of the one learning experience I'd had that had changed my life in a truly profound, lasting way—a summer in a University of Texas class called Shakespeare at Winedale in which I lived in the countryside with eighteen other students for two months, struggling to create honest performances of three Shakespeare plays. The class, taught by Dr. James "Doc" Ayres, a tough, brilliant professor with strong passions and a stubborn energy, was a true "sounding of the self" through ensemble work and the haunting poetry of Shakespeare's language—and it gave me, for the first time, an awareness of my own voice and my potential to create meaning with others. In the article I wrote, "In the end, they were our plays. We did these amazing things we never imagined we could do. What a gift to give another human being."

Sometimes I think that's why I became a teacher—to try to reach kids like myself who have some fountain of untapped resources just beneath the surface. And do you know which ones those kids are, the ones like me, with so much more to give than meets the eye or can be squeezed out in a test? It turns out that it's every one of them.

I still believe that. But almost two years later, a bit burned by what happened since then, I wonder anew how to pull it off.

When I get lost, I find myself working my way back home to Winedale—sometimes in my thoughts, as I recall a moment of discovery from my work out there, or physically, when I drive the hour and a half from Austin to see the new summer class's plays. It's a touchstone for me, and—to my great joy—for some of my former students. The last four springs I have taken Blackshear students to Winedale to perform Shakespeare at the program's Festival of Play, and each time it has been an amazing, joyful experience for the kids, myself, and the audience. One of my fourth graders, Cecil, who froze up before his entrance and wouldn't go on stage until I went up there with him (we ended up improvising a wonderful little scene together), wrote of his experience, "I felt like a true star in the hole world."

Inside the century-old hay barn at Winedale that served as our theater and classroom, Doc always came back to key words, key concepts. Improvisation and invention. Play as discovery, play as freedom. The world of the play, the world of the group, and how those two begin to inform each other. Discipline and responsibility. Role-playing and ritual and celebration. Doc didn't learn about these things at a workshop—he grew toward them over the years, following hunches, listening to his inner voice and to the words of a great playwright, learning with and *from* his students. And he often had to do all this alone, without much support, financial or otherwise, from the university administration.

When I think about the courage it takes to be a true teacher, I think back almost twenty years and see Doc alone in the barn at 7:30 on a summer morning, in his headband, shorts, button-down short-sleeved shirt, and running shoes, sweeping the wooden stage as we arrive for the day's work. His cup of coffee and his text are on a small stand, and he's already more awake and eager to work than any of us groggy twenty-year-olds. His presence makes it clear to us, as it will so many times that summer, that we all have important work to do and it is time to get up on our feet and get started.

In my darkest times that final year at Blackshear, I had called my closest mentors and asked for their insight.

STORIES OF THE COURAGE TO TEACH

My friend Dean in Seattle, the first elementary school teacher I ever saw who was fully present in the classroom, completely himself in each moment—who took his classes camping on the Pacific coast, where we watched bald eagles, explored tidal pools, and did scenes from *A Midsummer Night's Dream*—spoke of his own struggles and feeling of isolation in the school system, even after a decade of great work and happy parents. "I have found that keeping mindful of a 'higher purpose,' a 'heightened awareness,' and 'inner courage' is critical for my staying healthy in this profession," he wrote me.

My friend Linda, with whom I did my student teaching, who learned about fighting to survive while growing up in the projects of a small Texas town—and who adamantly refused to "teach to the TAAS test" yet had a phenomenal rate every year of kids passing the thing—listened to my litany of troubles and complaints and said, "You don't sound like Clayton. You sound like some *weak* person." Instead of joining me in a gripe-and-commiserate session, she was giving me a kick in the butt. "The kids are gettin' a piece, the administration is gettin' a piece—it's time for you to get a piece! Go on, tear you off a piece!" We laughed hard and I felt better. But the next day, without Linda actually beside me in the trenches, I felt overwhelmed, isolated, unsure of how and where to tear off that piece or what piece I could tear off without getting fired.

I hung on, hoping for a new principal who would offer encouragement and patience. Instead, the superintendent "restructured" the school and reassigned all but two of its teachers. It was time for a change, they told us. The handpicked incoming principal had been at Blackshear as part of a district "TAAS Team" the year before and had not looked fondly on my attempts to work on a class performance of *The Tempest* a week before the big test, so I knew my time was up even if I'd wanted to fight it out one more year. This family of teachers, many of whom had been at the school for more than fifteen years, was dissolved, and not without feelings of heartbreak and anger and bitterness. On the final morning, after I had carted out the last box of books and stacked the desks and chairs and swept the floor, I sat on the floor of my empty room and looked at the light pouring in from the windows and saw Cecil wiggling his ears *here* and Vanessa laughing *there* and I just lost it and buried my face in my hands and cried like a baby.

That summer I did a few interviews with principals who seemed interested in me until I started speaking too much about creativity and flexibility and not enough about planning and behavior plans and the infallibility of the state-mandated Texas Essential Knowledge and Skills. So I left the district, and after touring charter schools and a Waldorf school and not finding a match anywhere, I ended up teaching social studies and theater part-time at a small private high school.

The next fall, I was dying to visit the kids at Blackshear, but I didn't want to make a scene. So I waited until November. Then I pulled into the parking lot at 2:43 P.M., just before the final bell. My kids from last year were on the playground, and the second I stepped out of the car, I was crushed in a mob of hugs and shouts. We all talked and laughed and asked each other how it was going. I hadn't been there five minutes before a grim-faced man in a suit and tie strode down the steps—my old friend, the new principal. After a perfunctory greeting, he informed me tersely that former Blackshear teachers were being asked not to visit the school. It would be too much of a distraction for the kids and new teachers, especially in the midst of another year of public and district scrutiny over test scores. "If you want to keep up with the kids, that's fine; just do it off-campus," he told me. I pursed my lips, said, "That's too bad," and left stunned, and unsure of my next move. Should I blast him in a letter to the editor? Organize a protest? Or out of respect for the new teachers, whose job was plenty hard enough, should I let it go?

Again, I asked mentors for guidance, and a brilliant free school teacher with whom I'd had an e-mail correspondence gave me this splash of cold water:

> I beseech you to do something in response to what went down yesterday. Don't teach hopelessness to your twenty kids, that

the evil in their lives will always go unopposed. Write that letter, organize a visit in, call *60 Minutes* . . . This is the time to act, and act quickly and decisively. . . .

You probably won't be confronted with such an opportunity again. I regret that I don't live closer and can't do more than just preach at you.

Sorry if I came on too strong. This is my life.

I felt a hot flush of shame and fear. Was he right? Would such an action benefit the kids, or would it just seem like grandstanding on my part? Did I just want to "win" because things hadn't gone my way? What did I really want, anyway? I didn't want to go back there as a teacher; that was impossible. I couldn't take all "my kids" out and start a school of my own—I didn't have the resources or the vision yet for that. And this principal was clearly miserable, wound tight as a spring. Perhaps he too was caught up in the mechanical dance of the system; perhaps I should seek to find compassion for him, wish him and the new staff well, and keep up with the kids individually with home visits.

In the end, I waited. I had a friend teaching at the school, and she advised holding off; she was gaining some clout, she said, and perhaps in time she would have enough leverage to bring me into her classroom as a visiting Shakespeare teacher. I was looking for grant money for just such a project, and at the same time my schedule was filling up with work from my private school job. So I let the moment pass, choosing instead to contact individual children and organize a Saturday Shakespeare group for the spring and a pizza reunion at the end of the year. With another teacher, I attended the Blackshear sixth-grade graduation that May and gave happy hugs to Gordon and Dalisa and Jackie and other kids I'll never forget.

I rediscovered this e-mail recently and felt a sharp pang of regret. This teacher was right. It had been an opportunity, and I'd fumbled it. I could have done more, something, *anything*. Even in being compassionate to the tortured folks in the administration and in being respectful of the feelings of the new teachers who took the place of the old staff, I could have asked to meet with this man, face to face, and found a way to speak honestly and without anger about my desire to do something to help those kids. I could have stood up straight in the midst of my queasy fear of conflict and spoken up without anger or recrimination. Who knows, perhaps this principal and I could have both let go of some of our poisonous anger and found a compromise. Perhaps not. But why not try?

So, another failure. Forgiveness is the only thing that keeps me from giving up on myself as a teacher in self-disgust. The most powerful moments in Shakespeare come from this mysterious gift, which "droppeth as the gentle rain from heaven / on the place beneath," blessing both "him that gives and him that takes." We've all seen scared children lash out angrily in the classroom, and we usually find the clarity to forgive them because they are young. We sometimes forget, though, that we too need mercy—from ourselves. In seeking to help so many children in such constricting conditions, we will constantly come up short. We will fail; we will falter; we will slip into selfishness; we will become blocked by fear and think of self-preservation first. I am a lousy fighter; I get red-faced and defensive. The only thing to do when I chicken out is to forgive myself and try again.

And having seen this fear of failure and need for approval in ourselves, how can we not see it in our administrators as well? They too operate under ludicrous conditions and pressures. Perhaps, viewing them with compassion and speaking our truth to them without fear or anger, our words can do more good. And even if our words are still dismissed, we have spoken them. More and more, I see the boundary between "classroom" and "life" dissolving. The wholeness we are seeking in our lives, we must live out in our classrooms as well—and what a wonderful, living thing to model for a young person.

I almost think that the opportunity to grow in this way, as painful as I'm sure it will be, is the hidden reason I'm returning to a public school system that runs counter to every understanding and intuition I have about what is best for children. Can I return to the ground of compassion and be truly myself in the classroom while being directed to prepare students for a standardized test? Can I find my voice of calm leadership even when someone with a name badge and a clipboard arrives to see a math lesson at the very moment I'm lining up the class to go look at migratory hawks circling in the fall sky? Or is that just too steep a hill for these forty-year-old legs?

There's only one way to find out.

I was at Austin's once-pristine spring-fed pool, Barton Springs, on a hot summer afternoon yesterday, and I couldn't let something go. It was the loss of something precious—the natural beauty of this place. The water, once clear and aquamarine, is still cool and re-freshing, but it has now taken on a greenish tinge. Clumps of algae float on the surface. The pool has to be closed all day Thursday so lifeguards can hose the greenish-brown muck downstream, through the dam, and toward the Colorado River. It makes me sick, and it makes me angry.

I tried pretending in the sparkling sunlight that Barton Springs was as beautiful as it had been, but I finally realized I couldn't do it. We—we human beings, all of us, with our cars, our malls, our office buildings, our golf courses, our housing develop-ments—had fouled the aquifer, and this sacred spot, once a Co-manche watering hole, where Austin's first settlers swam, was now clearly suffering the consequences.

I felt the reflexive fury toward the faceless real estate devel-opers; then I thought: no, it's not that simple. I too feel greed and desire in my heart; I too want success and the good things in life; I too want things that will distract me from the reality of death for a while. For me, it is a beautiful swimming hole; for them, it is a beautiful home and a nice golf course.

Looking at the blue-green water, a phrase popped suddenly into my mind: "forgiveness and caretaking." It reminded me of a phrase I'd discovered recently in a book by the iconoclastic Zen teacher Kosho Uchiyama: "vow and repentance."

When I acknowledged that all of us, in our hunger to live and work near beautiful places, in driving on new roads traversing the aquifer that feeds the springs, had played some part in damaging this natural place—not just an anonymous "they"—I allowed an opening to feel my own shame and regret. My lazy hypocrisy and arrogance in simply seeing myself as one of the "good guys" who loved the pool and would never do it harm was a self-serving fiction. Caretaking meant cherishing the pool as it was, pollution and all; forgiveness meant accepting our human foolishness without hatred and seeking to remedy it wherever I could. The pool's integrity or wholeness had been damaged, but perhaps I could meet that with an integrity of my own.

Then it occurred to me that in an indirect or parallel way, I was also trying to work out the puzzle of how I feel about the school system.

Learning, in its purest form, runs as clear as spring water; it is the joy of discovery, the satisfaction of a deep curiosity. We have befouled it with our desire to control things, to shape them in our image, to tell others what is best for them. As John Taylor Gatto has pointed out in *Dumbing Us Down,* the loose thread that unravels all progressive fantasies about public schools is that they are compulsory; make attendance optional, and even the "creative" classrooms would be empty until something more authentic and interesting took their place. I realized that I was dreading returning to the public schools because I wasn't sure I could live with the painful knowledge of how far the schools were from what I wanted them to be. Then I saw that I wanted them to be that way *for myself.*

Suddenly my exchange with Margarita—how it sank me— appeared in a new light. I realized I had felt not just despair and anger over how little I had done for Margarita and the class but also a deep sense of shame.

Yes, I had taken the kids outside—no other teachers were having their kids write about sights and sounds in the middle of the afternoon—but in so many other moments that year, I had given in to fear of reprisal; I had let a queasy dread of disapproval from administrators dictate my actions. The kids had paid for that. I had most often "modeled" not courage but a kind of frustration at not getting my own needs met for security and ego protection—a natural enough response, given the pressure-cooker atmosphere, but not something that really helped others in any lasting way.

The strange thing was, it was a great relief to finally recognize this.

That same day I read a quote from Pearl S. Buck that kept popping into my mind: "All birth is unwilling." That rang a bell with me. We resist the new insight that brings on change because change is scary. But this birth is also liberating—a new start with a more honest perspective. Caretaking and forgiveness, vow and repentance, regret and renewal, again and again and again.

Until I can start my own school, or find the grant funds to do Shakespeare with my former Blackshear students and others, I have to stand up straight in the midst of the reality of the school system as it is and do what I can, one student at a time, one moment at time. Some children may blossom under my leadership; others might really benefit more from a teacher whose passion is organization and skills. I have to be ready for what that present reality is and find the strength in the midst of less than ideal conditions to keep offering an open hand to others and to myself and to friends and enemies alike.

"All birth is unwilling." We don't want to be the one who, openly facing shame and fear, stands up tall and speaks the truth each day in the classroom or the faculty meeting. And we don't want to be the one who tells the truth to ourselves, about how selfish and impatient we have been. But someone must. I used to think that courage was some sort of substance that people either had or didn't have. It isn't. Courage is simply having the clarity to realize that *someone* needs to draw on up to full height and lead the way, speaking the truth and taking the risks for those who can't—and how scary it is, and what a relief it is, to find that that someone is you.

✍

Last spring, while working part time, I received grant money through the Winedale program to do an outreach program in a public school. I couldn't go to Blackshear, obviously, so I checked with my former colleagues, and one paved the way for me to visit his school. His principal eagerly embraced my idea, and soon I was working with fifteen fifth graders two afternoons a week on scenes from *Midsummer.* On our performance night at an end-of-the-year PTA meeting, the kids, wearing a motley dash of leftover Winedale costumes, pushed through their nervousness and impressed parents with how much they'd accomplished in such a short period of time.

Before the performance, a third-grade girl I'd never seen before, the daughter of the PTA vice president, had appeared backstage and thrown herself eagerly into helping costume the actors. When the scenes were over and the kids had taken their bow to a shower of applause, I stepped off the cafeteria stage to visit with parents. Suddenly this third grader appeared in front of me. She held out her arms as if to stop me in my tracks; then she locked her eyes on mine and said in a direct, deliberate voice, *"How do I get to do this?"*

Later I wrote down her words so I wouldn't forget them. There was something beautiful in the sound of them, an almost poetic simplicity: *How do I get to do this?* "This" was everything, it was something I had to offer, something I often lose sight of, and she had helped me see it again. She was reaching out directly, spontaneously, to a line in my life that began almost twenty years ago in that old hay barn at Winedale.

"What am I doing here?" Maybe, I thought, this is your answer. *I'm here because I have something to offer.* And even here, in a place where I'm not sure I belong, within a system that so often leaves me feeling numb, dispirited, and powerless, there are children who reach out to what I'm offering with open hands and remind me why I try every day to become a teacher.

Clayton Stromberger teaches fourth grade at Widén Elementary School in Austin, Texas. He also teaches an after-school Shakespeare performance class for third, fourth, and fifth graders at Widén. Earlier, he taught for a year at a private high school and before that at Blackshear Elementary School in Austin, where he developed and produced a Shakespeare performance program for Blackshear students that culminated in annual performances at the Shakespeare at Winedale spring festival at the University of Texas. Before becoming a classroom teacher, he shared his love for theater with young people as an artist-in-residence in several schools in the state of Washington. In 1999, his "20 Kids," published in the *Austin American-Statesman* and detailing his experiences in the classroom, was honored as the article offering the "most insight into modern education" in the *Austin Chronicle's* 2000 "Best of Austin" issue. He describes feeling most alive in his teaching when "the kids feel like they're doing something great out of their own power and energy and imagination and forget I'm even there."

Making Change

Reformers, administrators, and pundits are always after teachers to change the way they teach. The assumption is that a teacher's way of teaching can be easily altered because it's merely a matter of adjusting an individual's technique or reengineering an individual's pedagogical method. The flaw in this logic is that so much of our teaching is an expression of who we are. This means that real change can be accomplished only if it is attached to genuine changes in way we experience, understand, and believe the world. After thirty-one years in the high school English classroom, Katherine Kennedy attends a Courage to Teach program, where she encounters a learning community in which she feels safe, listened to, and honored. Inspired by the approach, she returns to her own classroom determined to transform herself as a teacher and the community of her classroom. Weaving the voices of her students through her own story, we experience the travails and triumphs of a teacher reaching out to her students in a new and challenging way.

—S.M.I.

The Risk of Teaching and Learning Differently

Katherine Kennedy

FALL

Today I began my thirty-first year of teaching—how can that be? This year will be my third year of teaching in a circle seating. After experiencing listening circles through the Courage to Teach,[1] I knew I wanted to—I *needed* to—bring circles into my classroom so that my students could have what I had been given, allowing them many more decades than I will have for understanding myself and others. I wanted the students to have the same opportunity to challenge themselves, to know themselves, to finally honor themselves as wonderful, thinking, feeling people who could challenge, know, and honor others—even those they could not understand.

I think I have learned the dynamics that this structure entails. It takes my willingness to let go of some control, to sit in silence and let the conversations emerge from the students. Yet paradoxically, to maintain the safe space, I must be very visible and in charge. It is a delicate balance, one that I renew and the students learn anew each year.

Only the honors class is able to start in a circle because the other classes still test to see who will really run the class, the clowns or me. The honors class seems less fragmented as a group than last year's class. The students still consider *discussion* and *debate* synonymous, but at least no one is openly aggressive this year. Another year begins—we will sow the seeds in September and hope to have a June harvest.

> "Circle up, Class." These words will forever ring through the memory of my senior Honors English class. In early September, the call to circle initiated feelings of discomfort and frustration for both myself and my peers. Disregarding formality, the structure of Honors IV English transcended the atmosphere of anything that we had ever known. . . . Many of us longed for the straight rows where we could escape from expressing ourselves.—Grace

Students must accept that their peers, not to mention they themselves, already have many of the answers to the questions they address to their teachers. I believe that with all my heart, but they have to cope with not being told exactly what to do, when to do it, and how to do it. Each year in the fall, I realize how far the last years' classes really traveled, and I must remember that they will do the same this year, too. The students will learn and gain confidence, but right now they get very angry because I, the teacher, will not teach them in ways that feel familiar and routine to them.

Today a student asked me how many times a student had to speak in a discussion to get an *A*. The concept of discussion still mystifies them. The students who have been successful in classes that emphasize one right answer seem particularly distressed when I tell them that there may be many right answers in literature and writing.

Note: Excerpts of student writing are from the class's year-end writing project.

We wanted Mrs. Kennedy to feed us and tell us what to do, when to do it, and how. Personally, I just wanted some reassurance that I was doing the right thing. . . . My motivation for speaking came from fear of the silence; however, I never wanted to speak until I felt sure that what I said would measure up to the intelligence of the others in class.—Lisa

We had several class arguments that involved a great deal of defending ourselves and very little listening to other people. We were just beginning to learn that things were going to be different this year, and most people in our class found the breaking of our four-year routine very uncomfortable. When sitting in our often uneven circle, we'd wait for Mrs. K. to feed us information, and we furiously scribbled notes on her words awaiting an impossible multiple-choice test.—Anita

Two girls stopped in after school today to talk about the fact that they never know the right answers. After listening to them express their frustrations, I reminded them that each day, I tie their major discussion topics together and summarize the main points of the day, even adding a few ideas. Of course, they thought that they still might not have the "right" information, just because a fellow student brought up the concept rather than a teacher. Tomorrow I must go over the purpose of the discussions again and remind the group that I will add things they may miss. Maybe they can come up with ideas about how to organize the discussion better; I know this must be their process of learning, and I know it scares them.

I felt like a freshwater fish might feel if it had to adapt to life in a salty ocean—unsure of my abilities, prior knowledge, and acceptance within the group. The old devices that I used to use for survival the year before were not working, and I knew that the time had come to create new methods of working to survive in this new space as well.—Mara

Personally, I found this type of learning environment very difficult. I am used to being told everything, and I like to be given facts.—Ben

I have been thinking about how much the honors students are improving; I don't think they realize it yet, but I see signs of real listening here and there. We are ending our fall—both in nature and in my classroom. I can feel the shift. The students in honors now feel very uncomfortable in the traditional rows of desks (we tried it one day and they protested!). Still, they don't really feel comfortable in the circle either, and they often challenge each other and debate rather than just allow ideas to flow. The football team unexpectedly lost the "big game," the students with problems at home dread Christmas, and the reality of winter can no longer be avoided.

WINTER

Winter came with a burst—both with the snow and the seniors' struggles with college choices and all the other human dramas of any high school. I watch them grow and learn and struggle, but it is not easy. While they learn to discuss ideas in class, they also write challenging papers and do research outside of class. Their writing has improved geometrically (those twice-weekly "twenty-minute writes" really do pay rich dividends). While I see their growth, they grow impatient; they cannot see any change yet.

Long nights and cold days bring a slowing of group energy. This is a quiet time to be used in reflection. . . .

. . . rest, look inward, find awareness
Within myself, I find that my flowing river has turned icy
I can no longer maintain my frantic speed. . . .
Attempting to keep a rapid pace, I lose track of life's true
meaning

When one refuses to surrender to winter's cold, quiet
stillness,
One must struggle.

A definite cold season has settled in our class. . . .
But we refuse to go within
Instead, we force more energy out and go up against each
other
We argue about everything. . . .
Simply trying to sort out our own opinions.

But the beauty of winter still prevails
in its isolated crystal snowflakes
and clear, crisp starry nights
. . . We surely need this season. . . .

The seasons change,
we change;
when we resist the flow . . .
. . . we encounter difficulty.—Chris

Some of the students' inner conflicts come out sideways, making them frustrated with the reality that many different types of
people and different types of thinkers exist in the world and need
to be accepted. A major conflict occurs as students who feel comfortable looking at literature and making applications to different
works or "real life" clash with students who want everything to be
right or wrong, black or white—even the works of Shakespeare
and other great writers. Some of the students may be being contrary on purpose, just to stir things up. I never like this stage of the

process of students learning to interact with each other in different ways. They want to argue and blame rather than listen and
accept. Each day, I end the discussion by tying the loose ends and
showing how very different ideas can either fit together or all be
right; sometimes I ask the students to do this for me, but they still
struggle. But this too shall pass—at least, it has every other year. I
wonder what the catalyst will be this year. I wonder if I will know
when it happens or if it will slip by us unannounced.

> Although more people chose to participate and we spent
> less time staring at Mrs. Kennedy, the environment still did
> not feel safe to us as a whole. Those who chose to share
> personal stories got shot down, ignored, or attacked. One
> main argument that frequented our circle concerned
> emotions. The concrete thinkers of the class believed
> strongly that emotions only complicated the discussions
> and should be removed from conversation. Most of the
> class, however, felt that emotion is an integral part of us
> and cannot be separated.—Zoe

Though still far from nature's spring in Michigan, I think a
change may be on the horizon. The students write in their journals about their "fighting." Really, they are learning to deal with
conflict, or at least to sit with it. The honors students really need to
do something together, but we have no field trips. I have decided
to give them "extra credit" points for going to a basketball game
with the rival school. They must create and take "pep" signs that
included quotes from The Hobbit or Macbeth and relate them to
the game. Their family sociology class is teaching about the responsibility of having a child, so a number of them have these life-
size babies that cry—taking them to the game will add to the
hilarity. I hope it connects them in a different way.

Almost everyone decided to go; they jumped at the points,
not the opportunity. They had a grand time for a pittance of

points—and it did begin to change them. Their signs were so funny and creative; the parents and coaches loved the idea.

> This seemed to be a bonding time for us. Everyone who went had to ride on the bus. It took about an hour to reach the game, so our group had the opportunity to get to know each other better. Many students had to bring along their mechanical babies for one of their classes. That experience brought much laughter from our group. We enjoyed seeing the boys having to act fatherly toward the mechanical babies. The bonding experience started uniting our group and showing us that spring will soon come.—Miranda

The turning point, the catalyst, truly came this week; this year, that moment will not go unnoticed. Mara and Charles had a strong disagreement—gentle Mara and the very strong-minded, opinionated Charles. I really pushed the envelope, as they say; certainly, what occurred does not exist in the curriculum, but I believe it will be one of their most profound learning experiences of the year. I asked Mara to tell Charles how she felt after he strongly criticized her; as they began to speak and listen, I focused only on them, knowing the other students were watching me as carefully as they were listening to their classmates. We all stayed in the circle, and we all stayed present. When Cassie asked them to try to just "get along," I acknowledged her fear of conflict, and I told her (and the class) it was going to be OK. And I held my breath and we stayed in the circle. As Mara and Charles worked through their differences, I knew that what occurred had nothing to do with teaching English, but it had everything to do with honoring others and learning how to do that. Perhaps all "teachable moments" hold a risk, but not all risks create teachable moments. What happened this time was wonderful, intense, and true learning. I'm breathing normally again, and I'm smiling, too.

Making Change

In my winter, I found myself arguing and disagreeing with many people. When I wanted, I said things just to start an argument, whether or not I actually believed what I said. I justified this by saying that I wanted to make people think, and when I disagreed with them, they thought about what they said. Sadly, I did not think that this might be hurting people. One conflict that greatly affected the class occurred between Mara and me. It started when I made a statement about how her personal experience did not matter to the discussion. In so doing, I hurt Mara's feelings, and I did not even know it. The next day, Mrs. Kennedy brought this fact to my attention, and personally, this event started the path toward summer.—Charles

. . . Charles and I communicated and worked the problem out. This, I believe, tore down the barriers in our class between the concrete and abstract thinkers, which had been the main conflict between members during the winter. It melted the icy barriers and made way for spring, both for me personally and for the class. . . . I finally felt comfortable in our space and felt as though I were accepted into the mold of things. Sharing my ideas did not send my mind whirling, and I felt connected with the rest of my class and Mrs. K. in a new way. We suddenly were all on the same plane, working together with the same goal and same visions. While I did not feel as though we were a unit yet, I knew at that time that we were on the right track. Learning, reflection, and listening were all parts of spring in my mind and heart. I know that I will take the valuable tools of communication and sensitivity to others' needs wherever I go. People cannot always use poetry analysis, processes, or objective facts from various novels in their lives, but they can always use people skills. We learned in spring to work with people, not just faces, and continued on in that light until summer finally shone its face in our windows—Mara

Spring

A former student sent me an essay she studied in college on "how to seminar," saying it reminded her of my class. The essay includes descriptions of discussions in many ways, from "beauty pageants" (where people displayed their ideas) all the way to "barn building" (where individuals build on the ideas of each other to create a totally new and beautiful concept). I will share it with the students; I think it will help them see themselves and move to where they all really desire to go but don't know how. It will also be a safe topic after the raw emotions that occurred between Charles and Mara.

Today I know I am a very lucky person to be a teacher; it thrills me to see these young people go beyond my wildest hopes.

> Our conversations began to slow down, and we were getting more comfortable with silences. No longer did finding the deep, hidden meanings behind every line in a poem matter so much as finding some way to apply what we had read to our individual lives. In my own personal life, spring led me to uprooting and replanting. I faced the renewal of my spirit as I came to new convictions about my beliefs and my identity.—Cassie

> Gerry and Reena worked on not interrupting each other.
> Anita felt comfortable sharing personal things again.
> Mara was able to talk.
> I felt better, no longer tense and unsure,
> no longer afraid to share my ideas and contribute.
> Ms. Kennedy talked less but still helped us keep on track
> when we wavered.
> When she did talk, we were able to respond
> and work off of her.
> There was no longer a prolonged silence after she spoke.
> We forgot about points.

We found relaxation and renewal in discussions
rather than anxiety and intensity.
The air outside got warmer,
we opened the windows,
we read poetry and discussed it without too many
outbreaks.
Then came the reading of Parker Palmer.—Valerie

The whole seminar concept brought us together in our
discussions and spawned a departure from the traditional
academic discussions. Instead, we found a safe haven in
which we could open up our personal lives to a group of
caring individuals, rather than just another English class.
From this came what I like to think of as the beginning of
the "journey class." In this class, we began evaluating our
own personal journeys: how far we've come and how far we
have yet to go. This change allowed me to evaluate myself
on a higher level, which then helped me out of the winter
of my life, giving me a sense of hope and even euphoria at
times with how everything appeared. Nothing is ever
perfect, but there have been times this year when I feel that
perfection does in fact exist.—Paul

Teaching has now changed for the year; all my classes have
had the transformation that the honors class had, but each one got
to this stage in a different way. Now I get the best part of the year,
and I plan to enjoy it thoroughly! In spite of the fact that the administration rarely allows field trips, I managed to get permission
to take some of the honors class to see a workshop by Parker J.
Palmer. It will be the final activity before the students begin their
senior thesis in the middle of the month.

The summer season of the class was greatly influenced by
our reading of the chapter from Parker Palmer's book.
When we read his ideas about "listen to yourself" and

"simplify your life," we called him idealistic and unrealistic. Overall, we thought that the ideas were wonderful but would be impossible to live up to in this society. All of this changed when almost all of our class went to the Parker J. Palmer retreat. There the students saw that Parker, a real person just like us, was living the life that he talked about and that it wasn't impossible at all.—Cassie

SUMMER

So many teachers struggle with this last month of the year, but it is my best month. Today the students turned in their final project. Though the papers take all my time to read, that time really pleases me because the pride they have in the project cannot be ignored. They write about their own journey during the year by including their journals, papers on their favorite poetry, and discussions of the novels they had to read during the last six weeks.

> We have experienced all of the seasons in our class. Our summer season has been marked by understanding. Sharing and relating to one another has helped us along our journey. I feel that our class has come full circle.—Delfina

> The culmination of all I worked for in the spring, all I fought against in the winter, and all I didn't say in the fall, brought me into summer. From the point when I learned that I could look inside myself without even trying, I found a greater ease in following my path.—Gerry

The pride they show in that last big assignment carries over to every day until school ends. My days are easy now. It seems that all the students, no matter what level, realize that they have changed and learned and grown this year.

I feel that we should also credit the change in our classroom to writing our senior thesis. For many, the thesis stands as the first opportunity to examine one's life and growth so closely. The impact of this English class becomes apparent as everyone has grown so much as a person. While writing my thesis, I learned so much about my journey and the turning points for me this year.—Serena

I wish that we could have realized our problems and fixed them sooner, however, the path that we took was very important for the future experiences we will have while working in groups. I believe that the path she took us on became crucial for future learning experiences. She did not always give us the answers that we looked to her for. When our class got into an argument, she usually let us work it through. Throughout our lives, we will not always have someone to go to give us all of the solutions. The journey that she took us on became beneficial for our whole class. For that journey, I am grateful.—Miranda

The different seasons came and went, and we survived. We survived the intimidating newness of the fall. We survived the harsh solitude of the winter. We survived the difficult transition of the spring. We survived. We even grew; we learned about ourselves in the context of the class. . . . —Rose

The seniors have gone, and school is almost over. This year it all came together as I had hoped. It makes me realize why I decided to come back to teach this year and why I will come again next year.

Summer
Summer Daze
Endless Craze
Starry Gaze
and so we see
the profit in her plan
as we look at ourselves
—we are amazing.—Jocelyn

NOTE

1. For more information on the Courage to Teach professional
   development program, see the essay by Marcy and Rick Jackson (pp. 282–308).

Katherine Kennedy has been teaching at Mattawan
High School in Mattawan, Michigan, since 1970. Active
in professional organizations, she has presented at the
Michigan Council of English Teachers and the National
Council of Teachers of English. "I feel most alive in my
teaching," she writes, "when my students begin to show
the pride in the work that they do—especially work that
they initially considered far too advanced for them.
When they realize their own ability to go beyond self-
imposed limitations, they have a look in their eyes that
makes all the frustrations worth my effort (and theirs!)."

The heart of the school reform movement for the past two decades has focused on promoting students' learning and growth. A vast array of curricular innovations and institutional reforms has been devised in an effort to improve student learning and development. Only rarely do these school reform initiatives consider how the reforms affect the adults who work in the institution. Teachers are expected to embrace and enact the reforms even though they're rarely given the opportunity of growing along with the reform efforts. Teacher, reformer, and administrator Chip Wood reminds us of the strength and power that come from building trust and spirit within our teacher communities and the benefits to all when supportive adult communities take into account the mental, physical, and emotional health of the faculty.

—S.M.I.

Lift Every Voice

Chip Wood

Remember what it feels like to really be alone in the class-room? Nearly forty years ago, as a first-year teacher, I had an experience that indelibly etched in my memory the degree of compassion and support every teacher needs to sustain a ca-reer in education. In my combination first and second grade, the children were learning to read. We were using the basal reader. It was winter and bitterly cold outside our midwest-ern school. The basal story this particular morning showed children chasing their shadows on the sidewalk (the *sh* sound?). To capture their shadows, the children in the book decided to draw with chalk (*ch*) around the shapes (*sh*) of their bodies. To capture the essence of this scene for my young readers, I had them draw with the chalkboard chalk on the sunlit floor of our classroom, desks pushed asunder. Enter my principal, who stood and watched, arms folded across her chest, and then left without comment. At the end of the day, she returned to my room and told me in no uncertain terms that my lesson was unacceptable (we were not to draw on the floor) and wasted valuable time (the point was made in the picture in the basal, after all) and not to do any such thing again.

You can imagine how I felt. And there was nowhere to turn; no mentor teacher, no critical friends, no study team, not even a grade-level group; just the teacher's room and a hole in my stomach. What I did not know then in that sun-drenched primary classroom was that the secret to becoming a high-quality teacher would finally emerge through my discovery of and participation in strong adult community activity in the schools where I would teach. Today I advocate that every adult working in a school (from first-year teachers to veterans to cafeteria workers) needs this gift of a supportive adult community in order to have access to the intellectual, emotional, and spiritual strength that will sustain them in their life-giving work.

Throughout my career, I have been fortunate to find such a community. Gradually I discovered ways to talk about my teaching with my colleagues and my superiors, to listen to their experiences and observe their best practices. In my elementary classrooms, children not only drew on the floor, they waded in streams, collected specimens for microscopes, built block cities, and could tell you what the sun's shadow meant about the movement of the earth. They also cleaned up the floor, the buckets of pond water, and the block cities and helped solve the problems of classroom life. I took the time such teaching takes and was supported by the adults around me in my conviction to help children learn both to master their academics and to live together peacefully and productively in a democratic society.

I had the unique experience of being a nearly full-time teacher and the principal of two K–8 elementary schools that featured discovery-based curricula during my teaching career. This made me worry a great deal about test scores being worse in these schools, but they never were. In both schools, we worked together to understand testing and its place in improving achievement and tried to make test scores useful for parents and our teaching without being driven by the numbers. We sustained our adult community by engaging in lively self-evaluation of an instructional approach full of inquiry and collaborative activity. We also spent a great deal of time on staff development and new learning as adults. The central focus of this work was observing in each other's classrooms and deepening our knowledge of child development—two things that the science of education virtually ignores today. We also worked together to invent or learn the collegial structures and supports we needed from and for each other as we went. We devoted a lot of time to conferencing with parents and listening to what they wanted most for their children. Needless to say, we worked long hours and spent endless time preparing our lessons, the way good teachers always have.

As someone who has spent more than thirty years in schools, I am unsettled by the new, cold, statistical analysis and the increasing use of American education as political blood sport. Today the American metaphor for education has become a computer model of artificial intelligence. It is a chilling shift, further distancing us from a relational model of learning. Adults who work in schools are being made to believe that they are more responsible for raising test scores than for raising children. The constant call for more and more evaluation of students and teachers, with punishing effects for those not living up to artificially inflated standards, is actually having the unintended consequence of reducing time for teaching, diminishing the depth of acquired knowledge, and compromising the moral character of the next generation.

Political blaming and shaming is also having a chilling effect on the teaching profession, as we witness a steady early exodus of veteran teachers and the rapid exit of new teachers in high numbers. Principals and superintendents are increasingly transient and scarce. I see the increased demoralization of the adult community of schools where dedicated grown-ups have worked tirelessly for years against significant odds, only to be told that their efforts do not measure up. Respect, support, and appreciation for those who work in schools seem at an all-time low. And for those working in poor communities, the situation is often more difficult.

In disproportionate numbers, poor children receive a poorer education, in poorer facilities with fewer ancillary supports than their wealthier neighbors. This is true for both the urban and rural poor. While poor students obviously have the same potential intelligence as rich students, holding them to the same rigorous and punishing standards of achievement without providing resource advantages to poor schools is cruel and cynical governmental practice. Simply applying skill drills, teaching only through so-called direct instruction, and beefing up testing is no replacement for legislative action and compensatory funding that could provide teachers and administrators of high quality and diverse backgrounds for *all* our schools.

Needed also are humane personnel practices for the adults in these school communities. High-quality teachers and exceptional communities of learning are not created in environments of fear and intimidation, nor do such schools need to rely on artificial instructional practice or microwaved curricula. High-quality teaching is built on relationships, connecting students' learning experiences to their life experiences.

Sadly, we now find that students often cannot apply what they learn to solve real problems, let alone the problems on tests designed to measure what they have been taught. The reason they cannot do this is not because their minds are incapable of problem solving. It is, rather, that in our rush for results, we are short-circuiting the ability to think. The volume of schoolwork completed is equated with accomplishment. School schedules are crammed, and time is seldom available to process thinking and consolidate learning—to reflect, ponder, revise, discuss, debate, explore, wonder, observe, and make connections. Time to listen to the children, the essential ingredient in good teaching, is now at a premium.

In schools where rigor and informed inquiry are both valued and protected for students and grown-ups alike, where it is safe to make a mistake, where strengths and weaknesses are appraised honestly, where the goal is both academic excellence and a caring community, learning thrives and measured achievement is not compromised. Such schools, I am convinced, depend on the vitality of the adult communities that direct and nourish them. But to create and maintain a vital adult community is not a simple matter. It requires intentional structures and specific strategies that build communication and support, reinforce collaborative activity, and provide the time to make it all possible.

The Latin root for the word *education, educare,* meaning "to nurture, bring up," implies an adult community leading the process of learning. Over the past several years, as a Courage to Teach facilitator and in my work as a leader of the Responsive Classroom approach to professional development, I have encouraged the adults working with children in schools to pay closer attention to their adult community interactions. I have increasingly seen the impact such attention can make on the mental and physical health of these adults, their longevity on the job, and their ability to nurture and instruct with more skill, energy, and sheer joy.

High-quality teaching cannot be sustained by the teacher alone, no matter how idyllic the classroom. It requires the trustworthy space of a true learning community. I have witnessed many school communities as they attempt to build these spaces.

• In one urban middle school, homeroom time has taken on a new meaning for the teachers. Inspired planning by the principal and a small group of teachers led to the creation of "adult community meetings." These happen at the same time as homeroom, first thing in the morning, and coverage is provided through creative scheduling so that each teacher can attend an adult community meeting each week. Gathering in small groups across grade levels and subject areas, teachers have a chance to share insights and experiences about their lives and their work, engage in fun activities relevant to their teaching, and pursue the same kind of community building they are creating with their students in their own homerooms.

• In many schools I have worked with over the past several years, there are no longer any "substitute" teachers—at least they are no longer referred to that way. In these schools, "guest teachers" replace staff out sick for a day. An orientation session and reception are held for guest teachers at the beginning of the year, and students and teachers plan and practice together how to make a guest teacher's experience in the classroom positive and productive for teacher and students alike. In one school, guest teachers pick up a name badge in the office inscribed "guest teacher" before heading to their assignment. In a number of these same schools, staff titles have changed too, as the adult community comes to realize that every adult in the building is a teacher through the ways they work and model what it means to be an adult in this world. Playground and lunch teachers now work where aides and paraprofessionals previously labored. Service learning in these schools takes place in the office, in the cafeteria, and with the custodian, not just in projects outside in the broader community.

• In a large elementary school, faculty meetings now often begin in "home groups." These small, heterogeneous groups also cross traditional grade levels and friendship lines. Teachers meet for the first fifteen minutes of each faculty meeting to explore a common theme affecting everybody in the school. "How is recess going?" "What should we do to support our coworker and her family now that she is in the hospital?" "What are some strategies that are working for you to deal with classroom interruptions?" Ideas are sometimes reported out when the whole faculty reconvenes, and sometimes they are reported back as a written summary.

• A teacher engaged in a two-year cycle of Courage to Teach retreats reports on a way she found to offer time and space for reflection with her colleagues. Every Monday, after school, she serves tea in her classroom to anyone who chooses to show up. No expectations, no agenda. What has emerged has been an ever-changing stream of people and conversations, adding respite for the adult community.

• Putting chairs in circles works not just for morning meetings for children but also for staff conversations. In a circle, adults feel known and acknowledged, just as children do. In the first elementary school where I was a principal, the staff gathered in a circle five minutes before the students' buses arrived each morning to check in about the day ahead, to offer support for colleagues in special need of it that day, and to feel the strength of our teaching community. This daily circle continued through several subsequent administrations.

• Many schools have adopted the strategy of having the adults in the building wear name badges all the time for security purposes. This proves to be a good device to help the grown-ups get to know each other at the beginning of the year, as children do in classrooms by wearing name tags. Especially in large schools, getting to know everyone is no easy task, and staff solidarity is extremely important to the strength of the school community.

• On designated days during the school year, a principal in a rural K–8 school, along with some of his teachers, cooks breakfast for the entire student body so that paraprofessionals can participate in staff development programs at the beginning of the school day.

• Everyone on a large school staff is given a book at the end of the school year and asked to read it over the summer. In the fall, small study groups meet at different times to pursue the book's relevance to the school community and to decide on some new strategies to try out together that the book has suggested about discipline.

• Peer coaching is made an approved "professional day" activity for teachers, allowing them to visit in each other's classrooms and provide feedback through an agreed process while being given coverage for their own classroom and time to confer among themselves.

• In more than one school, I have witnessed a kind of "buddy system" for teachers. Teachers next door or across the hall from each other work together to know and help each other's students, and practice discipline procedures that are consistent and supportive of the agreed expectations of the adult community for students and respectful of the dignity and differences among children. These efforts have often grown out of yearlong study and planning by committees of parents, teachers, administrators, and staff who are listening to each other and are seriously invested in increasing social responsibility as well as academic performance. Schoolwide discipline begins with a disciplined adult community.

The more we are connected, the better our schools will be. Our individual voices matter, but what matters more is the gathering of our voices as we help each other teach with courage in our classrooms and cafeterias. To understand and utilize the power of our adult community requires courageous collaboration. We must take the time to gather with each other not only to honor our daily acts of courage but also to acknowledge our mistakes. If every day we help each other teach together a little better, we will increasingly be able to provide and defend for children the basic social and academic skills they truly need to become productive adults and caring and involved citizens. And we will all be the stronger for it. Taking the time we need for each other in the midst of the currently perceived educational crisis of accountability is an ultimate act of teaching courage. By gathering our voices, we model hope for ourselves, the children we teach, the parents we serve, and the policymakers we seek to inform. Our gathering voice is an old hymn of democracy's promise: "Lift every voice and sing."

Chip Wood began teaching in a combination first- and second-grade classroom in 1965. For the next six years, he worked in the field of social work before returning to

STORIES OF THE COURAGE TO TEACH

the classroom in 1972 as a teaching principal of a rural K–8 school in western Massachusetts. In 1981, he cofounded the Northeast Foundation for Children (NEFC) in Greenfield, Massachusetts, and taught in its demonstration school while cocreating the Responsive Classroom approach to professional development for teachers and schools. Today, for the NEFC, he teaches teachers, consults with schools and school districts, writes and lectures on education topics, and collaborates with other national organizations on educational reform issues. Wood has written two books on education: *Yardsticks: Children in the Classroom, Ages 4–14* (1996) and *Time to Teach, Time to Learn: Changing the Pace of School* (1999, both published by NEFC). In 1999, he was awarded the President's Medal for service in education from Fitchburg State College, Massachusetts. He describes feeling most alive in his teaching with children "when I am listening to their ideas, leading them in song or outdoor play. I feel most alive in my teaching with teachers when I see ideas we have explored in workshops come alive in classrooms."

D espite the fact that teaching occurs in a public forum where we are constantly surrounded by students and others, many teachers describe feeling painfully isolated and emotionally alone in their work. The culture of teaching and the routines of the institution rarely provide opportunity for teachers to come together for the appointed purpose of talking honestly and openly about our teaching. The distrust of genuine conversation about our teaching leaves us feeling insecure and vulnerable. Robert G. Kraft acknowledges the toxic nature of our isolating ways and then describes a seminar program he designed that promotes conversation about the questions central to who we are and what we do as teachers.

—S.M.I.

Teaching Excellence and the Inner Life of a Faculty

Robert G. Kraft

> Good teaching comes from the identity and integrity of the teacher.
>
> PARKER J. PALMER, *The Courage to Teach*

In the fall of 1998, two of my English department colleagues died suddenly within weeks of each other. They were active men, barely middle-aged. One died of liver cancer, the other of meningitis.

In discussing their deaths, my doctor spoke of compromised immune systems, and he prompted me to speculate about what factors could have caused these breakdowns. Both men were active, respected professionals. Keith had recently been through a divorce. Bill was single and the most isolated man I knew. His neighbors reported that he never had guests.

Note: An earlier version of this essay was published in *Change,* 2000, *32*(3), 48–52. Copyright © 2000 Heldref Publications.

His body was found in his room several days after his death. In his last days, he was totally alone.

Perhaps this is a grim way to open a discussion of the inner life of a faculty. We can't know for sure what caused these deaths, but in both cases there may have been chronic trauma with psychosocial factors involved. To put it simply, stress may have been a root cause—hardly a new idea in modern mind-body medicine.

Over the past fourteen years, I've taken a close look at the emotional landscape of faculty life, and these deaths triggered an observation that's been stirring in me for much of my thirty-five years in higher education.

ISOLATION AND EMOTIONAL STERILITY

The isolation and emotional sterility of faculty life can be dangerous—perhaps toxic. That isolation and sterility are even present seems paradoxical considering that faculty are involved in what is widely regarded as a most rewarding enterprise and are usually surrounded by people.

But I was not surprised to hear about a tenure-track professor who recently quit her job because, she said, it was so dreadfully lonely.

Loneliness is only part of the problem. What I will report on here is an experiment that began fourteen years ago to improve the quality of teaching at my university and eventually led to a program that addressed the emotional factors in teaching.

Eastern Michigan University (EMU) is a large, comprehensive university in southeastern Michigan. It serves a suburban, diverse population and is the largest producer of professional education personnel in the nation. It has colleges of arts and sciences, education, business, technology, and health and human services. If you think of the varying sizes and functions of American colleges and universities, ours falls somewhere in the middle of the spectrum—large but not the largest, with a teaching emphasis and lots of research. You could describe us as "typical." Thus I believe a similar experiment would have similar results at most American institutions of higher education.

Our state has three large "research" universities. Because we are a "teaching" university, our provost decided we should have a teaching and learning center. He asked me to set up and direct such a center because I had written about pedagogy and was a senior professor with the right credentials. In 1986, the Faculty Center for Instructional Excellence (FCIE) began offering workshops to faculty members about teaching at EMU.

THE DESIRE TO CONNECT

The workshops were surprisingly well attended, and two full-scale conferences we sponsored attracted almost one-third of our 660 tenure-track colleagues. We wanted to think we were succeeding, but I had no reason to believe that teaching was getting better at EMU.

In candid moments, faculty would tell me that what they heard at these events might apply to other teachers but was not appropriate for their own teaching. However, they did want to hear their colleagues talk about teaching. It became clear that the chance to talk is what drew them in surprising numbers. Above all, they wanted to connect, and teaching was what they all had in common. One senior professor of music wrote that the FCIE was "a lifeline for me . . . a chance to interact with colleagues from other departments which created for me a sense of belonging to the university community." Over and over again, faculty spoke of "an opportunity to network with faculty."

That a senior professor would call our center a "lifeline" was beyond our expectations. Apparently, he had felt he was drowning. I had no idea faculty felt such distress. I believed they wanted to be better teachers, but I had not imagined that the feeling of being isolated and submerged was so acute. Why wouldn't faculty find a "lifeline" in their own departments?

Initially I had no answer to that question. But as the person in charge, I felt I had to respond directly to the clear need for connection. So I set up a seminar called The Scholarship of Teaching and Learning. We met every Friday for ninety minutes throughout most of the fifteen-week term. With no released time, no encouragement from administrators, and no promise of credit toward tenure and promotion, 240 faculty enrolled in this seminar over a period of eighteen semesters.

This seminar continues at EMU and is open to all who teach in higher education. It is advertised throughout the university as a forum "not about methods but about the larger questions out of which methods might emerge. What is genuine learning? When, why, and how does learning happen? What do teachers do to enhance or retard learning?" Participants use a coursepack to "explore the primary literature about teaching and learning in the context of their experience as teachers and students."

Faculty joined up, about a dozen per term. Several showed up term after term. Occasionally we had faculty guests from neighboring campuses who had heard about the seminar, but we did not advertise beyond our own campus. It became immediately clear that they mostly wanted to talk. (At times the talk became so intense I had to establish ground rules.) In their own words:

> Talking about my [teaching] problems openly has been like a breath of fresh air, as it is very difficult to find understanding and sensitive help in academe.

> I got to know many faculty members on a one-on-one basis, which is quite important for me.

> We could speak freely about our failures and learned that others had done things equally awful and survived.

> I felt at ease with these people and I was intellectually challenged in the open give-and-take.

> It was heated and intensely personal, but always provocative and enlightening.

Inhospitable Departments

One theme emerged consistently in these conversations. There was no room for such talk within departments. As one participant put it, "No other forum in the university addresses the types of issues covered in this seminar." Faculty find their own departments inhospitable places to talk about teaching.

As another participant said, "Too often discussion [about teaching] within departments produces little more than preening. Competition to be best tends to override honest discussion or disclosure of difficulties." The theme of inhibiting competition was constant. You didn't share your playbook with department colleagues, nor did you discuss difficulties openly.

And there is an even deeper problem in departments: a reluctance to share feelings of any kind. One faculty member said, "It's useful to be able to share both the good feelings and the frustrations [of teaching]. It's difficult to do that with faculty in your department—too much hinges on such discussions. But in the freer environment of the seminar . . . ideas can be expressed more freely."

What exactly "hinges on such discussions"? Why is the atmosphere outside departments "freer"? One participant cited the seminar's lack of compartmentalization: "Since the seminar is made up of faculty from a range of disciplines, it offers a kind of open, unpredictable forum. In such openness, many opinions about the classroom experience emerge through a form of constructive, intellectual explosion."

The seminars featured a lot of honest agreement and disagreement, but that is how people build intellectual communities—through real dialogues in which people listen to each other rather than speak past one another. Sometimes this atmosphere is hard to achieve within one discipline, where a kind of compartmentalized reality may exist.

Why are there no "intellectual communities" featuring "real dialogues" in departments? What is the "too much" that "hinges on such discussions"? What I heard from faculty, added to my own three decades' experience in a department, yielded insights that I am still testing.

Our faculty (along with our many adjunct professors) come from graduate schools nationwide. Pursuit of knowledge in their discipline has been largely isolated. Their scholarly writing must be objective and impersonal and characterized by the scientist's distance (for example, "Do not use *I* in your writing"). Despite the fact that these notions are obsolete in "new" science, their protocols continue in higher education. As graduate students, our faculty breathed in the research values of their disciplines. And departments are the home of these disciplines and therefore the home of their research values.

Research requires dispassionate observation. And whereas teaching, for those who truly care about it, is full of feeling, feelings reflect bias. In research, bias must be avoided at all costs. The conclusion thus made by many faculty members is that departments are not places to celebrate feelings of any kind, much less the intensely personal ones about teaching, a role in which relationships—full of emotional dynamics—are central. Those emotional dynamics are instead "compartmentalized," walled off from the values of the discipline. Faculty separate their lives into segments: home life, teaching life, department life, and research life. Feelings belong in the first two segments and only there.

I don't mean to overstate this point. Of course, some departments are warm, friendly places, including my own. They're "home" in many ways, and faculty make friends there. Yes, they often chat about their classes. Expressions of frustration with students and administration are a hallowed tradition. But those expressions tend to be superficial chitchat. Sustained, in-depth conversation about teaching—especially in a public forum—is seen as taking teaching too seriously. Furthermore, a persistent and not-so-subtle undercurrent suggests that the uninhibited display of feeling is undignified and inappropriate in a "disciplined" department.

208

It's widely understood that department discussions of curricula, policy, and promotion must be dispassionate and conducted from a broad perspective. But teaching excellence is passionate. There can be no discreet distance between the teacher and his or her subject and students. Feelings are constant, and supportive environments that honor feelings of all kinds are central to teaching excellence. In fact, a math professor reported, "I was surprised by the almost unanimous belief that emotions are the most significant factor in learning." And excellent teaching is highly personal; how can it be otherwise?

Therefore, teaching may be at home in a university but not in a department.

Yes, teaching is the department's primary business, so we must talk. But we talk about curricula, not about teaching. Teaching is hardly worthy of talk.

"Worthy" raises an even more central issue. Despite Ernest Boyer's landmark book *Scholarship Reconsidered*,[1] teaching is not regarded within disciplines as a serious intellectual pursuit. It is simply functional, operating knowledge.

Knowing how to teach is knowing how to run the copy machine. Yes, we need copy machines, but we don't need to know their hows and whys. They may require some chat, but they're hardly worthy of sustained, earnest conversation. Copy machine know-how is not scholarship. You don't do research about copy machines.

But teaching is what faculty actually do—day in and day out. It's where they live. It's where their emotional energy is going. But it's not what you talk about in department meetings, where important work must be done.

So how does this suppressed emotional energy find release? When it's high, how does it find celebration? When it's low, how does it find compassionate support? Where are the outlets? If there's no comfortable place for expressing emotional energy in departments, what happens? Is it too dramatic to say "death"?

Making Change

A final point about inhospitable departments. Faculty consistently confess that they feel like frauds in their teaching. No one prepared them for teaching. A computer science professor wrote, "Most of us felt like professorial imposters." They feel constant doubt and vulnerability. But they have no such feelings about their disciplines. Their subject knowledge is certain and confident. That confidence makes all the difference.

In three department meetings about teaching that I was part of, one clear pattern emerged. To one another, department members wanted to talk about what they teach, not why or how. Since they were talking to an "inside" audience, the eagerness to exchange knowledge—their confident command of their subject matter—persistently overcame the more vulnerable and tentative conversation about the hows and whys of teaching. As one seminar participant observed, "disclosure of difficulties" is not what goes on in departments.

THE EMERGENCE OF TEACHING EXCELLENCE

So how does teaching excellence emerge from these emotional deserts? I'm tempted to say it doesn't. Complaints about poor teaching are endless. Listen to student talk in the hallways. But my and probably every university has many excellent teachers. Where do they come from?

No one explains the source of excellent teaching better than Parker J. Palmer in *The Courage to Teach*, a breakthrough book and a survival manual for college professors. (Palmer's work is the centerpiece of our seminar.) "Good teaching," he writes, "comes from the identity and integrity of the teacher."[2]

Good teaching comes from the heart, from a deep center of caring for subjects and students. A teacher with such a deep center—with integrity, with wholeness—is likely to be effective with most any method. A teacher who is split—or disconnected from subjects, students, colleagues, and his or her whole self—will likely fail with any method. Therefore, method, while important, is peripheral to teaching effectiveness.

Good teachers emerge when there is primary attention to the heart of it all, to the whole person of each teacher and student. Every teacher must ask, "Who and what am I? Why am I doing this? What exactly am I trying to accomplish and why? What effect does my personhood, my mind and heart as expressed in my personality, have on my teaching? Can I relate to these students?"

These highly personal questions are full of danger, uncertainty, and fear for the teacher who seeks to answer them honestly. Listen to the remarks of a psychology professor:

> I have approached every teaching opportunity with great enthusiasm and great trepidation. My enthusiasm is rooted in my love for learning and the belief that this passion is contagious. My trepidation arises from my insecurities as a teacher. I fear that I do not know enough to be expert. I fear that my approach may fail to capture the students and spark their curiosity.
>
> There are many approaches to a body of knowledge, and I fear that I do not know them all and thus cannot employ them. I want to accommodate all types of learners and reach all levels of intelligence in the classroom. I want to be a seasoned teacher. I fear that I am not.

Where can we go with our fear? To a safe place where there are no bosses. To colleagues who listen, who are not competing with us, and who understand and will admit that they feel the same fear. That is where the reach for teaching excellence begins.

INCREMENTS, NOT METHODS

From this beginning, how does genuine improvement happen? First, as the seminar underscores, teaching methods must be compatible with personalities and goals. No two teachers have exactly the same goals or understand those goals in the same way. Effective methods must evolve for each individual teacher.

Second, teachers improve in small increments in response to felt inadequacies that are personally troublesome. We do not change unless we feel some discomfort and are looking for relief. Those highly rational and learned discussions in workshops and conferences, however stimulating, may have little effect unless they respond to felt needs. I'm reminded of a remark by Carlos Castaneda: "Conclusions arrived at through reasoning have very little influence in altering the course of our lives."

And we do not change because we are criticized or because someone tells us we should.

Finally, change is a huge risk, especially when it must be done in public. We tend to teach—and live—the way we were taught; only because it's familiar and comfortable. We tend to do what our own teachers did, what other teachers do, and what students expect—however ineffective. Departing from the familiar requires constant support and reassurance. So there must be a safe place for free and open talk. There must be a place to connect with other struggling minds and, above all, hearts. There must be a place to be reassured.

Some remarkable things happen in such a free and open place. I have a flood of reports from my many participants. Here are a few. First, faculty talk about the effect of the seminar on their emotional health. The seminar, they said:

> Had such a strong healing effect for my soul that I was
> charged to go for another week to try new things.

> Was worth its weight in gold for my psychological well-being.

It carried me through a difficult semester.

Made me feel better to learn that I was not the only one experiencing problems.

Was my Friday afternoon fueling for the week to come.

Enhanced my willingness to be bold and try new approaches.

Gave me a sense of renewal from the readings. And I realized I needed a support system of my peers.

Helped me leave my comfort zone, explore new frontiers, and be a risk-taker in the classroom.

I mentioned earlier that I saw no evidence that teaching improved after most one-stop workshops and conferences. In contrast, this seminar made a difference. By the end of it, all participants had made or were planning changes in their teaching:

I have begun to embrace a new paradigm in education—one that stresses connections and relationships over facts and right answers, that honors participation over competition, and that welcomes critical thinking without abandoning the affective side of the learning process.

I walked away with a new approach to teaching my classes.

It sensitized me to the many factors that may go on simultaneously in the classroom.

I learned to modify some of the ways I interact with students.

I learned that cognitive self-awareness is the most critical attribute I can help my students develop.

I became much more aware of the ways my actual teaching violated my own beliefs about doing good teaching.

I've been experimenting with group activities in my

classroom. There has been a distinct improvement in the attitudes of the students.

I've changed some of my classroom procedures as an experiment. I'm writing about them for publication. I have been introduced to participatory learning, am convinced of it, and will work to integrate it into my teaching.

After the seminar was over, faculty reported on their class-room experiments. (One of them invited me in to watch.) Two seminar participants wrote textbooks about teaching. We have become a university laboratory of teaching scholarship. Other programs have sprouted. And we have communities. One participant remarked, "In isolation, each of us has been reinventing a good many wheels."

These results do not emerge from focused attention on various aspects of teaching. There are no lectures, no "presentations" by "experts." Instead, the focus is always on a community of peers in conversation. Much of that conversation turns out to be a kind of problem storytelling. The storytelling seems to happen inevitably and spontaneously. Because they've just stepped out of their classrooms, faculty have all kinds of issues on their minds, and they want to talk. Here is a typical conversation among four colleagues:

"Today I caught three of my students cheating on my exam."

"Yeah, that's happened to me over and over. So I started using exams that are 'cheat-proof.' I give them problems to solve and tell them to cheat like crazy. Which means, get whatever help you can to solve the problems."

"I stopped giving exams entirely and went over to lots of papers, short ones, long ones. I think it's more valuable for learning."

"I still haven't figured out what to do about cheating. But I'm getting away from stressing memorized information. I'm going to try something different next term."

STORIES OF THE COURAGE TO TEACH

Many possible responses to the exam problem are given. Invariably, participants find new ways to approach their own concerns. Over the course of the term, most of the common teaching problems emerge out of these random conversations. And while the seminar readings draw positive responses, the talk invariably goes to immediate and concrete problems. It may start with remarks like "A student blatantly lied to me today." Because such issues are what's on faculty's minds and in their hearts, they insist on getting them out, not because they want advice—some kind of "fix"—but because the intense feelings cry out for expression.

HOW IT HAPPENS

It's simple and inexpensive to create this seminar. It requires only an experienced faculty peer-leader with some released time, some passion for teaching, and some familiarity with teaching scholarship. Such a leader must be a kind of servant-guide who can organize and facilitate and has the capacity to be quiet, listen, and let the group form a community on its own terms.

Such a leader must start the group off with community building, such as the personal "Who am I and how did I get into this?" storytelling. The leader keeps the focus of the talk on the daily experience of the classroom and gently discourages excessive complaining and keeps the group from going off into irrelevance. The leader must also set a tone by being open about his or her own teaching fears and failures. Then the leader must shut up.

Above all, the leader must avoid being the answer person or advice giver. Connection, after all, is what faculty are after, not someone else's "right" answers. Faculty won't return weekly for patronizing advice. In fact, "seminar" may be too serious a descriptor for these meetings. They are more focused and purposeful, but they're also TGIF parties. Coffee and cookies fit right in.

The seminar may sound very informal, almost frivolous, but some frivolity together appears to be what faculty are craving. The informality encourages honesty and warm feelings, and the genuine exchanges that result generate forceful connections and powerful learning.

The High Price We Pay

The barriers to teaching excellence in higher education are far deeper than evaluation problems, time allotments, and the reward system. Research values—cognitive, cerebral, narrowly focused, exclusive, highly deliberate, and solitary—actively work against the values implicit in teaching excellence—those that are intuitive, relational, inclusive, spontaneous, impassioned, and communal. These opposites can be mediated, but only with a sustained and focused effort.

Such efforts are rare and sporadic in higher education because they require that we shed our masks and mantles of expertise—what faculty call "preening"—that serve as a kind of armor against honest exchanges. Such exchanges appear to be essential to our emotional well-being, to any kind of community, and to genuinely new thoughts and new possibilities. We often resist such exchanges because they celebrate spontaneous feeling, a source of embarrassment and discomfort for many of us.

As for my own university, we can't know if the emotional malnutrition in faculty life contributed to the deaths of my colleagues Keith and Bill. But I do know that faculty are often without the nourishment they need to support the ideals they seek to serve and to live fulfilled lives. This lack weakens their enthusiasm and commitment. It lessens the joy of service that is essential to teaching excellence and to the whole range of faculty duties.

As playwright Arthur Miller says of his emotionally desolate and dying salesman Willy Loman, "Attention must be finally paid."[3]

NOTES

1. Boyer, E. L. *Scholarship Reconsidered: Priorities of the Professoriate.* Princeton, N.J.: Carnegie Foundation for the Advancement of Teaching, 1990.
2. Palmer, P. J. *The Courage to Teach: Exploring the Inner Landscape of a Teacher's Life.* San Francisco: Jossey-Bass, 1998, p. 10.
3. Miller, A. *Death of a Salesman.* New York: Viking Press, 1949, Act I.

Robert G. Kraft is professor of English at Eastern Michigan University (EMU) and the creator and first director of EMU's Faculty Center for Instructional Excellence. He teaches courses in American literature and in professional and technical writing. He has received all the major faculty awards EMU offers, including the 1982 Distinguished Faculty Award for Excellence in Teaching. In 1986, he was awarded the State of Michigan Distinguished Faculty Award by the Michigan Association of University Governing Boards. Among his many published articles, "Bike Riding and the Art of Learning" won the 1978 Exxon Foundation award as the year's "outstanding article on college teaching." He is also the founding publisher and executive editor of *Issues and Inquiry in College Learning and Teaching.* He serves on the editorial review boards of *The Teaching Professor* and *Innovative Higher Education.* He says, "I feel most alive in my teaching when I first notice that the student has made a personal connection to me as a person—beyond my role as the teacher."

We seek opportunities for growth throughout our professional life. We seek clarity on who we are as teachers, we seek to understand our subject matter more deeply, we seek to build our storehouse of techniques and methods, and we seek closer relationships with our colleagues. Despite our genuine hopes for professional development that provides the time and mental space to promote continuous inquiry and growth in our professional roles, it rarely happens in public K–12 education. Most teachers suffer through teacher training programs that focus narrowly on their techniques without acknowledging their personhood. In this essay, Kelly Chandler-Olcott describes a professional development retreat that brings the strands of heart, mind, method, and relationship together.

—S.M.I.

Journey into the Wilderness
A Teacher-Researcher Group's Retreat

Kelly Chandler-Olcott

In *Undaunted Courage*, his best-selling book about the Lewis and Clark expedition, historian Stephen Ambrose devotes an entire chapter to the supplies taken by the Corps of Discovery on its cross-continent journey. That commander Meriwether Lewis laid in a large stock of ink powder for journal entries and sketches suggested his commitment to the scientific aspects of the mission. That he took so much powder and lead suggested confidence in his men's ability to hunt game as well as trepidation about the welcome the corps might receive from native peoples. As Ambrose puts it, what the captain chose to transport, as well as what he chose not to, reveals a good deal "about Lewis and the point of view he held."[1]

In the summer of 1998, ten members of the Mapleton Teacher-Research Group and I embarked on our own journey into the wilderness—only this time, the trek was not over the Continental Divide but into the deepest recesses of northern Maine. With the assistance of a Spencer Foundation

Practitioner Research and Communication Mentoring Grant, we were able to plan and participate in a retreat intended to improve our own teaching as well as contribute to knowledge in the field of literacy education. For five days in late June, our schoolwide team explored data analysis, reflection, and rejuvenation in a stunning natural setting.

The story of the retreat began several years before that June, however. Convinced that classroom-based inquiry could be one of the most generative forms of professional development, teachers at Mapleton Elementary School in Mapleton, Maine, decided to start a research group, and they enlisted me, a university-based teacher and researcher, to be what member Judy Kenney called their "outside facilitator." The group's core activities included monthly meetings, held after school on a voluntary basis, and informal research conferences with each other and me. Both of these endeavors featured the discussion of professional readings, the development of research questions, and the sharing of data from classrooms. During our first year together, we conducted case studies of struggling readers; the following fall, we turned our attention to the teaching and learning of spelling, a curricular area that had frustrated many of us for a long time. Not only were Mapleton students' test scores in spelling significantly lower than their scores in reading and writing (a matter of considerable concern to the community), but many students' attitudes toward spelling were laissez-faire at best and apathetic at worst (a matter of greater concern to the faculty). Something needed to shift, and Mapleton teachers hoped their inquiry would help make it happen.

It didn't take us long—no more than a few months—to realize that spelling was a more complex topic than we expected it to be. Nor did it take us long to identify some weaknesses in our research design: important insights were being generated during monthly meetings and conferences, to be sure, but neither structure provided enough sustained time for deep data analysis, the kind that could drive lasting change. That's when we decided to try a summer retreat, a model we first encountered in *Engaging*

Families,[2] a book about collaborative teacher research into home literacy practices. Like those authors, we felt that a few days of concentrated analysis would benefit us greatly.

After researching various local sites for the retreat, we settled on Libby's Camps, a family-owned sporting lodge located in an unorganized township fifty miles from Mapleton. Accessible only by logging roads or air, the camps were remote enough to create a feeling of isolation that would help us focus. Nestled on the shores of pristine Millinocket Lake, they were picturesque enough to stimulate reflection and inspiration. Equally important, the hearty and delicious meal package we selected freed us from having to cook or clean throughout the week—chores that group members, all of whom were women and nearly all of whom were mothers, usually had to juggle with their teaching and research. In retrospect, we believe this combination of factors was crucial to our positive outcomes.

WHAT WE TOOK TO CAMP

The week before our departure brought intense preparation, including a whole-group shopping trip to Wal-Mart that eventually sent two full shopping carts through the checkout. The remoteness of our destination, underscored by our predeparture discovery that the camps lacked reliable cell phone reception, led us to engage in a flurry of consumerism. All joking aside, however, what we eventually stowed in the bed of the pickup truck reveals as much about the aims of our mission and the culture of our group as Lewis and Clark's supply list did about them. Wise to the changeability of northern Maine weather and the voraciousness of early-season black flies, we packed predictable items such as raincoats and insect repellent. We also took a variety of items that were specific to our particular mission.

First, and perhaps most important, we took Post-it Notes in assorted colors, sizes, and shapes because we knew that these tools, more than any others, would help us analyze what several of us eventually dubbed our "truckload of data."[3] Included in those data were writing samples from all students in grades one through five, observational notes taken by teachers during writing workshops, and surveys completed by Mapleton parents about their attitudes toward and expectations for spelling instruction. Analysis of these artifacts took a large chunk of each whole group session in the morning and frequently spilled over into the afternoons, during which individual members pursued inquiry-related work of their choice in addition to recreation opportunities. Working in pairs and small groups, we used Post-its to tally survey responses, mark quotations to read aloud, and identify themes and patterns across the data. By the end of the week, most of the documents we brought with us had primary-colored strips of paper protruding from their edges. The scribbled annotations on those notes would have been cryptic to an outsider, but to members of the group, they represented key insights we gained from reading, rereading, and discussing the data we collected over the space of a school year. Without the Post-its, we would have had a difficult time organizing our ideas, not to mention sharing them with one another.

We took stacks of notebooks, legal pads, and composition books because we believed writing to be one of the best ways to reflect on and learn from experience. In our classrooms, each of us helped students use writing as a tool for thinking, but we weren't always so consistent about using that tool ourselves. For this reason, we deliberately built reflective writing into our retreat schedule, beginning each morning session with ten minutes of silent drafting in response to an open-ended prompt or question about spelling or teacher research. When the time was up, we shared our ideas with a partner, a trio, or the entire group. According to Lynne Brabant, these activities were a "really valuable experience" because she didn't initially see herself as a writer but came to realize that "by freewriting every day, we could get a lot down on paper."

In the afternoons, individuals used writing for various purposes. Some members wrote short pieces, often collaboratively, to contribute to the book we were coauthoring.[4] Fourth-grade teacher Kim Wright wrote a first draft of a piece[5] about her weekly spelling workshops that later appeared in *Language Arts,* a leading literacy journal. Other members wrote simply for themselves, to make sense of their teaching over the preceding nine months—and in some cases to make sense of their lives outside the classroom. Some of these pieces in progress were read aloud at the sharing sessions we held each day at 5:00 P.M.; others remained private, with the writer as their only audience.

We took an easel and several pads of lined chart paper because we knew from our research group meetings that some of our best thinking was done together, through collaborative talk. Each morning session during the retreat included time for discussion, with key issues and ideas recorded by a scribe on a chart. Sometimes we noted ideas raised by individuals' writing; at other times we jotted down responses to questions such as "Having conducted classroom inquiry for two years now, what advice would you give a novice researcher?" Recording and saving our brainstorming on charts allowed us to reflect on it at a later date, as well as to "share the tracks of our thinking," in Martha LaPointe's words, with others who weren't at camp with us. For example, a document we drafted on chart paper during the retreat eventually became a schoolwide rubric for spelling—an evaluation tool that helped us be more consistent in our approaches and communicate more clearly with parents what we valued about students' spelling. Other charts were useful to us in assembling chapters of our book and in planning presentations for the miniconference on spelling we hosted several months after the retreat for educators in our county. The sheer number of chart pages we generated in a week contributed to our feelings of productivity and accomplishment during the week.

Our packing wasn't limited to professionally oriented gear, however. We also took items whose purposes were more personal: to sharpen our senses, enhance our personal reflections, or heighten our enjoyment of our surroundings. Although these supplies might have seemed less essential to our funders than writing or analysis tools, we're convinced that they were pivotal to the retreat's success.

We took collections of poetry by authors such as William Stafford,[6] Naomi Shihab Nye,[7] and Mary Oliver[8] because we knew that their work would feed our minds just as much as professional resources about literacy would. Each morning session began with reading out loud a few poems—some focusing on nature, others on writing, and others on relationships. We talked only briefly about the meaning of these poems and their implications for our inquiry; mostly, we allowed their rich language to hang in the air and inform the rest of our days in subtle ways. Throughout the week, the collections sat on a window ledge in the main lodge, and group members often borrowed one or another to browse in the afternoons when we scattered to pursue independent activities. Nor were we the only visitors who appeared to appreciate a snippet of poetry in each day. By the end of the week, we noticed that the other guests at the lodge, mostly out-of-state sportsmen and families on vacations, hushed their breakfast conversations when readings began so they could hear the poems too. For all of us, poetry served as a way to focus what Oliver calls "the rich lens of attention."[9]

We took hiking boots, sneakers, and swimsuits because we knew that exercise in the cool water and clean air of the northern Maine woods would be healthy for us, both emotionally and physically. During the school year, teaching is a job that punishes the body. Educators, especially those who work with small children, bend down hundreds of times a day, lug heavy bags of hardcover books, and deny their bladders for hours. In contrast, the retreat was about rejuvenating the body and spirit as much as the mind. During free time, members swam back and forth to a stationary float, paddled in the camp's kayaks, and wandered logging roads in hopes of seeing a moose or deer. One evening after dinner, the entire group traveled a narrow footpath through the woods to visit a dam at the lake's western terminus, where we took photographs and identified local wildflowers before returning to camp. As hiker-writers like William Wordsworth, Henry David Thoreau, and Barry Lopez have long known, such physical exertion also helps stretch mental muscles, and a number of us, myself included, found that our treks led to clearer and more creative thinking when we returned to work.

We took graham crackers, marshmallows, and Hershey bars because we knew making s'mores around a campfire would build connections among us, as well as feed our cravings for chocolate. One evening near the end of our stay, these expectations were realized when our host, Matt Libby, lit some brush in a ring of stones on the beach. We sat on driftwood logs in a semicircle facing the fire and looked out across the moonlit water to Beetle Mountain, a cone-shaped peak in the distance. Several members skewered marshmallows with sharpened poplar branches and toasted them to a crusty golden brown. Later, our mouths sticky, we sang songs together, including a few about the group with lyrics adapted by Lois Pangburn, who had plenty of practice leading songs with her first graders. These experiences helped us discover the truth of Sapon-Shevin's claim that "singing together is a highly cooperative act" because it encourages "everyone to 'have a voice' and participate, creating a sound that no one person could make alone."[10] For us, the joint creation of music served as a fine metaphor for the kind of cooperative research we were engaged in, reminding us that all of our voices were needed to develop trustworthy conclusions and create a more consistent spelling curriculum for students.

WHAT WE TOOK HOME

When we left Libby's five days after our arrival—our stock of insect repellent depleted, our supply of Post-its diminished—we took some things home with us that didn't fit neatly into suitcases, crates, or tote bags. Different people carried different things away from the retreat, ranging from restored confidence as a writer to a new desire to spend more time in the outdoors. Across the group, though, there were some definite finds.

First, we took home a better understanding of the spelling process, particularly a clearer sense of what we wanted students to learn and how we needed to teach to facilitate that learning. At the beginning of our inquiry, our expectations for spelling were inconsistent and our approaches myriad; after a year of data collection and a week's worth of intensive analysis, it was much easier to articulate what we valued and why. As a result of conversations begun during the retreat, we wrote and piloted a schoolwide rubric for spelling evaluation that served as a supplement to the district report card. Instead of a single letter grade representing their child's achievement in spelling, parents received an annotated rubric, sometimes even a paragraph-long narrative accompanying the rubric, that discussed their children's strategies, strengths, and needs. We also established a list of spelling concepts, brainstormed during the retreat, to be introduced at each grade level. For instance, first-grade teachers agreed to teach children that all syllables need a vowel, and third-grade teachers agreed to teach the four regular spelling rules discussed by Wilde.[11] Because the list was more context-specific than a scope-and-sequence chart (and much briefer, with only three to five concepts per grade level), it helped individual teachers see where their work fit into a schoolwide picture without creating a lockstep curriculum they needed to follow.

These opportunities to calibrate our expectations and develop a common language to talk about spelling were important for us because we had learned, from both our reading and the parent surveys, that few curricular areas come with as much baggage and "conventional wisdom" attached to them as spelling does.[12] To make the kinds of curricular changes our data suggested were necessary, we would need to work against that conventional wisdom—and we would need to present an articulate, united front about why such changes were necessary. The retreat helped us prepare for that challenge.

In addition, we took home a renewed commitment to professional development that attends to individual differences and permits teacher-learners to be in community with one another while working toward personal goals. Unlike the infamous whole school in-service meeting run by an outside expert, the retreat was designed by the group with members' specific needs in mind. Its flexible schedule allowed the pursuit of activities that made the most sense for each of us given our learning trajectories, interests, and experiences. As Lynne Brabant observed, "You'd see people in groups, and then at another time people would be working on their own. It was so neat that people were comfortable doing what they needed to do."

Having seen the effectiveness of a professional development model that balanced social and independent learning, we became dedicated to lobbying for similar opportunities in other settings.

Gail Gibson, Mapleton's principal, worked to carve out time during faculty meetings and other school-sponsored activities for teachers to pursue their own agendas as well as to participate in community conversations. First-grade teacher Lois Pangburn, a member of the district's professional development committee, was a strong voice for building districtwide release days around teachers' expressed needs and interests. I later helped several other schools use a similar model of independent goal-setting and inquiry combined with collaboration and social learning when consulting on teacher research. We see these efforts as crucial first steps toward changing pervasive attitudes about professional development and teacher learning.

Last but far from least, we returned to civilization from the retreat with a renewed commitment to one another, as well as an appreciation of each other's gifts. As Martha LaPointe explained, it was important "for people to have the time to write and then share that writing. People you don't hear much from—it raised my respect for them and their thinking. . . . I guess I had never heard their thinking before." Lois Pangburn echoed this idea, saying that a number of members had "blossomed" during their time on the retreat. Just as members of the Lewis and Clark expedition emerged as leaders in various areas—hunting, tracking, identifying plants—so did members of our group discover new strengths in themselves and each other from our sojourn together in the wilderness.

NOTES

1. Ambrose, S. *Undaunted Courage: Meriwether Lewis, Thomas Jefferson, and the Opening of the American West.* New York: Simon & Schuster, 1996.
2. Shockley, B., Michalove, B., and Allen, J. *Engaging Families: Connecting Home and School Literacy Communities.* Portsmouth, N.H.: Heinemann, 1995.
3. Chandler, K., Gibson, G., and Pangburn, L. "A Truckload of Data: Focusing on Data Analysis and Writing in a Retreat for Teacher-Researchers." Paper presented at the annual meeting of the American Educational Research Association, Montreal, Apr. 1999.
4. Chandler, K., and the Mapleton Teacher-Research Group. *Spelling Inquiry: How One Elementary School Caught the Mnemonic Plague.* York, Maine: Stenhouse, 1999.
5. Wright, K. "Weekly Spelling Meetings: Improving Spelling Instruction Through Classroom-Based Inquiry." *Language Arts,* 2000, *77,* 218–223.
6. Stafford, W. *The Way It Is: New and Selected Poems.* St. Paul, Minn.: Graywolf, 1998.
7. Nye, N. S. *Words Under the Words: Selected Poems.* Portland, Ore.: Far Corner, 1995.
8. Oliver, M. *Twelve Moons.* Little, Brown and Company, 1974.
9. Oliver (1974), p. 21.
10. Sapon-Shevin, M. *Because We Can Change the World: A Practical Guide to Building Cooperative, Inclusive Classroom Communities.* Boston: Allyn & Bacon, 1999.
11. Wilde, S. "A Speller's Bill of Rights." *Primary Voices,* 1996, *4*(4), 7–10.
12. Chandler-Olcott, K. "Squaring Up to Spelling: A Teacher-

Research Group Surveys Parents." *Language Arts*, 2000, 77, p. 224–231.

✎

Kelly Chandler-Olcott, an assistant professor of reading and language arts at Syracuse University in Syracuse, New York, began her teaching career in 1992 teaching English and social studies at Noble High School in North Berwick, Maine. A recipient of the Meredith Recognition Award for Excellence in Teaching, she has served as the facilitator of the Mapleton Teacher-Research Group, a schoolwide inquiry group that was supported from 1998 to 2000 by a grant from the Spencer Foundation's Practitioner Research Communication and Mentoring program. She has written numerous articles and books on literacy teaching and learning, including one chronicling the story of the Mapleton Teacher-Research Group, titled *Spelling Inquiry: How One Elementary School Caught the Mnemonic Plague* (Stenhouse, 1999). She feels most alive in her teaching when she is "conferring with individual students—usually preservice and in-service teachers—about pieces of writing or plans for instruction that they see as worth our mutual commitment and effort."

Our best teachers weave dynamic connections among themselves, their subjects, and the students they teach. While the heart of teaching is centered on the relationship and interpenetrating connections between student, teacher, and subject matter, most teacher preparation focuses on each individual strand as a separate and isolated entity. Describing a novel and innovative approach to teacher education, Alison Cook-Sather details a program in which prospective teachers dialogue with high school students about teaching, learning, and youth development. She reveals that there is much to be learned about ourselves as teachers and the way that our teaching is experienced by students when we ask for their perspective and listen to what they have to say.

—S.M.I.

Teachers-to-Be Learning from Students-Who-Are

Reconfiguring Undergraduate Teacher Preparation

Alison Cook-Sather

My job is to prepare college students to be high school teachers. As a former high school English teacher, I know something about what it takes to teach at the secondary level. But it's been a while since I have had my own high school classes. Times, teachers, and students change. So when I became director of an undergraduate teacher certification program, I knew I wanted to develop an approach to teacher education that did not rely solely on my own past teaching experience and the published perspectives of well-known educators. I also knew that I wanted to represent but not speak for those who have the most direct and immediate experience of precollege classrooms: high school teachers and students. I wanted to make learning to teach through the Bryn Mawr/Haverford Education Program an inclusive and dynamic conversation.

During my first year as director in 1994, I had regular conversations with a high school teacher friend of mine about the pedagogical questions preservice teachers raised in my courses. She often noted that her high school students had a lot to say about these same issues. As we talked, we realized that her high school students' perspectives could add an essential and missing dimension to my preservice teachers' education. We decided to create a project that would give high school students and preservice teachers the chance to interact directly with one another.

The project we created is called Teaching and Learning Together, and one of its central goals is to position high school students as teacher educators.[1] The project is based in the Curriculum and Pedagogy Seminar I teach at Bryn Mawr College, the last education course preservice teachers complete prior to their student teaching semester. Through Teaching and Learning Together, each preservice teacher is paired with a student who attends a local high school. The pairs exchange weekly letters focused on issues of teaching and learning. This written dialogue is complemented and informed by weekly conversations between the preservice teachers and me in the college classroom and weekly conversations between the high school students and my collaborator at the high school.[2] The conversations at the high school are audiotaped and made available to the college students. The high school students and the preservice teachers meet once at the beginning of the semester to establish a relationship on which to base their correspondence and once at the end of the semester to conclude that correspondence. Throughout the semester, in class discussions and in formal written analyses required at the end of the semester, each preservice teacher is challenged to interpret and learn from the exchange with his or her own partner and to learn from all the high school students' perspectives.

In creating Teaching and Learning Together, I reconfigured who participates in the conversations that constitute undergraduate teacher education. Through this project, I include those who are generally excluded but who are most directly affected by the pedagogical choices we make. Not only do I include high school students, but I also treat them as people with expert knowledge.

232

Just as I would pay guest speakers or adjunct instructors, I pay the high school students for their participation. I believe this is significant. It sends a message to the administrations at both the college and the high school, to teachers at both levels, and to the students themselves that student perspectives are valuable in the preparation of teachers.

Inviting high school students to be an integral part of preservice teacher education has meant that all of us—preservice teachers, high school students, and me—need to reposition ourselves. In other words, within the shared project of teacher education, we all need to realign ourselves in relation to one another and in relation to the knowledge each of us brings. To illustrate what this reconfiguring can look like, I offer a glimpse into the dynamic among one preservice teacher, Marianne; her dialogue partner, Chris; and myself.

It's the fall of 1995. An English major at Haverford College, Marianne has exchanged one round of letters with her high school partner, Chris. At the second class meeting of Curriculum and Pedagogy, she tells her classmates and me that Chris has asked her how she would prepare students for an Advanced Placement exam in English and, specifically, how she would structure the first few writing assignments that constitute that preparation. Marianne recounts to us her answer to Chris: before giving students the first assignment, she would go over what she was looking for in an essay and also probably brainstorm with them to try to define what a good essay is and how they could go about writing one. Marianne then shares Chris's response to this approach:

> He just basically wrote back that he disagreed with me and
> that [my approach] wasn't appropriate, implying that students
> wouldn't be in the AP class if they didn't already have good
> writing skills. And he was very dismissive and didn't want to
> talk about it anymore; that was pretty obvious. And I didn't
> know whether I should take him up on it again or what to do,
> because I disagree with him.

Although Chris is not in the room with us, his perspective informs our discussion. Resounding through Marianne's repetition of his words are the thoughts of a high school student who has both experienced an AP English class and has strong opinions about what is and is not appropriate to such a class. Speaking to us, Marianne is also speaking to him: "I still thought, especially because they're high standards, that's why it's important to go over them."

Proceeding with her narrative, Marianne tells us:

> I was typing this in my letter to him, and I was a little
> frustrated and a little mad, and then I didn't think it was
> appropriate to send because in some ways it was his opinion
> that helped me clarify how I felt. And I felt that I was just
> being argumentative or that he didn't really want to talk about
> it anymore. And I just didn't know to what extent . . .

Marianne trails off, no more certain about how to respond now than she was when she first received Chris's letter.

As Marianne is talking, many possible responses flash through my mind. Thinking about my own experience as a teacher, I can identify with Marianne; I know that as teachers we may not hear from students directly that they think our teaching methods are ridiculous, but of course they will and do think that. I remember that as a teacher of AP English, I often took an approach like the one Marianne describes. In fact, I still use it in the college courses I teach. Did my former students share Chris's perspective on this approach? Do my current students? As a teacher educator, I have a whole other set of responses. I want to applaud Marianne's tenacity in thinking through her own beliefs, her recognition that Chris's opposition helped her do that thinking, and her sense that there are appropriate and inappropriate moments and topics around which to interact with students. In addition, I want to say something that will encourage her to take away from this exchange a willingness to continue to listen to students.

My response to Marianne includes all of these elements. And as I say these things to her, I am aware that we could not be having this conversation in this way if Chris weren't a part of it. It is his direct challenge that pushes Marianne to clarify her thinking, but even more fundamental, it is because she is interacting directly with him that she not only thinks about but also *feels* these things. Although I could speak for a student with Chris's perspective, I could not reach Marianne or other preservice teachers the way an actual student's voice can.

By making space for Chris's input, and encouraging—indeed, requiring—Marianne to listen to him, I am both repositioning myself and repositioning Chris. Both of us are teacher educators, but my role is to create a space for him to play his role. To do that, I have to displace myself—create a forum within which Chris can express himself without my mediation. I also have to re-place myself. I do that not necessarily by standing behind what Chris or the other high school students say, although that is often the case; instead I stand behind the students in a metaphorical sense as they share their perspectives and by insisting that the preservice teachers take those perspectives into consideration.

These shifts reposition Marianne as well, making it more difficult for her to fall into the traditional us-them dichotomies education perpetuates—teacher-student, theoretical-practical, college–high school. With a greater variety of voices speaking to her about teaching and learning, Marianne can engage in more informed reflection and perhaps remain open to wider variety of perspectives in the future.

Even in the course of the semester, such openness to different perspectives is apparent in Marianne's participation in the project. A few weeks further into the semester, when Marianne and Chris again disagree about a pedagogical approach—literature circles—she listens carefully to his critique. Then she explains, "I made a list in my journal of reasons why I thought literature circles were valuable. Writing this list was very helpful. I had not thought about the reasons I like literature circles before Chris challenged me." Just as when Chris questioned her approach to teaching writing in an AP class, in this case Marianne writes out and clarifies for herself what she believes and why. It's as though she continues the conversation with Chris in her head; his voice shapes her evolving sense of her pedagogical approaches and herself as a teacher.

Unlike the first conflict they had, however, this conflict does not make Marianne angry or defensive. Rather, she moves directly to processing what he has argued and clarifying her own perspective with that input in mind. But she also goes a step beyond that to consider the educational experiences Chris has had that might have shaped his values and beliefs. Thus Marianne considers at once the pedagogical approach itself, the reasons she values it, her presentation of it to Chris, Chris's reaction, and the larger educational context within which all of these variables operate. Marianne concludes that

> Chris has been raised (and he has succeeded) in a school system which taught him to value the individual. He has not been encouraged to question this system. When I introduced something that did not fit with the system, he did not see the advantages. I realize now that when I introduced Chris to literature circles, I needed to place them in a context: I needed to tell him more about my philosophy of teaching. I also realize that it was a mistake not to tell Chris about the advantages I saw to using literature circles. He is not used to valuing this kind of program. Finally, I should have been able to answer Chris's concerns. I had expected Chris to do the analysis himself, but that was not realistic of me.
>
> This whole experience with Chris made me rethink how I would introduce new practices to my classroom. I realized that I should be prepared to explain why I think something is worthwhile. Students are not going to instantly recognize why a different approach might be beneficial, especially if it does not fit in with their view of schooling.

Marianne and Chris did not always disagree, and there were times when she revised rather than reinforced her thoughts on pedagogical approaches in response to his and the other high school students' input. I tell these parts of the story, in which Marianne fortified her beliefs but imagined how she might change her approach to practice, because they offer the most vivid illustrations of the moments at which Marianne reflected deeply and learned important lessons that I would have had a harder time teaching without Chris's participation. As the only teacher educator in the class, I could have told Marianne that it is important to consider students' previous learning experiences, to contextualize and explain a new pedagogical approach, and to respond to student questions and concerns when they arise. But I believe that she learned these lessons much better from her interaction with Chris and her reflection on that interaction. By making a space in this teacher education course for Chris, I better facilitated Marianne's preparation than I would have by filling that space myself.

Of ongoing concern to me as a teacher educator is whether or not the lessons preservice teachers learn through the Bryn Mawr/Haverford Education Program stay with them once they enter their own classrooms. Does this reconfiguring of their teacher preparation—the positioning of high school students as teacher educators—change precollege education as well? Marianne, for one, has internalized her experience and integrated the lessons she learned from it into her classroom practice. Looking back on her exchange with Chris after teaching for two years in a middle school language arts classroom, she writes that Teaching and Learning Together "taught me to value students' opinions on approaches to teaching. I don't think it always occurs to teachers to ask students about this. But after my experience, I do it as a matter of course in my classroom." Like many of her fellow participants in Teaching and Learning Together, Marianne continues to think of students as teacher educators and the project of teaching and learning as a shared one.

The kind of reconfiguring of undergraduate teacher education that I describe here poses both systemic and individual challenges. The systemic challenge is that of refusing the schisms that are so deeply inscribed in education and educational institutions—between teachers and students, between theory and practice, between precollege and college classrooms—and the accompanying assumptions about who has valid knowledge about teaching and learning. This is a challenge not only within the education program but also for graduates of the program. When they enter classrooms and school systems that not only do not value but also actually discourage students' perspectives on teaching and learning, it is difficult to continue to solicit those perspectives. Does it do participants in the Bryn Mawr/Haverford Education Program a disservice, then, to take a programmatic stance that not merely encourages but actually requires the integration of student perspectives? This is a question with which I continue to struggle, although my belief in working toward better communication and more reciprocal teaching and learning tends to overpower my doubts about the challenges I pose to prospective teachers.

The individual challenge to me as teacher educator is to embrace the seeming paradox of displacing myself to re-place myself in order to make spaces for and facilitate dialogue among those differently positioned in education. Sharing authority on teaching and learning with high school students requires that I continually reexamine my theory-into-practice in light of input from two groups: the high school students and the preservice teachers. Thus I must face the same challenge I pose to the preservice teachers.

There is much in education, and thus in teacher education as well, that pushes us to isolate ourselves and one another—to divide ourselves into separate groups and arrange ourselves in hierarchies. Formal learning and promotion for both students and teachers is measured in terms of individual accomplishment. Yet I have found that reconfiguring the Bryn Mawr/Haverford Education Program has not only enriched undergraduate preservice teachers' education but high school students' and my own as well. By creating a more inclusive conversation and sharing the responsibilities of teacher preparation, our accomplishments and our potential are deepened, not diminished.

NOTES

1. The project also includes experienced teachers as teacher educators. I focus in this essay on the inclusion of high school students because they are the more uncommon participants in teacher preparation. Grants from the Ford Foundation and the Arthur Vining Davis Foundations supported Teaching and Learning Together between 1995 and 1999. Bryn Mawr and Haverford Colleges now support the project without external funding.
2. From 1995 to 1998, I facilitated this project with Ondrea Reisinger, at the time an English teacher at Springfield High School, Delaware County, Pennsylvania, with whom I also designed the project. Since 1998, I have facilitated this project with Jean McWilliams, assistant principal at Lower Merion High School, Ardmore, Pennsylvania.

Alison Cook-Sather began her career as a high school English and writing teacher. She is presently an assistant professor of education and director of the Bryn Mawr/Haverford Education Program at Bryn Mawr and Haverford Colleges. She is a recipient of the Rosalyn R. Schwartz Teaching Award, which is given to Bryn Mawr faculty members who have made a distinctive difference in teaching and leadership at the college. She has written extensively about the relationship between student teachers and their students and pioneered several programs in which high school students have worked closely with preservice teachers in exploring questions of teaching and learning. She recently edited (with Jeffrey Shultz) a book of essays written by middle and high school students in collaboration with teacher and researcher adults, titled *In Our Own Words: Students' Perspectives on School* (Rowman and Littlefield, 2001). Cook-Sather feels most alive "when my students and I are learning something new or relearning something from a new angle. It is this shared sense of discovery—shared in the sense that all are learning something, not necessarily the same thing—that I find most vitalizing about teaching."

This story celebrates how listening to each other with deep attention can power authentic and enduring school reform. Instead of tampering with the curriculum, cranking up the pressure on students and teachers by raising standards, or mandating new programs, David Hagstrom inspires school reform by modeling a way of relating that begins with asking open, truthful questions and listening with reverence and intensity to what parents and students say.

—S.M.I.

Honor the People;
It's the Leader's Work

David Hagstrom

Not long ago, I traveled to Alaska to spend some time with my son and his family on the occasion of the birthdays of my grandchildren. Bruce; his wife, Cathe; and their two daughters live on an island in southeastern Alaska. I could have easily flown there, but instead I elected to take a more leisurely route. I made journey by ferryboat through the Alaskan coastal waterway known as the Inside Passage, a thirteen-hour journey that gave me an invaluable chance for recollection and reflection. I will forever be grateful for that magical day out on the water when I reclaimed my birthright.

During my long wait in the ferry terminal that morning, I overheard two young people talking about their jobs. "I have a wonderfully joyful job," said one. "I'm a flight attendant, and I do these short hops and serve everyone on board all by myself. I'm really at their service, and I love it. But what I really want to be is a teacher. If I were a teacher, I'd truly be able to make a difference in this world. I'm such a believer in people; teaching would give me the chance to give young people the sense that they're truly valued and appreciated."

These two continued to talk, but my thoughts were suddenly drawn back to my own early days as a teacher, when I too really wanted to make a difference.

In 1953, as a senior in a Chicago area high school, my after-graduation plans did not include college. I planned on getting a job in the building trades or perhaps as a cabinetmaker. Many members of my family were painters and carpenters, and I looked forward to opportunities to work with my hands.

That all changed in an afternoon. I was called down to the dean's office by Mr. Fritzmeier, the senior dean. "What are your plans for college, David?" he asked. Caught off guard, I blurted out, "Well, Mr. Fritzmeier, I'm not planning to go to college. No one in our family has ever gone to college, we don't have a lot of money at home, and I'm really looking forward to becoming a carpenter or cabinetmaker." Mr. Fritzmeier looked at me for a very long time and said, "Well, we'll see about that, son. Please come back here again tomorrow at the same time. Understand?" I thanked him for his time and said, "Sure, I'll be back tomorrow, same time."

When I returned to the dean's office on that Wednesday in late March, now almost fifty years ago, Mr. Fritzmeier asked me if I had anything planned for the weekend. What a peculiar question, I thought. "No big plans, Dean," I answered. "Good," he said with a smile. "Be here in my office with a bag packed for the weekend on Friday by one o'clock. And by the way, you won't need any money. Just tell your parents that I've arranged for a special weekend of travel for you. Are you comfortable not knowing how you're going to spend the weekend, simply knowing it's going to be just downright terrific?" Well, what are you going to say to the dean in response to a question like that? "Of course, Mr. Fritzmeier; I'm just fine with that!"

On Friday, Mr. Fritzmeier hurried me off to his car and drove me downtown to Chicago's Rock Island railroad station.

"You're traveling to Grinnell, Iowa, my boy. Grinnell College is located there, and when you get off the train, someone will meet you. Here are your tickets. Have a good time. As the miles go by this afternoon, just rejoice in the adventure of it all, knowing all the while that I appreciate who you are. Oh, and there's one more thing—be prepared to say, 'Yes, thank you.'"

When I arrived at the Grinnell train station that evening, a representative from the college admissions office met me and took me to a dorm room for a rather unsettled "settling in." For the next day and a half, I sat in on classes, went to a dance, and talked to folks in the admissions office. As I boarded the train to return home on Sunday afternoon, the admissions officer said to me, "David, we'd like to have you as a student at Grinnell for the next four years. All of your expenses have been arranged for—you'll work as our night telephone switchboard operator three nights a week, and we've assigned you to Clark Hall. We strongly appreciate who you are, David, and we want you to be with us. So what do you say?" There was only one response, as far as I was concerned. As Mr. Fritzmeier had earlier directed, I said, "Yes, thank you."

I later learned that the dean paid for that train trip with his own money and completely arranged for my admission to Grinnell. Today, almost fifty years after receiving Mr. Fritzmeier's gift, I realize that my own entry into teaching was motivated by a similar desire to make a difference in the life of at least one other person, just as Mr. Fritzmeier had made a difference in my life. I wanted to value others in the way that Mr. Fritzmeier had valued me. The various stops along the way—YMCA camp work, teaching in middle school and high school, becoming an activities director and later a principal—all of this work was the result of one person's special gift to me. My initial move toward teaching was clearly motivated by someone who had chosen to make a difference in my life. How could I *not* choose to make a difference for someone else?

During my long ferryboat ride, with bald eagles circling overhead, I found myself thinking about what I've now come to call the "turning point" of my teaching career. My most joyous days as a teacher came, I realized, not from what I'd taught but from what I'd learned. While gazing out upon the waters of Frederick Sound, I acknowledged that the most important lesson I'd ever learned about teaching was taught to me by the children, teachers, and parents of Denali School in Fairbanks, Alaska, where I once worked as principal.

In the mid-1980s, while working as a college professor at the University of Alaska, I'd come to believe that as a teacher of "principals to be," I needed to be an Alaskan principal myself. I'd been a principal before in the Midwest but never in Alaska. How could I be considered relevant and knowledgeable if I'd never been an administrator in the North Star State? This thought motivated me to begin pleading with superintendents and personnel directors: "If you ever need a substitute principal for one of your schools, even for just a week or two, please consider me. I truly would appreciate the experience. It would give me an opportunity to blend theory with practice. I'd be a much better professor, don't you think? And besides, as a principal, I'd be out there in the real world, making a genuine difference with my life. Please help me do what I simply must do."

Years of pleading, however, brought me no results. I was becoming resigned to simply carrying on as a college professor, unable to "walk the talk." I'd do my best, I told myself, and bring practical everyday school issues into class discussions as much as possible, and make the very best of it.

Then, toward the end of August 1988, Jerry Hartsock called. I was sitting at the back of the library at Ryan Middle School in Fairbanks, listening to the new principal greet the staff on the occasion of the first in-service session of the school year. "I'm really pleased to be here," she told the teachers, "and we're going to have a great year. However, I'm really sad that school is going to be starting at Denali Elementary, where I taught for the past eight years, without a principal."

On hearing that news, I thought, Yes, absolutely! It's too bad that there's not a principal at Denali Elementary. That school really needs a good principal. It was the first school built in Fairbanks, and over the years the building had become a bit shopworn and forlorn. The school is also downtown, and as the town grew, the more well-to-do and more fortunate residents gravitated to the outlying schools. Denali had became home to many Alaska Native children and young people from the adjacent army base. A place like Denali really needs a fine principal, I said to myself. But I forgot about all of that as I got into my car and headed back to my office at the university. There was a faculty meeting awaiting me that afternoon and a million other things.

When I arrived back at my office, my phone was ringing. I picked up the phone and heard a voice announcing: "David, we're calling your bluff." It was Jerry Hartsock, the associate superintendent of the Fairbanks school district. "For years you've been telling us all that you want to be a substitute principal and be out there in the real world making a difference. Well, you're going to get that opportunity. We want you to be the acting principal at Denali Elementary—until we can find a real principal." I practically shouted: "Jerry, that's just great! I'm so pleased!"

Putting down the phone, I bounded on down to our dean's office and barged in on him with the news: "We've just had a great opportunity drop in our laps. I've been asked to be the acting principal at Denali Elementary. Isn't that just the very best news? Won't that be a really fine opportunity to build better school district–university relationships? What do you think? Isn't this just terrific news?"

The dean's response rather surprised me, but I was in such a state of ecstasy that I didn't pay much attention to it at the time.

"That's good news, David," he said. "You know, I think you can carry on with both jobs and make this work. Let's see, the public schools start up at 7:30 in the morning and go till about 3:30. As a graduate school, we offer our courses beginning about four o'clock and go until ten. Seems like the perfect arrangement to me. Work there until 3:30, and be here by 4:00. Good work, and congratulations."

The next day, very early in the morning, I was at Denali Elementary School. As I entered the building, I found myself murmuring: "OK, David, just what have you gotten yourself into now? Wanting something is one thing. Now that you've got it, what are you going to do?" Reality was beginning to set in. But this was just the beginning of "real life." It was also the beginning of what was to become one of the finest learning opportunities of my life.

The next few weeks were very difficult for me. I learned that there was a world of difference between having "good ideas" and simply doing what needs to be done in a school for children and teachers on a day-in, day-out basis. Early on during what I came to call my "days of baptism," I would often mutter to myself, "David, you're out of your league. Just cut your losses and get out of here. Get yourself on back to where you belong. You can probably make a difference back at the university. This is just way too much to handle." Of course, one of the contributors to this "way too much" feeling was that fact that I was working two jobs. I was exhausted at the end of the first job and almost a basket case by the end of the second. By Halloween, I was just about to throw in the towel.

But then, at the end of the school day on a Thursday in early November, I found myself in the hallway just outside the office, resting for a moment before setting off on my drive to the university. I noticed two teachers and two parents in the hall and walked over to them, expecting to make small talk or perhaps simply to say hello and to make my presence known. By that time in the school year, I was almost completely worn out and felt completely incapable of instigating much intelligent conversation. So I just opened up my mouth, wondering what words might tumble out. To my surprise, I said, "What do you folks want for your children here at the school?"

For a really long time, the four of them just stared at me in silence. Finally, one of the parents, Sue, spoke up: "You know, no one has ever asked me a question like that, but if you can handle the truth, I'm going to answer the question." She went on to explain that her two children really appreciated living in Fairbanks. "It's a real outdoors kind of place, and my kids enjoy building forts along the river in the summertime and snow houses in the winter. They can be true adventurers in their free time," she declared. "But then they enter this dark, dank school, and there's not a hint of that exploring fun that gets them so excited. This is really a pretty dreary place for children. I want my children to be the same kinds of explorers inside the school as they are outside. I'd like school to be an exciting experience for them."

The other parent agreed enthusiastically: "You sure got that one right! But there's something else I'd like. Somehow, I'd like the school to teach the concept of giving, not taking. For years and years, outsiders have been taking from Alaska. Fishing folks come up from Washington State and take the fish out. Forest products people come in and take the wood out. Gold miners used to take the gold out. And of course, the oil tankers take the oil out. To add insult to injury, now, in the process of taking out the oil, Exxon has spilled the oil all across some of the most pristine beauty of Alaska! It's simply ridiculous! And because it's so ridiculous, I want my kids to learn to be givers, not takers."

The hallway conversation went on in this way for about two hours. At the end of the time, I was really quite energized. "This has been good," I said. "Do we want to continue this talk at another time?" Everyone agreed, and after a rather frustrating attempt to figure out a convenient next time, Sue extended this invitation: "Here's an offer you can't resist. I'll make breakfast next Tuesday morning if you'll all come. What are you all doing at 6 A.M. next

Tuesday? I can't imagine that you've got a lot scheduled at that hour!" We all laughed as she continued, "So be at my house at six. We'll live with this question some more and talk."

Tuesday morning at 6 A.M., the five of us were there, and we continued to live with the question: What do we want for our children here in this school? Interestingly, the answers given in the hallway remained the same. At the conclusion of the breakfast meeting, the people in Sue's kitchen strongly indicated that they wanted the children to be explorers—maybe even discoverers—and givers, not takers. So as we were about to part company that morning, I asked, "Shall we meet again?" It was quite clear that the group wanted to meet again, so Sue issued a new invitation: "Come on back next Tuesday, at the same time. But here's the deal: Each one of us has to bring someone. It doesn't matter whether it's a teacher, parent, child, or neighbor. You all have to bring some-one—as your ticket to eat. Then, with ten of us, let's see if others have different answers to the question that's before us. See you next week with a child, friend, or colleague. Remember, be here at six!"

And we were there the following week at six. And the fol-lowing week, and for many weeks thereafter. As the months went by, the breakfast became a potluck and our numbers swelled. The question remained the same, and so did the answers. What do we want for our children here in this school? We want them to be-come explorers—and givers, not takers. Over the weeks and months, it became clear that we wanted to create a math-science magnet school with a strong character component that stressed the importance of service to the community.

During the following year, the entire school community be-came involved. We enlisted the aid of the science department fac-ulty at the University of Alaska, engaged the support of the Alaska Department of Education, and mobilized the neighborhood that surrounded the school. Parents became teachers, children became discoverers, and I—the "substitute principal"—became totally caught up in the adventure of it all. Where earlier I had been ex-hausted, I was now amazed and invigorated.

As the adventure grew exponentially before my eyes, I recalled (and endorsed) words that the theologian Henri Nouwen shared with me years ago: "Lose yourself in the work of the group, David, and then find yourself again, revitalizing the group." Without a doubt, I had lost myself in the work of these children, teachers, parents, and neighbors. They—*we all*—had become like eager little kids discovering things together for the very first time. As we went about our work of learning earth science ideas, the laws of physics, and Alaska Native ways of understanding the world, we were becoming a learning community, and we were coming to strongly value the contributions of each and every human being in our midst.

In the six months since we began living with the question "What do we want for our children here in this school?" the building we inhabited had become transformed from that "dark, dank place" to "Alaska's Discovery School." The school had become a more exciting place. Perhaps even more important, we—children, teachers, parents, and neighbors—had become more exciting people in the process of creating that more exciting place.

The more we invested ourselves in the Discovery School project, the clearer it became that we were in truth involved not so much in a school change project as in an "honoring the people" project. We were about the work of identifying, supporting, and celebrating the unique and special talents of each person in the school community. More and more, I began to hear people saying to one another, "Thank you for your very good work. We really value and appreciate you. It's an honor to be working with you."

At the end of a staff meeting, one of the first-grade teachers stood up and said, "Thank you, David, for being who you are with us. Please continue sharing your gifts with us. We need who you are. You value us, so we value others. You appreciate us, so we appreciate others. You believe in us, so we believe in others. You honor us, so we honor others. We've learned how to be with those who inhabit this place because of how you are with us. Thank you so much."

It was at that moment that I felt I'd learned the lesson that they, not I, had taught. This is what I'd come to this place to learn, a lesson simple yet profound: Honor the people; it's the leader's work.

In response to the first-grade teacher's compliment, I told the staff the following story, which they later told me hooked them completely into the affirmation activity that was our work: One evening at the university's ice rink, I noticed a father teaching his disabled son how to ice-skate. I was simply amazed at the father's persistent patience. I was particularly impressed because I knew that this youngster had experienced very little success in school. So while his son was in the locker room changing into street clothes, I asked the dad, "What's your secret, Jim? You're so patient with Scott. How'd you learn to be so good with him?" Looking ever so intent, Jim quietly said, "There's so little that Scott cares about. But he loves to collect bottles, and he loves the ice. So I help him collect bottles. And since his main goal in life is to learn to skate, I spend every spare moment I have with him on the ice. I've simply learned to notice what he's passionate about, and then I just pour it on. This shows I honor Scott; I affirm him by supporting whatever it is that he wants to create."

The Denali staff elected from that time forward to find out what they—children, parents, and neighbors—were passionate about and then pour it on. This became our mission. "This is how we will honor our people."

That is how we worked. And as we honored each person for who he or she was and what he or she had to offer, we truly became "one people." We had become united around a wish to provide a wonderful education for our children, and in that uniting we had identified the contributions that each of us could make that would make that wish come true. As I reflect now upon our journey toward becoming the school that we wanted, I realize that each of us had become the persons we had always wanted to be.

This is David Hagstrom's forty-third year as an educator. In every position he's occupied, from elementary school teacher to principal to associate superintendent to college dean to graduate school professor, he has always described himself first and foremost as a "teacher." His first job in education was as a middle school teacher in Evanston, Illinois, in 1958. He has written extensively about a broad range of educational issues. A recent article published in *Educational Leadership* was titled "Keeping Teachers Fresh Through Metaphor." Of the many honors and awards Hagstrom has received during his four decades of work in education, the one he particularly cherishes was a letter of commendation from Alaska's governor Walter Hickel on the occasion of his school's receiving a national New Century School award. The letter recognized his work as principal in bringing the community together and serving as "a teacher to all of the people in the community: children, teachers, parents, and even the people who live in the neighborhood." He feels most alive in his teaching when "I truly know my students and know what they're passionate about. Then I'm able to 'pour it on.' I'm able to support and encourage whatever it is that they deeply care about. I did this work in the 1950s, and I'm doing this work today."

School reformers often approach the challenge of making change as a clinical or simulated problem they have to solve for the good of other people. Locked in this mind-set, reformers grope to find the external levers and technical fixes that will set the system right. Writing from a unique stance as a psychologist, teacher, school reformer, and organizational consultant, Linda C. Powell challenges educational leaders to rethink the logic of most school reform efforts. She rejects the technical logic of most reform agendas and compels us to imagine a theology of school improvement in which leaders acknowledge how their own feelings and projections affect what they see and propose. She suggests school leaders draw on their faith, wisdom, and discipline to address the complex adult relationships at the heart of the school system.

—S.M.I.

From Charity to Justice
Toward a Theology of
Urban School Reform

Linda C. Powell

THE ACCIDENTAL EDUCATOR

When I left the corporate world to pursue my dream of being a psychologist, I imagined helping individuals and organizations make important changes. Although psychotherapy is a powerful form of learning, I never saw myself in the traditional role of "teacher," in front of a class. Two outstanding mentors dramatically changed my plans. Echoing my father, Leroy Wells Jr. relentlessly reminded me that African Americans who were fortunate enough to earn doctorates had a responsibility to teach at the university level. His own career at Howard University was an inspiration and a prod. Then, in 1989, Michelle Fine invited me to join the mammoth effort to improve Philadelphia's public schools.

Those two mentors completely shifted my professional direction. Suddenly, I found myself in a classroom filled with midcareer educators pursuing graduate degrees. All were committed to improving education, and most to something called "systemic reform." I was simultaneously learning and working with teachers and students inside urban schools to change their governance structures, improve their school culture, and raise academic achievement. I was also researching the challenges of improving urban education for the children we have most persistently failed. For real contrast, I continued coaching corporate executives, elected officials, and NASA scientists. Each of these experiences fed and illuminated the others, as stories and experiences from my multiple "classrooms" collided and interacted.

Systemic school reform is fundamental change for improvement. To make a genuine difference, reform requires both individual and organizational behavioral changes. Creating the scaffolding to improve *all* the schools in a district, not just an individual school or a select group of children, is daunting work. These complex and expensive efforts bring up knotty problems of values and scale. Issues of equity—sometimes framed as closing the achievement gap between poor students of color and more privileged students—reveal the profound and historic differences among adults. Grappling with these issues with different audiences profoundly affected my teaching, research, and consultation. Over time, these multiple and sometimes jarring experiences provoked a shift in my thinking from what we can do "for" students, teachers, and schools to what adults must do "within" and "among" ourselves to improve education for all children.

Given the special ecology of the learning life, nothing is ever lost or wasted. Personal, professional, and political experiences merge to create new knowledge. My skills as a psychologist have proved especially useful in identifying the individual, internal experiences that affect group and organizational functioning. This essay traces the development and interaction of a set of midlife experiences as a teacher, learner, and researcher—which inexorably revealed the "limits" of organizational theory and psychology. When they failed, I began to wonder whether a theology—an attempt to "see God" in urban school reform—might come next.

256

GETTING DEAD

I am a member of a team of researchers investigating the impact of school size on the poorest children in a major city. One morning, my colleague and I are interviewing a group of middle school children about their plans for high school. Their comments are predictable: they want to go to a high school that will get them into college, to one with a good sports teams and cute boys. Then the young woman who had been identified as the "special education" student says that in her opinion, the most important thing about choosing a high school was to go where you "wouldn't get dead." Each member of the group nods in agreement. Their conversation grows lively as they recount in vivid detail the death of a young man many of them knew. He had been shot in the head at the neighborhood high school while going to class. Then, with barely a pause, they turn to considering the differences between their school and Catholic schools, which they assume would be better.

Something was profoundly wrong in this discussion. Later, I realized that I had been offered a nanosecond of their genuine experience of school. This was not the carefully constructed world that students collude with us to create when they respond to our delicately crafted questions. This was a wild moment, an out-of-control poetic beat. My academic "objective" researcher-self was caught off-guard. Even though I had led groups for almost thirty years, I couldn't find a single way to intervene and say, "This shouldn't be how you make your decision. The world we have created for you is unfair, and you deserve better." I said nothing. In fact, my research colleague didn't even take note of this moment because it fell outside the parameters of our interview protocol.

Even more startling, the students didn't expect us to comment. I was suddenly aware of a tremendous divide yawning between these children and us. In their view, personal safety must be considered before other issues of education. But we adults have not demonstrated serious concern or effectiveness in these life-and-death decisions. In fact, we appear to display a studied lack of interest as we plan standardized testing schemes or implement interdisciplinary curricula or fight power battles over our turf while they work to simply "not get dead." Children no longer expect adults to offer anything useful because they assume we are responsible for the conditions in which they find themselves.

In the days and weeks immediately following this encounter, I could not write up my notes or think clearly about the overall project. Something had happened that I could neither make sense of nor push away. It took a while even to connect my inner paralysis with this encounter. Finally, the head of the research team confronted me: I was not carrying my share of the responsibility for the project, and this was having an adverse impact on the study. As a middle-class professional, accustomed to "doing well" and "being a success," this was a humbling and sobering experience. In a single group experience, these young people had created what psychologists call "parallel process." They had created in me what they feel within: a rage, sadness, and helplessness that makes it difficult to think or perform intellectually. Under this burden, I was not working up to my potential. I was actively participating in the creation of an "achievement gap" between myself and my colleagues on the project.

This was a tiny example of the power of projective processes—complex psychological mechanisms that individuals and groups in organizations use to "communicate." Most of us are familiar with the power of these projections from our families and interpersonal relationships. We reduce complexity by splitting issues and people into all good or all bad, black or white, eliminating the "messy" and the shades of gray. Unfortunately, we cannot actually rid ourselves of these complexities; group psychology suggests that we "project" or associate these split-off qualities onto other individuals or groups. (We see this politically when certain individuals or groups are demonized.) This process actually contributes to strong forces within an organization as people come to take on the roles and ideas we project onto them. For example, during this period I started to "believe" that I was not a good writer or researcher. I avoided opportunities that might somehow confirm that fact. On an organizational level, these psychological dynamics intensify the already impenetrable politics that swirl within urban school districts.

NEW QUESTIONS

This was certainly not the first time that I had doubts about my work. I questioned myself each time I faced my leadership class or conducted professional development for teachers. But this experience was an internal crossroad. Hearing these children so casually consider violent death as a possibility of school life stunned me. It was a slap that shattered an internal sense of "rightness" that I hadn't known I possessed. Unwittingly, I still unconsciously considered my own positive, safe schooling experience as the unexplored backdrop for what school is like for all children.

Holding the faces of that group of children became my image for Gandhi's words:

> Recall the face of the poorest and most helpless whom you
> may have seen and consider if the step you contemplate is
> going to be of any use to him. Will he be able to gain anything
> from it? Will it restore him to control over his life and
> destiny? In other words, will it lead to *swaraj,* self-rule for the
> hungry and spiritually starved millions of our countrymen?
> Then you will find your doubts and your self melting away.[1]

I continued to teach and consult, but now I did it through the lens of these children and their schools. I saw my own efforts with far more humility, and I began asking new and dangerous questions. Would what I was teaching make any difference to those children? What was the actual quality of the leadership and educational professional development programs that I was providing? Why was it routine to invest thousands of dollars in a bank vice president's development and outrageous to propose that for a third-grade teacher? Could the structure of higher education allow Gandhi's "melting of the self," or did it somehow require the inflation of the self? And what about "spiritual starvation" in education? What about the hunger for depth and meaning and hope that I often encountered?

This new lens brought three realizations into sharper focus. First, systemic reform requires adults to look at their own issues. Most of us came to education to work with children. We often find adult processes unexpected and unsettling and employ our own damaging projective processes to manage our discomfort. We need more sophisticated help to productively manage these organizational processes of splitting and projection. It is absolutely crucial that we be professionally anchored and supported as we change our practice with children. The public focus is on improving children's learning, but the unspoken challenge is to accelerate adult development, to somehow mine the untapped knowledge in our inner conflicts and anxieties. As adults, we must improve our ability to take on tough tasks, to make difficult decisions with insufficient information, and to learn about how systems change as we change them.

Second, despite the concrete language and dizzying numbers, systemic reform is filled with ancient and unexplored feelings. Whenever we open big questions of systemic reform—like curricular reform or teacher preparation or school finance—we hear autobiographical stories in response. Every policy question is linked to individual experience. Teachers describe why they chose education as a career. Principals recount their hopes and desires to make a difference. Superintendents talk about teachers who made a difference to their lives. As adults, we have powerful feelings about our own childhood experiences, as well as about schools as symbols of the future. One maladaptive way we manage these feelings is to

STORIES OF THE COURAGE TO TEACH

move away from the real experiences of current students and teachers. We push the strength of our reactions and associations outside of our immediate awareness. But these unexpressed feelings continue to operate, making it even more difficult to harness our passions for genuine change.

Finally, I realized that while we may disagree on the strategies and priorities, we know what we need to do to improve education for all children. We know the large levers that have to be moved. We just refuse to move them because we are frightened about the dislocation these changes will cause among adults. We resist the uncharted nature of much of what we know must be done.

Educational researchers routinely comment that school systems are "dysfunctional" and "irrational." Some say we lack political will; others say we lack courage. Still others believe we are "addicted" to low-performing public schools. All of these diagnoses acknowledge the central challenge: technical questions of "what" are not the primary obstacles in systemic school reform. But these researchers rarely go beyond description to propose any set of principles or actions that would help us be more effective in those kinds of systems. This may be because the answers are "beyond" their current paradigm of technique or legislation or policy. At least part of the solution now resides in the world of spiritual matters: questions of justice, will, perseverance, and hope.

To be ruthlessly honest, little of what I did was intense, sophisticated, or complex enough to influence the intrapersonal, interpersonal, and organizational level dynamics in most school systems. Nothing I was teaching was substantial enough to enable educators to work through the genuine challenges of adult development, fear of change, and addiction to low performance. At best, my teaching inspired a small percentage of individuals to take on this more painstaking internal work of reform. At worst, I was contributing to a growing sense of futility and despair around school improvement. And I worried that I was helping to maintain a false sense of "progress" toward ambiguous goals that would make no discernible difference for the students that I met in that group.

TOWARD A THEOLOGY

I am teaching an experiential course called Community and Diversity. As a way of getting to know the group, we are "doing crossover." Participants stand on one side of a large room and walk to the other side in response to a series of statements: "If you went to private school . . . ," "If teaching is your second career . . . ," "If there has ever been a racial incident at your school . . ." In a flash of inspiration, I add to my planned list, "If a religious practice is important to you as an educator . . ." After a brief skirmish over "religious" versus "spiritual," all but two or three students cross over. There is a moment's stunned silence as we take in the implications of this question and its answer.

Not surprisingly, talking about a "theology" within the education community has provoked strong reactions. After presentations on this topic, colleagues of all faiths swamp me with stories of their own classrooms, students, and districts. They insist that we need a new language of purpose and community, one that links our profound yearnings for wholeness with our daily activities in schools and district offices. They say we need to be able to talk about how systems behave as well as what individuals do. They worry with me about the dynamics of pride and ambition that infect even our best efforts. Their religious values keep them effective in their classroom and often in efforts to improve their school. However, their deepest commitments remain hidden in their daily work.

Others react more cautiously. *Theology* is a scary word in the same context with public education. It raises the specter of school prayer and fundamentalist assaults on intellectual freedom. It provokes painful stories of unhealed harm by faith communities. These concerns are a legitimate hurdle to a theology of urban school reform, which will require tolerant, thoughtful dialogue among people with differing opinions.

In 1995, the Servant Leadership School (SLS) in Washington, D.C., provided a unique laboratory to begin such a dialogue. SLS—a "people's seminary"—was the perfect place to explore a potential "theology of school reform." The students in this class were diverse, including some who thought of themselves as "religious" and some who did not. Many already worked with children as educators or advocates; others were simply interested in the topic. School reform and children's issues in general were starting to be framed as "the new civil rights movement." Many students were interested in articulating the kind of powerful theological foundation for children that the "freedom movement" had. There was an amazing chemistry as we read, fought, and prayed together about the needs of children and our responsibility as adults. Three practices emerged that might form a theology for systemic school improvement: presence, silence, and nonviolence.

Presence. Reading reports and attending meetings is insufficient involvement for the difference we need to make. We must be physically present as both a witness and a support to the students, teachers, and administrators. But being present can be difficult and unsettling. It is easier to maintain our certainty and opinions at a distance. In the actual presence of poor children, stressed and unsupported teachers and administrators, and schools overwhelmed by the daunting set of tasks before them, we run the risk of seeing and feeling things that will change us, that will lead us to question our assumptions. We may find that our "answers" fall short and that the only thing we can do is to be present, to show up.

Silence. We must learn more about our projective processes by holding on to our inner life in a disciplined way. The busyness of modern life encourages rather than constrains projective processes. Our public conversation about education is often too loud with too little substance. Lines are drawn, enemies and allies identified, using child-centered rhetoric to cover serious adult-oriented interests. We talk too often to those with whom we agree, and we listen too seldom to those with whom we disagree. Silence creates a clear space that harnesses the power of the human spirit. Dialogue processes, quiet days, and retreats not only strengthen the individual teacher but can strengthen the system's ability to manage the new and complex information that school reform initiatives generate.

Nonviolence. An underlying commitment to nonviolence is a requirement of this theology. The philosophy and practice of nonviolence joins us across our differences in a deep faith in the future. We can cultivate the belief that difficult (even evil) organizational processes can be overcome. Nonviolence provides a human way to disagree and to resist oppression. It is a political tactic as well as a self-development strategy. And it is a crucial intervention in an irresponsible culture that promotes violence to young people as entertainment. The study and practice of nonviolence leads us to see ourselves as more than pawns in "central office " processes or consumers of the ideas of others but as change agents with commitment, potential, and perseverance.

THE MORAL ARC OF HISTORY

We often talk about public education as if it is the center of a story. Putting it at the center, we speak from our roles as parents and teachers "as if" government and culture were directly influenced by children's needs. Those of us in the field of education are especially prone to this tendency. But in reality, there is another "story that is telling us." In that story, education is an increasingly minor character with less influence and value. "Entertainment" and "leisure" are huge industries in our culture, promoting a powerful set of values that are often at odds with the demands of human development. Young people are often deeply disenchanted with the work of schooling and see it as increasingly irrelevant. Many adults despair that public education is not designed to serve the needs of children, especially poor children of color. And the huge profits to be made from the failure of public education, an $880 billion industry, exert their own pressures.

As my personal religious path has become clearer, colleagues have expected me to leave education and do "something in the church." However, many of my deepest values have not developed in a religious context. I have seen the faces of good and evil while involved in systemic education reform efforts. My religious beliefs and my commitments to public education are hardly at odds with each other. On the contrary, perhaps this search for justice in how we organize schools to educate all young people is the next right development in education and in our civic life.

Without question, this is complex work, requiring intense exploration of three notions. First, this theology is not about school prayer for children. This is a theology that strengthens adult efforts to improve education. This theology supports and enhances the faith, wisdom, and discipline of adults involved in systemic change. It addresses the "spiritual starvation" Gandhi describes by placing a cadre of vibrant and committed adults in children's lives as educators.

Second, our commitment to religious freedom should not inadvertently lead to valueless education. As long we fail to agree about the purpose and importance of public education, we leave a vacuum to be filled by another set of ideas: the relentlessly effective "curriculum" of individualism, materialism, and violence-as-entertainment that is routinely available to young people. Finally, within the discourse of "faith-based organizations," our desire as people of faith to be involved in education should not limit our responsibility to be the "conscience" of the democracy that provides that education. The question of equity is squarely before us, and developing individual schools does not answer the larger systemic questions.

As in India under British colonial rule, among black workers in Montgomery, Alabama, and in postapartheid South Africa, the cards seem stacked against the dramatic transformation schools surely need. We could reasonably move on to a more "promising" social problem, bemoaning the impossible circumstances of urban schools. Or we can dedicate ourselves to using every resource available—including a willingness to face ourselves, each other, and maybe even God—to resisting and overcoming these internal and organizational obstacles to authentic school change.

NOTE

1. Attenborough, R. *Words of Gandhi.* New York: New Market Press, 1982, p. 25.

Linda C. Powell brings an interdisciplinary set of skills as educator, organizational consultant, and psychotherapist to groups and individuals working on issues of power and change. Almost thirty years ago, she began her career in the not-for-profit sector, working with caregiving organizations before moving into the corporate sector, where she created and managed a number of executive development programs at American Express and Marine Midland Bank. In 1989, she became involved in efforts to reform and transform urban public education. During her tenure on the faculties of the Graduate School of Education at Harvard and at Columbia University's Teachers College, she developed a series of courses using techniques more typical of schools of management to prepare urban school leaders. Her course Understanding Authority and Exercising Leadership is unusual and controversial in that it requires an intensity of feeling, thinking, and action rarely found in academic settings. She has written several articles and book chapters on leadership and urban school reform. She is also the coeditor of *Off-White: Readings on Race, Power, and Society* (Routledge, 1996).

We demand much from our educational leaders. Principals, college presidents, and superintendents must answer to many stakeholders, each lobbying with complicated, impatient, and often conflicting agendas. There are buildings to be built, achievement scores to be raised, curricula to transform, grievances to negotiate, and jumbles of other critical duties to execute. At the center of this fray, Wellesley president Diana Chapman Walsh asks one of those basic questions that stills the tumult: What can I do as an educational leader to support teachers so that they can be their best and do their best work? Her answer is as inspiring as the question: educational leaders must develop a leadership of peace that creates and protects space within our institutions for growth and self-discovery to flourish.

—S.M.I.

Toward a Leadership of Peace for the Twenty-First-Century Academy

Diana Chapman Walsh

Everything we know about human behavior underscores what social beings we truly are. The social environment shapes our actions, indeed, our beliefs, in profound and subtle ways. Peter Berger's pungent insight that we "choose our gods by choosing our playmates"[1] reminds us of the potency of social reference groups. We make important decisions in communion with people we trust—and sometimes in reaction to others whose values we reject. Even if we are locked alone in a room to resolve an important question, we invent a dialogue.

THE INESCAPABILITY OF ORGANIZATIONS

We know from public health research that altering the environment—by mobilizing economic incentives, applying legal

Note: Many of the ideas developed here were incubated in conversations with Richard S. Nodell, a longtime organizational consultant to my senior management team at Wellesley College and to me.

restraints, or shaping social norms—is demonstrably more effective than counting on personal motivation and force of will[2]. Organizations like Alcoholics Anonymous create a whole new social support system to replace the one in which the person developed the addiction. Ulysses had his men lash him to the mast because he knew that when he heard the Sirens' call, he would be powerless to resist.

"The difficulty of being a good person in the absence of a good society" is illustrated poignantly by Bellah and his colleagues in the example of the uncomfortable and all-too-familiar experience of passing a homeless supplicant and wondering whether to give or withhold the change many of us can easily spare, knowing that "neither personal choice is the right one."[3] Social structure affects us more than we like to admit, even those of us fortunate enough to occupy its safer niches.

And so it is with the places where teachers do their work. It's hard to be a good teacher in the absence of a good school. Teachers can retreat for a time from the pressures of a hostile or indifferent world to listen for the stirrings of their own hearts. Any of us can, and should, take time away to retap the wellsprings of our motivation. When we do, we renew a vital resource without which we are less than fully alive. And that inner teacher we find by opening ourselves to its leadings enables us to listen better to the longings of others' hearts. If in that mutual listening we can name those common things that are worthy of all our care, we can begin the chain reaction that starts, in Marge Piercy's poem "The Low Road,"[4]

> when you say We
> and know who you mean, and each
> day you mean one more

We each make daily choices about where we will stand and fight, about where our vocation lies at any moment or stage of our lives. The teacher who rescues one child has accomplished a life's work, a work that stands by itself as an unequivocal good. But the odds of that miracle occurring—and recurring—would be substantially improved were Piercy's multiplying "We" more creatively engaged in shaping the social environments in which we ask teachers to do their difficult work.

My charge from this book's editor was to reflect on "what we can do to transform our organizations so that they can be places for the self to be expressive." How have you worked in your role at Wellesley College to come closer to that ideal? I was asked to ask myself—in two thousand words or so. A tall order, that—both the doing and the telling.

In response, I want to argue (1) that in order for teachers to be effective, inspiring, and impassioned by their work, they must be connected—to themselves, to one another, to their material and their students, to their schools, and to the larger and deeper meanings of their work; (2) that to create and sustain settings in which teachers can be so connected, we need managers and leaders who are themselves working self-consciously to avoid powerful forces that tend to drive *them* into isolation; and (3) that we can understand this purposeful work that seeks to preserve connection as a leadership of peace.

THE PRECONDITION FOR INSPIRED TEACHING: STAYING CONNECTED

First, let's reflect for a moment on what teachers need so that they can be their best, most present, and most expressive selves and do their best, most inspiring, and most transformational work. A Maslow-like hierarchy of need is an obvious starting point. If teachers lack the most basic material and instrumental necessities—as far too many in our country do—then little else will matter. Teachers must have decent compensation packages; adequate space, equipment, and materials; job security and mobility;

attentive, respectful, and supportive supervision; collegiality, enough time to give each student the attention he or she deserves; and regular opportunities to learn and to grow in the role. All this is necessary but far from sufficient, as we all know from our own experience.

Robert Levering discovered in many interviews that workers who loved their jobs spoke less of the extrinsic rewards—salary, vacation, fringe benefits—than of the more intrinsic satisfactions in the work itself. He concluded, in *A Great Place to Work*,[5] that a deeply satisfying job is like a deeply satisfying marriage in that the metrics we naturally apply are more subjective than objective. If you ask a friend how her marriage is going, she's unlikely to recite to you her family's net worth, the number of children and pets they have, and the make and year of their automobiles.

What she will describe vividly are a variety of connections, and as Parker J. Palmer has so eloquently taught us, it's the ubiquitous sense of *disconnection*—the profound sense of isolation— that is strangling our schools and our teachers. If we hope to transform this new century into one we can survive, the world is going to need young people who themselves are able to make durable connections: connections between various domains of knowledge; connections between thought and action; connections between competency and ethics; connections across generations, across cultures, across town, and around the globe; connections that honor our radical interdependence with all living things.

If we want our teachers to guide our young people in developing the skills and habits of mind they will need to make these kinds of connections—the ability to read critically, write persuasively, speak cogently, and reason quantitatively; a knowledge base from which to think historically, spatially, cross-culturally, comparatively, and (not least) with empathy—we will need them to engage in a style of teaching that emphasizes context, relationship, and creativity. And teachers who are themselves isolated and dispirited are unlikely to be able to summon the personal resources to inspire those leaps of faith.

WHAT LEADERS CAN DO TO FOSTER CONNECTION

To keep teachers connected, then, we need schools that seek to integrate individualism and interdependence; that promote a communal spirit and a sense of common purpose; that encourage and appreciate everyone's contributions and accomplishments; that address human needs for both solitude and solidarity; that attend, in the words of Jane Tompkins, to "social excellence as well as personal achievement."[6] That's all well and good, I hear you muttering now, but how do we achieve such a remote ideal?

Virtually everyone who writes about leadership emphasizes the importance of (1) holding and conveying a vision of the organization's future, one that expresses everyone's best hopes for it, and reflects its history and values; (2) catalyzing a realistic and fluid assessment of its current reality; and (3) aligning and mobilizing all the resources at its command (especially the human and intellectual resources that are so indispensable in our information society) to close the gap between the vision and the reality.[7]

Jean Lipman-Blumen argues further, as others have, that a fundamental shift has taken place in our understanding of the style of leadership that will be capable of this demanding work. She identifies two contradictory forces—interdependence and diversity—that she says are "pulling in opposite directions" and "rendering traditional leadership behaviors obsolete." In *The Connective Edge,* she offers a most intriguing set of strategies for tempering the inherent tension between those two competing forces and channeling them into a sense of community and mutual purpose.[8]

What I've come to believe after eight years of experience as a college president—and much reading in the literature on leadership and organizational change—is that the leader's most crucial and most exhausting challenge is to maintain his or her *own* connections (to self and to others and to the purpose of the work), to resist relentless pressure from the system to be driven into isolation. In a small, intense, and highly critical intellectual community, the assignment of blame for things that go wrong can become so heightened and personalized, while the levers of change are so diffuse, that it is natural for people with managerial responsibility to become guarded and defensive of themselves and the status quo.

As the combatants scramble for their foxholes, the possibilities for connections fade. So it often falls to the leader to establish and carefully tend a series of key working partnerships—partnerships that are honest and effective, solid and self-conscious. Calling others into partnership, then, becomes a major part of the leader's task: exploring together what happened when things have gone awry; mending tears in the fabric of relationship; helping others integrate and digest the ways in which what they are doing is enabling them—and the organization—to learn and to advance, guiding them in maintaining their own connections to their roles and tasks, to one another, and to their own inspiration.

A LEADERSHIP OF PEACE

The president of a college or university is constantly beset and besieged by competing claims for resources, attention, and validation. The same can be said, I suspect, of educational leaders at all levels and in all settings. Often the claims manifest as invitations to go to war or to mediate wars in which others are engaged. But to participate in war is inevitably to sever connections. With this in mind, I've tried to develop and enact what I've begun to think of as a leadership of peace.

Toward the end of his riveting and all-too-relevant book, *The Plague,* Albert Camus has his hero say this: "All I maintain is that in this world there are pestilences and there are victims and it's up to us as much as possible not to join forces with the pestilences."[9] This is akin to the Hippocratic injunction *primum non nocere,* first do no harm. Surely this would be the foundation for a *de minimis* leadership of peace. And yet it is not trivial to carry out by any means.

To offer a leadership of peace would involve, first and foremost, declining all invitations to go to war—sending people back to find their own creative solutions, never forgetting, not even for a minute, that the most important job a college president (or school superintendent or principal) can do is hold open a space in which a community of growth and self-discovery can flourish for everyone.

Unlike an organization whose function is to produce a product efficiently, in education the process is inextricably bound up with the product. And learning is nothing if not a process of discovery and unfolding. So how we do our work in schools and colleges— where we put our emphasis, what values we embody and express— is tightly intertwined with the outcomes we seek to produce. We teach as much by the example of what we do and how we do it as by what we actually profess in the classroom. We teach a silent curriculum not detailed in the catalogue, syllabus, or lesson plan.

This is a humbling realization for an organization (like any human arrangement) that has its imperfections, has gaps between what we say (our expressed aspirations) and what we do (the lived reality of the place for everyone there). I'm constantly being called to account by students, faculty, staff, alumnae, and even strangers for gaps that they see between what they think we ought to be or what they think they heard me say we are (or what they did hear me say) and how they are experiencing us. And those gaps matter if we are serious about protecting a learning process that has constancy and integrity. That is a challenge I face every day—more effectively some days than others. It can be daunting.

But the good news is that human creativity arises in just this gap between vision and reality, in the disquieting but galvanizing structural tension we experience between where we are and where we aspire to be. Holding that tension in active consciousness is the first step in the creative act. Holding it with reverence is a movement toward peace. Creativity is stifled, voices are silenced, and people are devalued when we paper over the tension with self-delusion about where we are or, conversely, when we lower our ambitions rather than tolerate the tension.[10] Creativity and progress require the confidence to grant what we may not know and demand the courage to look failure in the face.

So if we are serious about this business of teaching and learn ing together— if we grant the importance of sustaining connections and maintaining peace—then one of the most important tests we shall always face is how we deal with our imperfections, vulnera-bilities, and inevitable mistakes. We can seize on them as learning opportunities without which we'll never stretch and grow to our full capacity. We can support one another in that sometimes painful process of self-discovery and growth. Or we can allow our-selves to be so chary of the anticipated humiliation of criticism and failure that we avoid the risks altogether and hold ourselves back from exploration, from creation, from self-invention.

And this work cannot be done well in the absence of the prac-tices described in Parts One and Two of this book—the inner work of self-discovery and self-development and the reaching out to oth-ers. People of diverse backgrounds will not come together and sus-pend their suspicions and hostilities, will not let down their guard to learn from one another, until they are secure enough in their own identities that they do not have to risk everything—fears of exposure, isolation, rejection—to open themselves to others.

This, it seems to me, is among the most pressing challenges we all share, as students, as teachers, as workers, as organizations, as the beleaguered "industry" of education, and most profoundly, as human beings whose nature it is to seek to know ourselves in all our messy complexity and whose life task it is to keep adapting to ever-changing circumstances.

At a time of confusion and conflict around the world—a time of mounting tribalism and ethnic hostility—our places of teaching and learning are among the few islands in our society where people from diverse backgrounds can come together and try to find ways to live in peace while learning from each other. This is crucially important work—delicate, sometimes painful, sometimes explo-sive work, but work that we as a society must do, and do well, if we are to pass on to our children a future worth having. The fu-ture begins in our schools.

NOTES

1. Berger, P. S. *Invitation to Sociology.* New York: Doubleday, 1963, p. 120.
2. Walsh, D. C. "Social Factors in Substance Abuse." In H. Freeman and S. Levine (eds.), *Handbook on Medical Sociology* (4th ed.). Upper Saddle River, N.J.: Prentice Hall, 1989.
3. Bellah, R., and others. *The Good Society.* New York: Random House, 1992, p. 4.
4. Piercy, M. "The Low Road." In *The Moon Is Always Female.* New York: Knopf, 1980, stanza 4.
5. Levering, R. *A Great Place to Work.* New York: Avon Books, 1988.
6. Tompkins, J. "The Way We Live Now." *Change,* Nov.-Dec. 1992, pp. 12–19.
7. Senge, P. M. *The Fifth Discipline.* New York: Doubleday, 1990.
8. Lipman-Blumen, J. *The Connective Edge.* San Francisco: Jossey-Bass, 1996.
9. Camus, A. *The Plague.* New York: Random House, 1948, p. 229.
10. Fritz, R. *The Path of Least Resistance.* New York: Fawcett Columbine, 1984.

Wellesley College president Diana Chapman Walsh is a leading expert in public health policy and the prevention of illness. Inaugurated as president in 1994, she was previously Florence Sprague Norman and Laura Smart Norman Professor at the Harvard School of Public Health, where she chaired the Department of Health and Social Behavior. Prior to joining the Harvard faculty, she was at Boston University, as a university professor and professor of social and behavioral sciences in the School of Public Health. As a Kellogg National Fellow from 1987 to 1990, she traveled throughout the United States and abroad studying workplace democracy and principles of leadership, as well as writing poetry. She has written and edited or coedited fourteen books and many articles. She feels most alive in her teaching when "I have managed to create and hold a space that is a true learning community in which we are engaging important questions together and supporting one another in a process of inquiry and exploration."

Part Four

Rejuvenating Heart
The Courage to Teach Program

The authors in this book have shared their stories, and here's what we know. They have been drawn to their work for reasons of the heart. They describe their desire to serve students, their mission to convey their passion for the subjects they teach, and the belief that through teaching they can awaken in students a zest for learning and goodness. They believe in the noble promise that when they come before a group of students, much is possible. They also believe that teachers, bound together by a mutual commitment for our students, can jointly create institutions where learning can flourish. They have faith, optimism, and an abiding belief that they work on the girders and beams of our society. These stories remind us that teachers believe in the elemental virtue of their vocation.

Parents, educational leaders, politicians, and philanthropists, should be heartened that our teachers step through the classroom doors eager and resolute in their verve to support students on journeys of growth and development. Yet those who purport to care about education must hear the anguish that runs through these stories as well.

The authors describe how they are drawn to this work by reasons of the heart, yet many feel they're losing heart. They speak simultaneously of the noble contributions possible in their work and the toxic conditions in which they do their work. Some have lost heart and left; more ponder leaving; others slog on feeling demoralized. All describe a mighty struggle to stay energized and whole despite difficult working conditions in our schools, excessive demands on their time, and intensified pressures heaped on by a society anxious and exacting yet strangely disconnected from its children.

The bind is clear: we need teachers to be present, alive, and connected, yet our institutions and systems smother and do violence to the energy and goodwill of our teachers. The questions we must ask are, What can be done to help teachers retain and sustain the fire and passion so integral to their work? How can educational leaders, policymakers, and a concerned public recruit promising teachers and then provide conditions that allow them to develop and flourish in their professional roles?

The single essay in Part Four describes an effort to provide a sustained programmatic response to these questions in the form of a professional development program. Established under the guidance of Parker J. Palmer, author of *The Courage to Teach*, and supported by the Fetzer Institute, the Courage to Teach program pioneers an approach to teacher professional development called "teacher formation." It is rooted in the belief that while technique and methodology are important, the source of good teaching emerges from the identity and integrity of the teacher. This program invites educators to reclaim their own wholeness and vocational clarity and to make connections between the renewal of a teacher's spirit and the revitalization of public education. This chapter explains both the principles at the center of the formation work and the practices important to the work, which may be understood as an attempt to promote professional growth by tending vocational development. The authors, Marcy and Rick Jackson, direct the Center for Teacher Formation and present numerous quotes from K–12 educators who have participated in Courage to Teach programs around the country.

—S.M.I.

For us to be inspiring and spirited teachers, we must stay connected with our colleagues, with our students, with the subjects we teach, and ultimately with our own hopes and ideals. When we feel isolated from colleagues, detached from our students, and removed from the subjects that we teach, we become disconnected and it is nearly impossible to teach well. Despite the profound but simple truth that teachers must feel connected and wide-awake if they are to engage their students deeply, this reality seldom guides the logic of educational reform. Most efforts at improvement focus on methods and techniques and on "fixing the teachers" rather than creating the space and time for teachers to make the connections to self and to fellow teachers that will sustain them in their teaching. Relying on the words of teachers who have participated in the Courage to Teach program, Marcy and Rick Jackson identify the principles of teacher formation and describe how the program supports teachers' effort to keep heart so they can give heart to their students.

—S.M.I.

Courage to Teach

A Retreat Program of Personal and Professional Renewal for Educators

Marcy Jackson and Rick Jackson

Twenty-five teachers and administrators sit in a circle, giving their full attention, as an elementary teacher speaks passionately and poignantly about her love for her students and her commitment to reach each and every one of them. She goes on to tearfully describe the personal toll this is taking on her own life—creeping guilt at not having enough time or emotional energy to give to her own family, bone-deep exhaustion, nonstop worrying about the safety of some of her students, the weariness of facing an always burgeoning mountain of papers and projects to grade, a sense of increasing isolation from friends and colleagues because there is simply no more to give. The listeners sit quietly, respectfully, as she finishes, each reflecting on his or her own version of the teacher's story.

Note: Excerpts of writing featured in this essay may also be found in the chapter "The Courage to Teach: A Program for Teacher Renewal," in *Schools with Spirit,* edited by Linda Lantieri (Beacon Press, 2001).

The next teacher speaks of the debilitating effects on the morale of his colleagues as more and more pressure is being placed to raise test scores at his school—or else! Whereas teaching was once a labor of love, it is now becoming an onerous task as the nearly singular focus on standardized testing dominates all communications among faculty and administrators. More silence.

The next person to speak, a newly appointed principal, describes her recent attempts to mediate an explosive situation involving a student, his parents, and a teacher. In helping the parties work through their threats and misunderstandings, she has become aware of the heavy burden of responsibility she carries. Yet in the telling of her story, she also recognizes a growing confidence and inner sense of authority, grounded not in her role as a new principal but in her personal integrity. And on around the circle it goes, one person after another relating stories and examples of how their complex journey as teachers and leaders has unfolded since the last time they were together a few months earlier.

What is this circle in which these teachers sit? Is this a group for "burnt-out" teachers and administrators? No. Then why have they come together in this way when their lives are already overfull with tasks, demands, and responsibilities?

This is the opening circle in a Courage to Teach retreat, part of a program in which the same twenty-five educators come together for three days four times a year. Through a process called "formation," educators are invited to reconnect to their identity and profession—their "soul and role"—through the creation of a circle of trust where they can reclaim their own wholeness and vocational clarity and find renewal. The formation process, as practiced in the Courage to Teach retreat program, involves the creation of an intellectual, emotional, and spiritual space in which participants listen and respond to one another with encouragement and compassion.

Why Teachers Need Renewal

Teaching is a calling, a vocation that requires constant renewal of mind, heart, and spirit. Teachers come to the profession inspired by a passion to help others learn. They are drawn to education by an ethic of service and a mission to make a difference in the world by contributing to succeeding generations of youth. Good teachers care, and they keep finding ways to connect with students. They do not check their hearts at the door.

Maintaining the passion to teach and lead wholeheartedly takes not only skill but also inner strength and spirit. Now more than ever, it takes *courage* to teach. A sampling of passages from applicants' essays attests to this deep need for courage:

> There are times when I'm not sure I can make it, when the pain of so many of the young lives I get wrapped up in threatens to swamp my own life and I fear I will be of no use to anyone. I also know that I reach children and that what I do is of value. When this [Courage to Teach program] brochure arrived, I was astonished. A renewal program for teachers? Inner life? Mine was far beneath my bed, gathering dust. (Elementary school teacher with eighteen years' experience)

> Friends urge me to move to an "easier" school, but I want to find a way to cope with the stress and enable myself to continue reaching out to these kids. I know that there are people out there who can do this and thrive. I want to be one of them. (Middle school teacher with fifteen years' experience)

> I want to be able to accept the realities of education without having to become disillusioned, bored, and disgruntled. I am a young teacher. Twenty years from now, I still want to say with passion that I am doing exactly what I want to do. (Elementary school teacher with five years' experience)

I seek the light to teach better and do more. . . . To develop collegiality is my main concern. . . . I find it natural to risk and be spontaneous with students, but it doesn't carry over to other teachers. Some are rigid and negative—psychic poison to me. Others are so overwhelmed and needy I hesitate to share much because they might start "living" with me. I have only a few teacher partners. I want some more. (Middle school teacher with twenty-five years' experience)

I don't need another in-service, nor do I need more opportunities to work on systemic reform. I'm already deeply involved in that! I need the chance to concentrate on my emotional and spiritual growth so that I am able to once again teach truly from the heart. (High school teacher with eighteen years' experience)

The American public continues to turn to our schools and teachers to better prepare our children for an increasingly uncertain world. But how do we better prepare teachers for this task? Typically, educational reform focuses on improving the curriculum and reorganizing schools. Yet while curriculum and reorganization are important, both solid research and common sense affirm that *what a teacher knows and how a teacher makes human connections* are the most dramatic influences on student learning.

Why does public education struggle with the difficulty of finding and keeping good teachers, principals, and superintendents? Perhaps what is missing is what is most essential: sustained and meaningful support for the persons who are doing the work, day in and day out, often under extremely discouraging circumstances.

To be an excellent teacher is to risk burnout at an early stage in one's career. The isolation from other professionals and the constant need to be "on" while teaching can exhaust and deplete a good teacher's inner resources. We simply cannot afford to lose good teachers through negligence of their need to connect with other teachers in ways that are respectful and trustworthy. (High school teacher with thirteen years' experience)

Is not quality public education the foundation of true democracy? Are not children our future? Do we really value all children? If public education is going to be a true road to a meaningful life and healthy community membership, we must nurture educators so they do not despair beneath overwhelming demands but maintain an inner gyroscope and persevere. We all need to be more attentive to the needs of the soul—our own and those of children. Without this deeper perspective, all the well-meaning reforms will wither along with the teaching staff. (Elementary school teacher with eighteen years' experience)

We need the power of collective spirit. We need opportunities for dialogue. We need to be affirmed, to ask important questions, to be in a community that challenges and supports our thoughts, that nurtures our deepest beliefs, that really helps us sustain and give meaning to the work that we do with students. We especially need these things at this critical time in public education. (Middle school principal with sixteen years' experience)

THE COURAGE TO TEACH PROGRAM

In *The Courage to Teach,* Parker J. Palmer invites us to go beyond the outer surface of structural reform and to summon the courage to explore the inner landscape of our own lives as educators:

The question we most commonly ask is the "what" question—what subjects shall we teach? When the conversation goes a bit deeper, we ask the "how" question— what methods and techniques are required to teach well?

Occasionally, when it goes deeper still, we ask the "why" question—for what purpose and to what ends do we teach? But seldom, if ever, do we ask the "who" question—who is the self that teaches? How does the quality of my selfhood form— or deform—the way I relate to my students, my subject, my colleagues, my world? How can educational institutions sustain and deepen the selfhood from which good teaching comes?[1]

The Courage to Teach program invites teachers and leaders to explore the inner landscape of their lives as educators by going back to the "deep well" of their calling. The program involves seasonal retreats spread over one or two years and focuses on the personal and professional renewal of teachers, administrators, and others in public education. The retreats are designed primarily for K–12 educators—on whom our society depends for so much but for whom we provide so little encouragement and support. Each three-day retreat focuses neither on technique nor on school reform but on the inner lives of professionals in education. In large group, small group, and solitary settings, concepts of teacher formation and "the heart of a teacher" are explored through the use of personal stories, reflections on classroom practice, and insights from poets, storytellers, and various wisdom traditions.

The Courage to Teach program builds on a simple premise: we teach who we are. Teachers who are disconnected from themselves cannot serve their students well—let alone invite each student's unique self into the teaching and learning exchange. Good teachers possess much more than information and technique. They possess a "capacity for connectedness." They offer up their own lives as the loom on which to weave a fabric of connectedness between themselves, their students, their subject, and their world.

Teachers are continually told what to do, how to do it, when, where, and so on. The results expected are fleeting and changeable. The methods are often contradictory. When an individual is unable to stop and reflect on the meaning of it all, that individual may become discouraged. Courage to Teach allows this reflection to happen in a variety of ways. You owe it to those, from whom so much is asked, to allow them to slow down and gather the courage to continue. (Middle school teacher with nine years' experience)

Students respect integrity and can sense hypocrisy. To be a valuable and effective teacher, one must know oneself. . . . Courage to Teach helped me gain and celebrate that knowledge. It is essential to be willing to share enough of yourself and to admit areas where there are challenges—to be able to teach from the heart. Students certainly respond and learn more from that safe space. (Elementary school teacher with nine years' experience)

We are guided in formation work by a clear image of the nature of the human soul. The soul is like a wild animal: it is tough, resilient, savvy, self-sufficient, and yet exceedingly shy. If we want to see a wild animal, the last thing we should do is to go crashing through the woods, shouting for the creature to come out. But if we are willing to walk quietly into the woods and sit silently for an hour or two at the base of a tree, the creature we are waiting for may well emerge, and out of the corner of an eye we will catch a glimpse of the precious wildness we seek.

As an African American woman, my voice was never fully respected. For so many years, I squelched my own voice as being not as important as theorists, professors, and principals. I would talk the way other people would expect me to so that I would be accepted. But it was destroying me. My Courage to Teach facilitator was the first professional person that actually listened and valued my voice. I realized that my voice had never been heard before and that my voice is valuable. Now with my students, I ask real questions, ones directed uniquely to them. I ask them to listen carefully to their own words. It is awesome what they come up with when they speak from deep within themselves. (Elementary school teacher with twenty years' experience)

Courage to Teach is not a Band-Aid. It deals with the very core of the issue of education—the soul of the teacher that touches the soul of the student. Without caring for the heartwood of a tree, the branches will fall off, the bark will peel, and the roots will rot. Without caring for the soul, the teacher will become frustrated and ineffective, and the students will fail. (High school principal with twelve years' experience)

This image of the "strong, shy soul" has practical implications for what goes on in a formation retreat. From the outset, teachers come to understand that this is not a "share or die" event. When working in small groups, a few simple and straightforward ground rules allow educators to sit quietly with one another: no advising, no fixing, no saving, no setting straight. Instead, they listen to one another at a depth that will "hear each other into speech"—a listening that can be enhanced by asking honest, open questions that might evoke more of what the speaker is trying to say. What each person most deeply wants is not to be fixed or saved but simply to be heard, to be received.

I've been involved in a lot of professional development programs at the local, state, and national level, both conducting them and participating in them. The thing that was so significantly different was that this retreat was for me. There was no other product than my own growth. Yet I've never worked harder or grown more in my life! I was there to rediscover myself and my lifework. (High school principal with twenty years' experience)

Almost all professional development opportunities are other-directed, looking at the skills that someone else has developed. Courage to Teach helped me understand that one of the most powerful things I can do to improve is to spend time going inside. There is enormous power, creativity, imagination, insight, perspective—all those things that I can bring to a class lesson. In trusting myself, I get the most true and authentic outcome with students. (Middle school teacher with twenty-six years' experience)

Courage to Teach is work that really exemplifies a very deep belief that I have about education, which is that you make the world better one person at a time, one student at a time. One principal renewed and reinspired and recommitted affects potentially thousands of people where they live and breathe every day. (High school principal with twenty-two years' experience)

Honest exploration of personal and professional beliefs demands trust, and trust requires boundaries. So one challenge in developing the Courage to Teach program was to find a way of bounding the formation space that would draw teachers into exploring their lives without giving offense or creating barriers in a society that is both secular and religiously pluralistic. To do so, we turned to the metaphors offered by the cycle of the seasons. The seasonal metaphors have proved to be powerful ways of framing the questions closest to the soul without making anyone feel trapped in a doctrinal or dogmatic box.

The Courage to Teach program begins in the fall, the season when nature is scattering seeds for the growth that is yet to come. In this season, we ask people to reflect on "the seed of true self," telling stories from their childhood or from their first moment of awareness that they felt called to teach—and from those stories they start to reclaim the birthright gifts and passions that put them on this vocational path. In the winter season, we raise questions about darkness and death, dormancy and renewal. Some of the seeds we brought into the world are now underground and may indeed have died. But others are lying dormant, awaiting a time of fresh possibilities. Spring is the season of rebirth, so in the spring, we reflect on "the flowering of paradox." It is a great paradox that what once seemed dead is now alive—and not only alive but quite beautiful! Summer is the season of embodiment and abundance. In this season, we invite teachers to explore who they are and who they are becoming.

> Facilitators talked about cycles and seasons. We focused on the seasonal themes of dormancy, renewal, paradoxes, community, abundance, harvesting, and gleaning. The themes were powerful ways to provide a framework to build wholeness and acceptance. For me personally, it was about learning to accept that I could not only plant and harvest but . . . also [take] time to stop and rest, even to cry. It's not just the "testable" or even observable work that you're doing with students. There are also intangible things important to the harvest of good teaching and learning, other things that can make a lifetime of difference. (Elementary school teacher with five years' experience)

For over a century, public education in the United States has been dominated by the "factory model." Standardization and uniformity of so-called measurable outcomes are the assumed hallmarks of good schools. But the work of human formation is much more akin to farming or gardening than it is to manufacturing. The manufacturer starts with "raw material" and adds value to it though a controlled and predictable process. But the farmer—who works not with raw material but with living organisms—must start all over each year through an eternal return of the seasons and must embrace the fact that not everything that happens in that

STORIES OF THE COURAGE TO TEACH

cycle is under his or her control: the rains may not come, or the hail may wipe out the crops.

Seasonal themes invite a different "way in" to education and professional development. The seasonal metaphors rid us of the hubris that we can control human growth. And they help us understand how interdependent we are with all the life forces around us—an understanding that can help us grow into the kinds of teachers who choose to spend a whole lifetime cultivating the young. A few lines from the poem "Seven of Pentacles" by Marge Piercy—a poem we use in formation retreats—speak to the way things grow in the natural world:

> Connections are made slowly, sometimes they grow underground.
> You cannot tell always by looking what is happening.
> More than half a tree is spread out in the soil under your feet.[2]

Elements of Courage to Teach Retreats

To provide a concrete sense of what happens in Courage to Teach retreat programs and how the formation process may differ from other approaches to personal and professional development, we will more fully describe six key elements of the formation approach: evocative questions, silence, paradox, birthright gifts, "third things," and clearness committees.

Evocative Questions

At the outset of a retreat and at various points in midstream, we offer a reflective question as a way of "checking in" with each other. The questions are designed to evoke a deeper level of sharing and to reveal the larger context within which we are working—and they often come in pairs to allow teachers to reflect on the complexity of the connections between their vocation and their selfhood.

For example, the question "What aspects of your identity and integrity feel most supported and engaged by the work you do?" is asked simultaneously with "What aspects of your identity and integrity feel most threatened or endangered by your work?" This paradoxical pair requires more depth and thoughtfulness than the question "What do you like most or least about your work?"

Before the teachers answer these questions in the large group, we invite them to take some time for reflection and journal writing. Then, rather than marching around the circle with each person speaking in turn, we invite people to speak only if and as they feel ready, and we invite silence after each person's reflections.

> I have experienced the practicality of setting aside time and space to address the deepest questions for educators (How can we nurture our personal powers so that we can be our best on behalf of our students?). The questions we are addressing have been at the edges of my mind since I became a teacher, but after more than a decade, I've let the questions take center stage and with the help of our Courage to Teach group have moved from the questions to strategies, to subtle—but I think profound—changes in my teaching (and family) relationships. (High school teacher with thirteen years' experience)

Silence

Words are not the only medium of exchange and learning in formation work. We share and grow in silence as well—not only because the silence gives us a chance to reflect on and absorb what we have been saying and hearing but also because the silence is itself a

STORIES OF THE COURAGE TO TEACH

sort of speech from the deepest parts of ourselves, of others, of the world. Though it is startling at first to teachers who are accustomed to being "task-oriented" and making "maximal use of minimal time," we often begin our group sessions with a few minutes of silence—and we invite quiet pauses in the midst of our conversations and activities. This helps create a slower, more reflective pace for discussion and enables participants to listen within themselves as much as they listen to the ideas and contribution of others.

> Silence. Going to a place to listen. Not saying anything. The quiet is so important, so soothing. I now use silence to center myself and to nurture my students. I make a greater effort to listen and connect on a personal level with colleagues as well. (Elementary school teacher with fourteen years' experience)

> I have continued the practice of silence and reflection in my daily life. I recognize the need for taking time to explore my inner thoughts and feelings so that I can be more helpful to my students and my family as well. I know and appreciate the close connections between seasonal cycles and human cycles as we live our lives. I feel more balanced. (High school counselor with twenty-five years' experience)

Paradox

Like the field that a farmer prepares in order to grow a crop, a formation space must possess several critical qualities if it is to respect and germinate the seed of true self. These qualities, like so much in the inner world, take the form of paradox—that is, the holding together of things that seem on the surface to be opposites or contradictions but that more deeply understood, complement and create each other.

Paradox is at the very center of the inner landscape of life: you cannot know light without darkness, silence without speech, solitude without community. And the poles of a paradox form a continuum along which almost anyone can find his or her current condition and thus find a level of comfort with what the group may be exploring at any given time.

In creating a formation space, we are guided by the following six paradoxes:

1. The space should be bounded and open.

2. The space should be hospitable and "charged."

3. The space should invite the voice of the individual and the voice of the group.

4. The space should honor the "little" stories of the participants and the "big" stories of the disciplines and tradition.

5. The space should support solitude and surround it with the resources of community.

6. The space should welcome both silence and speech.[3]

An illustration of one of these paradoxes—that a formation space should be both hospitable and "charged"—may be helpful. A hospitable space is one that people find not only comfortable but warmly inviting, not only open but safe and trustworthy, a reliably nonjudgmental space in which people can find the security they need to sustain challenging journeys. At the same time, the space must be "charged" if the journey is to be real and rewarding. There must be a sense of electricity, of risk, of stakes, of the danger inherent in pursuing the deep things of the human soul. This charge is not a "special effect"; it comes with the territory. We only need to bound or define the space with topics of genuine significance and refuse to trivialize them in any way.

These paradoxes are not captive, of course, to a formation retreat. They are also at the heart of all vital and engaging teaching and learning environments.

Paradox has been the essence, to reconcile discordant elements. There are so many dichotomies that I now play with rather than take sides on, playing on the edge between them and keeping that balance. As a high school teacher, management and containment were my goals. There were problems to be solved. Now it is more a mystery, and my job is to inspire kids to delve into that—instead of having them push against me, to have them pull me through these things. The hard work of teaching is easy again. (High school teacher with seventeen years' experience)

In our state, there is a huge pressure to meet the standards. As an administrator, it is my responsibility to make sure our school is right up there. It's a huge pressure on teachers. I ask them to remember: Why are we here? What are we doing this for? I hold out for my teachers that if we go for quality, our scores are going to be high. We teach to quality rather than the tests, and we have been successful. (Elementary school principal with twenty years' experience)

Birthright Gifts

Most of us have great difficulty acknowledging our strengths and gifts, but we have no trouble listing our weaknesses or failures. It's as if we have blinders on, especially to ourselves.

When we begin to explore "seeds of true self" in a formation retreat, it becomes crucial to uncover, or recover, *our own* particular gifts, strengths, and sensibilities. Referred to by the Quakers as "birthright gifts," these are not the skills we went to college or graduate school to get, nor are they the areas in which we have worked so hard to excel. Rather they are the qualities that are part of our essence, qualities that have often been apparent to others since we were young children but that we ourselves may have ignored, devalued, or simply taken for granted ("It's so easy for me, I thought everyone could do it")

To honor the individual teacher's soul, we must also honor each teacher's unique gifts. Given the beleaguered state of most teachers, and the teacher-bashing that too often goes on in the media and public forums, teachers often experience naming and claiming their birthright gifts as one of the most empowering aspects of the retreats.

> Courage to Teach seeks to honor the individual teacher by providing an opportunity to reflect and understand his or her own birthright gifts. We honor ourselves by taking the time four times each year to retreat to a place where it is safe to take risks. There we can examine our values, fears, concerns, and commitments. Best of all, we are accountable to ourselves, not to an outside entity. Being responsible to my calling to help kids is why I became a teacher in the first place. (High school teacher with thirteen years' experience)

> I am deeply concerned about the future of public education. It takes a lot of courage to be a teacher today—and to be a student. Much of the difficulty comes from a society and a system that ask teachers to be alienated from themselves. If there is to be any lasting revitalization of public education, it will come through encouraging teachers to be whole again and teach with their unique gifts. In natural response to that, they will encourage students to be whole and learn with *their* unique abilities. (Teacher educator with twenty years' experience)

> The concept of birthright gifts really came through. It was not only affirming but helped me look at children differently. It helped remind me that it's not just about what a kid can produce but [about being able] to go up to a child and say, "You are always fascinated when we talk about bugs" or "You

STORIES OF THE COURAGE TO TEACH

always know how to make people laugh and smile. That's really special!" (Elementary school teacher with five years' experience)

Why is this so important? Because when we are in touch with our own giftedness, we are much more likely to notice and draw out the gifts in others—the children we work with and our colleagues. By being more attentive to students' gifts and lifting them up, not only is the student-teacher relationship enhanced, but so is the opportunity for mutual respect and learning. We've found that when we ask people to talk about teachers that made a difference in their lives, some interesting patterns occur. One is that it is hard to get people to stop talking! The other is that the most memorable teachers seem to fall into two categories: those who ignited a passion for learning or for a particular subject and those who noticed and encouraged a person's unique gifts or skills and who recognized potential that the person couldn't yet see.

"Third Things"

In facilitating dialogues about vocation, about teaching, about the seasons in our lives and in our work, we use poems and teaching stories from diverse voices and traditions. Stories and poems create a mediating "third-party" presence by putting a subject in the center of the circle that establishes a plumb line for the dialogue that is owned neither by the facilitator nor by the participants. Its meanings can be imputed or interpreted but never controlled. Truth is not a point, or even a line made of many points. Instead, truth is a fabric, a quilt, a collage, a rich pattern of meaning that is generated by the whole group, a pattern in which every member of the group can find himself or herself.

In addition, this "third thing" helps us speak indirectly about things that we might have great difficulty saying head-on, to discover and speak important things about ourselves without referring to ourselves. The shy soul, we believe, appreciates opportunities to do what Emily Dickinson advises: "Tell all the truth, but tell it slant."

Take, for example, the first four lines of the poem "Now I Become Myself," by May Sarton, a poem we often use in the fall retreat to engage people with the "seed of true self":

Now I become myself.
It's taken time, many years and places.
I have been dissolved and shaken,
worn other people's faces.[4]

Even in those few lines, many people experience deep resonance with their own experience. The images draw them deeply into a dialogue about how long it takes to become ourselves, how much turbulence we encounter along the way, and how often we mask ourselves in someone else's image.

While we use some tried and true "third things" in Courage to Teach, this is not a curriculum-based model, and facilitators are also encouraged to discover and use their own teaching texts. Generally, good third things are relatively brief, accessible, and to the point. They also usually contain aspects of both the personal and the universal, allowing for exploration of the "little" stories of individuals while also being capable of expanding to encompass larger archetypal themes.

A poem about fear led to an amazing conversation about the fears in our own lives. Very capable and accomplished professionals shared openly and honestly. People with multiple graduate degrees and years of experience and awards in their professions shared their fear of being inadequate. Their fear of failure. Their fear of letting people down. Sharing that vulnerability, in a way I still don't completely understand, helped strengthen all of us. But somehow knowing we were all indeed quite human and quite apprehensive about being able to meet the challenge of educational leadership actually made us bold to keep on trying. (High school principal with twenty-six years' experience)

Clearness Committees

The clearness committee is a centuries-old practice invented by the Quakers to arrive at greater clarity or reach a place of discernment regarding a personal decision, an issue, or a dilemma. While at its heart a communal process of discernment, it is grounded in the belief that there are no external authorities on life's deepest issues. There is only the authority that lies within each of us waiting to be heard.

In the clearness committee, a small group of five or six people gather for the express purpose of asking illuminating questions to the person who is bringing forward an issue or dilemma seeking clarity. Committee members interact with the "focus person" only by asking open and honest questions—questions that are without a hidden agenda, questions that are real and honest and not intended to lead in any particular direction, questions that will help the focus person remove the blocks to his or her inner truth and to discover his or her own wisdom.

The benefits of this practice accrue not only to the focus persons. The members of the committee learn a great deal about deep listening—listening within themselves as they are forming good questions, attending to their own inner dialogue and attempting to keep their internal agendas at bay, listening with respect and caring to the unfolding story of another human soul. Most people emerge from a clearness committee having actually observed a person's "inner teacher" at work, often for the first time. The experience of the clearness committee confirms that human beings have an inward source of authority that does not need to be prodded with external answers and "fixes" but needs only to be given a chance to speak and to be heard.

> Clearness committees have helped us learn a way of being together that honors each person's way of knowing. We have seen the power that authentic questions, thoughtfully posed, have to help each of us get in touch with an inner teacher who is able to show us the way to the clarity we seek. It has been a challenge for teachers and administrators to learn to ask questions we don't know the answers to. We are told before each clearness committee that no one needs to be fixed, and we have learned the truth of those words. The clearness committee is such a powerful way of respecting and reinforcing a person's fundamental integrity. (High school teacher with twenty years' experience)

TEACHER FORMATION: A FOUNDATION FOR EDUCATIONAL REFORM

What difference does a retreat experience of the sort described in this essay make in the lives of K–12 educators, their students, their schools, and the larger public education system that is in such difficulty?

First, it is important to note that the principles and practices of the Courage to Teach program are not limited to the "hothouse" atmosphere of the guided retreat. Teachers who participate in the program often take the principles and practices that underlie formation and adapt them for a variety of settings, frequently with promising results. Here are several examples reported by Courage to Teach alumni:

> A high school English teacher begins her department meetings by inviting one faculty member to open the meeting

by talking for five minutes about his or her passion for teaching English or current areas of "aliveness" in teaching. The result has been a much greater sense of connection and collegiality within the department, as the faculty now have a space to share what matters most to them.

An elementary school teacher begins her fifth-grade class each week in a "community circle" by asking an evocative question to the group (for example, "How are the themes of the story we are reading—joy, loss, discovery, and so on—also happening in your own life?") and creating a sense of safety for the children to speak about what is really on their minds and in their hearts and to be heard by the other children.

A middle school teacher actively introduces seasonal metaphors in her teaching—drawing on what is happening in the natural world but also making the connection to the human cycles of change that the seasons represent. Using stories of nature, cultural stories from different traditions, and poetry and art activities that highlight the deeper meanings of the seasons, students are encouraged to see their lives as part of a larger whole.

A high school teacher introduces the concept of paradox to his class, explaining how two things that are seeming opposites can be understood as "both-and" rather than "either-or." Students are encouraged to look at paradox in their own lives—identifying personal paradoxes such as dependent versus independent, work versus play, student versus teacher, thinking versus feeling, active versus passive—and then to consider the larger whole encompassed by these paradoxes. This approach to introducing the notions of complexity and wholeness helps students move beyond simplistic and dualistic thinking.

A high school teacher works with students to help them identify their birthright gifts. Because it's often through the eyes of others that we recognize our own birthright gifts, the students are asked to interview two of their friends, their parents or grandparents, or another trusted adult or teacher who knows them well. The interview questions are open-ended and focus on stories or anecdotes that these persons share with the student. Some questions relate to what the adults have noticed about the student, not just what the youngsters are good at but "how they are in the world"— what's important to them, how they interact with others, the kinds of roles they play with their family or friends. Out of these interviews and their own journaling, the students begin to construct their personal "coat of arms," which includes a section on their birthright gifts.

A group of teachers come together for collegial support not only to enhance good teaching but also to create a place for deeper dialogue about what it means to be a teacher and why they do what they do. At each meeting, one or two teachers are invited to present an issue or a dilemma arising from their teaching, usually one that is at the intersection of their "soul" and "role." Using a modified clearness committee process, the other teachers respond by asking honest, open questions to help the individual uncover his or her own deeper understanding of this issue.

In addition to the compelling ways Courage to Teach approaches have been absorbed into participants' life and teaching practices, a further impact extends into the complex arena of educational reform. Two evaluation studies found the following lasting effects on the part of Courage to Teach participants:

- The Courage to Teach program rejuvenates teachers and renews their passion for teaching.
- Teachers who go through these programs undertake new leadership roles in education, often crediting their en-

hanced leadership skills and their capacity to assume new challenges and risks to participation in the program.

- Participants often report that their Courage to Teach experience led them to initiate more collegial relationships when they returned to their school site.

- Although the Courage to Teach program does not explicitly set out to change classroom practice, all of the teachers queried believe that the experience improved their classroom practice in significant ways through the development of genuine connections with their students and their "teaching from the heart." Most felt that their students had tangibly benefited by the changes.

- Teachers felt that the program helped them develop more reflective habits in their teaching practice, allowing them to become more critical practitioners who could stop and reflect on their own teaching.

- Teachers felt that they live more mindfully and more balanced lives.

These themes—passion for teaching, teacher leadership, collegial relationships, improved classroom practices, reflective habits, mindful and balanced living—are among those most often repeated in the education reform literature about what is most essential for good schools, good teaching, and good learning. Many observers of teachers have said that until we provide dynamic, supportive, and intellectually challenging conditions for our educational personnel, we will not be able to carry out our vision for creating dynamic, supportive, and intellectually challenging schools. Both research and common sense suggest that to be sustaining and renewing, we must provide opportunities for teachers and leaders to further develop, explore, and renew their core mission and purpose.

Why do so many carefully planned reform efforts fail to achieve their well-intended outcomes? Why is it that many initially successful reforms have difficulty enduring, often losing ground as their champions become depleted by overwhelming demands? Educators we have met through Courage to Teach are more than ready to shoulder the leadership tasks of change—*when they have reclaimed their sense of personal wholeness and vocational calling.* In teacher formation retreats, educators come together as colleagues, steadfastly reclaiming their identity and integrity as teachers. Enormous potential for positive change is rediscovered, leading to greater depth and vitality in student-teacher relationships, renewed collegial practices in schools, and the revitalization of teachers as leaders in public education.

> How do you get teachers inspired and invested, willing and wanting to give their best, able to dig into their hearts and intellects for a cause? You value teachers in a way they trust and believe in. This is delicate territory. Courage to Teach explores and maps this territory. It has profoundly altered my comfort-discomfort continuum. I see my job as a treasure and an honor and am uncomfortable with less than my best. In short, I am working harder and enjoying it more. . . . What difference does this program make for students? At first, my students are uncomfortable with the degree of earnest effort a class from me now requires. As time passes, they willingly, and with begrudging joy, "lean into" our tasks of learning. Courage to Teach instigated a renaissance in my practice of teaching. I remembered my idealistic self. For a profession having difficulty retaining talented people, the importance is obvious. (Middle school teacher with twenty-five years' experience)
>
> I consider myself a merchant of hope whenever I share my story about beginning my formation work. I can only testify to the impact the [Courage to Teach] program had on my life. I know that my teaching has become more humane. I have

found an authentic way to clear my thoughts of the many conflicting voices that deform rather than inform my work on a daily basis. I am not feeling burned out but "on fire" in terms of reaching out and embracing the many paradoxes of my teaching life. This program is a must for teachers who are so busy reaching out that they have forgotten the need to reach *in* and bring forth something worthy of their students' attention. This takes courage, and that is what the program provides. Courage to Teach provides a time to retreat, remember, and respond to the needs of your soul. (High school teacher with twenty-nine years' experience)

NOTES

1. Palmer, P. J. *The Courage to Teach: Exploring the Inner Landscape of a Teacher's Life.* San Francisco: Jossey-Bass, 1998, p. 4.
2. Piercy, M. "The Seven of Pentacles." In *Circles on the Water.* New York: Knopf, 1982, stanza 2.
3. The six paradoxes are explored further in chapter three of Palmer (1998).
4. Sarton, M. "Now I Become Myself." In *Collected Poems, 1930–1993.* New York: Norton, 1993.

Marcy and Rick Jackson direct the Center for Teacher Formation. The center prepares facilitators to lead Courage to Teach programs and to establish teacher formation programs around the country. The center is sponsored by the Fetzer Institute, a private operating foundation that supports research, education, and service programs exploring the integral relationships among body, mind, and spirit. Marcy Jackson has worked for twenty-five years with individuals, groups, and families as a therapist, teacher, and retreat facilitator. Rick Jackson's career has included a commitment to youth and community development, including ten years in campus ministry at the University of Minnesota YMCA and fifteen years as vice president of Ys in Minneapolis and Seattle and as a Kellogg Foundation Leadership Fellow. They teach and consult nationally around leadership formation with nonprofits, public schools, institutions of higher education, and foundations. She feels most alive in her teaching when "creating trustworthy spaces for learning and reflection in which others 'come alive' to themselves and their capacity to serve more wholeheartedly in their lives and work." He feels most alive in his teaching when he is "helping people reconnect with the passions and gifts that most deeply inform their life-work."

Afterword

What I Heard Them Say

Parker J. Palmer

In the Foreword to this book, I urged us to listen to teachers. I want to bring the book to a close by reflecting on a few things I heard from the teachers whose words are between its covers— things we need to know if we are to support teachers properly and provide the kind of education every generation deserves.

1. *Good teachers see young people as unique individuals, not as social types.* Instead of seeing "teenagers," they see Sarah and Sam.

As I read the essays in this book, I was struck time and again by the fact that every tale of good teaching is about a live encounter between *this* teacher and *that* student. There are no stories of teachers who deal categorically with kids, whose teaching is aimed primarily at "the brain development of the modal ten-year-old with respect to mathematical reasoning."

But when we train teachers, we often portray learners in the categorical terms of abstract theory, and we focus their training on theory-based techniques. Rarely do we help student teachers or teachers already in the field develop or sharpen the skills necessary to perceive and respond to idiosyncratic individuals.

Of course, the capacity to see the uniqueness in another person depends heavily on the capacity to see the uniqueness in yourself. If you view yourself as a replaceable part, you will view others that way as well. If we are to raise teachers who can discern individuality in their students, we must help both would-be and practicing teachers learn to discern their own natures. Moreover, we must help them learn to teach from those qualities, rather than simply from abstract theory and generalized technique.

Today, a major threat to teachers who want to help students develop their individuality is our growing national mania for one-size-fits-all standardized testing. We know that learning patterns vary enormously with individual gifts and circumstances; to prove it, all we need do is become acquainted with the educational autobiographies of half a dozen friends. As we do so, we will hear a great variety of learning experiences and personal paths to growth. What we hear will defy the notion that education can be improved by forcing all students to jump through the same evaluation hoops.

Standardized testing strategies, I am afraid, have nothing to do with the logic of education or genuine care for the young. They are driven, instead, by an old political ploy: propose simplistic solutions to complex problems in hopes of pacifying enough people to win their votes. As our obsession with testing deepens, this society needs a child to cry out, "The emperor has no clothes!" But since the children are often too busy being tested to get out on the street and shout, we adults need to do it for them.

2. *Good teachers see beyond the masks worn by their students—* they see more in the young than the young see in themselves.

One obstacle good teachers must surmount daily is the tendency of young people to present themselves in ways that either deny or distort their own gifts. Why do students do this? Because they are too young to know what their gifts are. Because they have had little help in getting their gifts named. And because when young people do see their gifts, they are embarrassed to claim them in front of peers or fearful of the challenge that comes from being gifted—the challenge to use their gifts wisely and well.

Many of us can remember a teacher who identified and called forth capacities that were dormant within us when we were young—so dormant that we had no idea we had them! We remember those teachers with deep gratitude, knowing that our lives would have been much the poorer without them. We may even remember how intimidating it was to meet a teacher who had high expectations of us, expectations that we did not believe we could fulfill—and how that teacher's confidence in us helped us rise to the challenge.

What we need to understand is this: the teachers who saw what was dormant in us could not have done so unless they had been well acquainted with what was dormant in their own lives. Not every adult can do this, for adults like to pretend that they are complete and fulfilled and have always been that way. It takes a highly self-aware adult to remember how incomplete one was as a youngster—and to see how much lies buried beneath the surface of one's life yet today.

As we train and sustain our teachers, we need to help them remember how unrealized they were when they were young—and help them explore how much more remains to be realized in them today. As teachers grow in self-knowledge of this sort, they become more empathic with the diamond-in-the-rough that each student is, and better able to help each student achieve authentic selfhood.

3. *When we listen to good teachers, they urge us to join them in listening to students as well*—for the young have much to say about what helps and what hurts in education and the larger world.

Teachers' voices have been muffled by our society, but the voices of the young have been very nearly silenced. Perhaps this is why the young often "speak" to us in words and images that strike the elders as offensive and outrageous, such as the words of rap music or the images of Goth culture. But these specters are like fearsome figures in a dream: they are trying to get our attention so that we will listen to something important they have to say. To mix

Afterword

my metaphors, we need to think of our young people as canaries in a coal mine. They are warning us about toxins in our culture, and in education, that will do us all great damage if we do not heed their alarms.

Listen, for example, to students talk about their fears of the future. You will not hear all the gory details of economic decline, political instability, and environmental degradation, though students are not unaware of these things. You will hear how little support and guidance young people are getting from the elders in this society—elders who have become too massively self-absorbed in their own needs to help raise the young. The bridge to the future for every generation has been the caring of elders. Without it, the young feel overwhelmed by the future and its threats.

Or listen to the young talk about education. While there are some things that not all young people understand—like the long-term importance of certain kinds of knowledge—there are other things that they understand better than many adults. They know, for example, the difference between memorizing information to pass a standardized test and studying in order to learn.

I know a family whose sixth grader was having problems taking the next step in math. When his mother asked him to talk to his teacher, he came back with this report: "The teacher said not to worry. We're dropping our regular math lessons to prepare for the state test, which is coming up in two months—and it doesn't include the stuff I'm having trouble with. She said if there's time later on, we'll return to our regular lessons. But I'm still worried. Maybe it will be harder for me two months from now. Maybe I never will learn what I'm supposed to learn."

We need to listen to what the young are saying. What they know could save us a lot of trouble farther down the road.

4. *Good teachers suffer because they wear their hearts on their sleeves*—but they learn how to suffer creatively, turning pain into self-knowledge, personal growth, and professional service.

To be a good teacher, you cannot barricade yourself emotionally and teach from behind the wall—though the temptations to do so are immense. Good teachers put their hearts on the line every day. Having done so, they often suffer the slings and arrows of outrageous students, colleagues, supervisors, and society at large.

If you doubt this, talk to a high school English teacher who has her senior seminar students deeply engaged with great literature and real human issues for the first time in their young lives—but whose fellow teachers ostracize her for being "too touchy-feely" or too enamored of "winning a popularity contest." Or talk to a fifth-grade teacher who in the midst of a crowded classroom reaches out instinctively to place a comforting hand on the shoulder of a distressed student—only to be reported to the principal for "inappropriate physical contact."

Insults to the spirit such as these, and others less dramatic, create deep and abiding suffering, the kind that wakes us up at three in the morning and keeps us churning until dawn, the kind that can, and too often does, drive good people out of teaching.

I do not know of any surefire fixes for suffering, and I distrust anyone who says he or she does. But I do know that our schools, colleges, and professional development programs can and should teach much more than they do about the tragic dimension of life—about the fact that no amount of intelligence and goodwill can wall us off from events that threaten to crush us; about the fact that such events, rightly appropriated, can enlarge our lives; about the fact that forgiving and letting go play a critical role in transcending our condition.

It was once the function of liberal education to help us understand these things. Schools of education and in-service training programs would serve teachers well by asking them to study Greek literature and Shakespearean drama right alongside "classroom management."

5. *Teachers sometimes work in situations where their colleagues are unsupportive or untrustworthy*—but good teachers find ways to transcend and even transform those situations.

When an entire class of people is abused by the larger society, its members cannot always refrain from abusing their own. As they internalize the abuse they receive from the outside world, they sometimes, tragically, turn on each other. Crime statistics show that the weak and the poor do not, for the most part, rob and kill the rich and powerful. They rob and kill each other.

A shadow of this sort sometimes arises among teachers. Teachers may feel unsafe not only with the general public but with their colleagues as well—unsupported in their struggles, unrecognized in their successes, "robbed and killed" in their spirit. But in the midst of this personal and professional pain, good teachers affirm two truths: they must find ways to transcend a fragmented and fearful peer culture and, if possible, find ways to help transform a cannibalistic collective into a community of mutual support.

The inner work of the teacher—or of anyone else who wants to do good work—is to find ground on which to stand that is more stable and supportive than the shifting sands of peer alliances, jealousies, and fears. Daily, people who work in settings of many sorts must learn how to stay centered on their mission and grounded in their own commitment to it, even when the cynicism or despair that surrounds them threatens to drag them down.

But trying to stay afloat by oneself while adrift in a sea of despond is exhausting, and one is likely to drown. So the people who care most about the work they do reach out to colleagues and try to make common cause. Not everyone will rally to the flag, but not everyone needs to; a few committed co-conspirators can make a huge difference in generating and sustaining energy and morale. Here is another subject that needs to be taught in our schools of education and professional development programs: how to build communities of professional and personal support in work situations that have devolved to the lowest common denominator.

6. *The integrity of teaching and learning is under siege*—threatened by powerful political forces that seem utterly unresponsive to the realities of education.

I refer again to our growing national mania to test every child regularly to find out "how well" teachers and schools are doing so that we can reward those whose students test high and punish those whose students test low. Apparently, this strategy makes great sense to more than a few people. But it makes no sense at all to the good teachers I know. They recognize that such testing will pit colleagues against one another, crush the neediest students and schools, and create endless institutional pathologies.

Deeper still, they see that the tests themselves are often a sham. John Strassberger, president of Ursinus College, tells the story of John Dewey's response to the IQ test—a story that should be retold during every debate on the merits of standardized testing: When Dewey was asked what he thought about the test, he likened it to his family's preparations for taking a hog to market. To figure out how much to charge for the animal, his family put the hog on one end of a seesaw and piled up bricks on the other until the two balanced. "Then we tried to figure out how much those bricks weighed."[1]

Every good teacher believes in standards, rightly understood. That is how a teacher becomes "good"—by aspiring and adhering to certain standards for oneself and by passing those aspirations along to one's students. Good teachers do not fear standards; they fear standardized tests that not only hold all students and schools to the same norms, regardless of variations in capacities and resources, but that operationalize those norms in a mechanistic "number two pencil" mode.

So what can good teachers do about the politically motivated juggernaut that is rolling over them? The same thing they can do to stay afloat in a sea of despond: form community with others—with like-minded colleagues, parents, and citizens at large—amplifying the teacher's voice so that it is more likely be heard inside those soundproof boxes where institutional decisions are made and national political life is conducted. Through community, teachers can become more engaged in the processes that shape education, can become leaders in helping to transform the settings of our professional and political lives.

All of this takes courage, of course. But good teachers possess courage in abundance, and I think I know why. Good teachers do not believe that they owe ultimate allegiance to the principal, the union, the school board, or the government. Good teachers pledge allegiance to their students, to the children and young people who have been placed in their care. Having made this commitment, good teachers find the courage to act on it in whatever ways become necessary.

We are blessed with many good teachers in our schools and colleges. We need to listen to them with deep respect, learn from what they have to say, and find our own courage to support them as they work to reform education and help raise the next generation.

NOTE

1. Strassberger, J. "Counting Quality." Fifth in a series of occasional papers by the president of Ursinus College, Collegeville, Pennsylvania.

Parker J. Palmer began teaching in 1961 when, as a student at Union Theological Seminary in New York City, he worked in a weekend program for fifth- and sixth-graders from Spanish Harlem. Since then he has taught undergraduates at Berea College, Beloit College, and Georgetown University; seminary students at the Pacific School of Religion; older adult students at Pendle Hill, the Quaker living and learning community; and seekers of many sorts during his long career as a "traveling teacher" in the United States and abroad. He has received several awards and honorary doctorates in recognition of his teaching and his books about teaching, including *To Know As We Are Known: Education as a Spiritual*

Journey (HarperSan Francisco, 1971) and *The Courage to Teach: Exploring the Inner Landscape of a Teacher's Life* (Jossey-Bass, 1998). He is the founder of the Teacher Formation Program for K–12 educators in the public schools. He says, "I feel most alive as a teacher when my students and I have a sense of community that allows us to take on tough questions, engage in creative conflict, develop mutual insight, and keep caring about each other and the world in the process."

Resources That Honor and Sustain the Teacher's Heart

Compiled by Helen Lee

Each of the authors was asked to cite three resources that inspire and sustain their professional heart. What follows is a list of their selections that we hope will be helpful in your own work.

Ayers, William. *To Teach: The Journey of a Teacher.* New York: Teachers College Press, 2001.

Barks, Coleman, and Moyne, John. *The Essential Rumi.* San Francisco: HarperSanFrancisco, 1995.

Bode, Richard. *First You Have to Row a Little Boat: Reflections on Life and Living.* New York: Warner Books, 1993.

Carrino, Deborah. *The Spirit of Children.* Amherst, N.Y.: Prometheus Books, 2000.

Chödrön, Pema. *When Things Fall Apart: Heart Advice for Difficult Times.* Boston: Shambhala, 1997.

Cohen, Rosetta M. *A Lifetime of Teaching: Portraits of Five Veteran High School Teachers.* New York: Teachers College Press, 1991.

Coles, Robert. *The Call of Stories.* Boston: Houghton Mifflin, 1989.

Dewey, J. *Democracy and Education.* New York, 1916.

Freedom Writers. *The Freedom Writers Diary: How a Teacher and 150 Teens Used Writing to Change Themselves and the World Around Them.* New York: Doubleday, 1999.

Freire, Paolo. *Pedagogy of Freedom: Ethics, Democracy, and Civic Courage.* Lanham, Md.: Rowman & Littlefield, 1998.

Freire, Paolo. *Teachers as Cultural Workers: Letters to Those Who Dare Teach.* Boulder, Colo.: Westview Press, 1998.

Gaines, Ernest J. *A Lesson Before Dying.* New York: Dramatists Play Service, 2001.

Gendler, J. Ruth. *The Book of Qualities.* New York: Harper Perennial, 1988.

Goleman, Daniel. *Emotional Intelligence: Why It Can Matter More Than IQ.* New York: Bantam Books, 1995.

Grant, Gerald. *The World We Created at Hamilton High.* Cambridge, Mass.: Harvard University Press, 1998.

Graves, Don. *The Energy to Teach.* Portsmouth, N.H.: Heinemann, 2001.

Hanh, Thich Nhat. *Peace Is Every Step: The Path of Mindfulness in Everyday Life.* New York: Bantam Books, 1991.

Hill, Kirkpatrick. *The Year of Miss Agnes.* New York: McElderry, 2000.

Hughes, Langston. *Selected Poems of Langston Hughes.* New York: Vintage Books, 1959.

Johnson, Keith. *Impro: Improvisation and the Theatre.* London: Methuen, 1994.

Kabat-Zinn, Jon. *Wherever You Go, There You Are: Mindfulness Meditation in Everyday Life.* New York: Hyperion, 1994.

Keizer, Garret. *No Place But Here: A Teacher's Vocation in a Rural Community.* Hanover, N.H.: University Press of New England, 1996.

Kornfield, Jack. *A Path with Heart: A Guide Through the Perils and Promises of Spiritual Life.* New York: Bantam Books, 1993.

Kozol, Jonathan. *Amazing Grace: The Lives of Children and the Conscience of a Nation.* New York: Harper Perennial, 1995.

Lamott, Anne. *Traveling Mercies: Some Thoughts on Faith.* New York: Pantheon Books, 1990.

LeShan, Lawrence. *How to Meditate: A Guide to Self-Discovery.* Boston: Hall, 1994.

RESOURCES THAT HONOR AND SUSTAIN THE TEACHER'S HEART

Levoy, Gregg M. *Callings: Finding and Following an Authentic Life.* New York: Three Rivers Press, 1997.

Louf, André. *Tuning In to Grace: The Quest for God* (Jon Vriend, trans.). Cistercian, 1992.

Meier, Deborah. *The Power of Their Ideas: Lessons for America from a Small School in Harlem.* Boston: Beacon Press, 1995.

Milosz, Czeslaw. *A Book of Luminous Things: An International Anthology of Poetry.* San Diego: Harcourt, 1996.

Nepo, Mark. *The Book of Awakening: Having the Life You Want by Being Present to the Life You Have.* Berkeley, Calif.: Conari Press, 2000.

Norris, Gunilla. *Sharing Silence: Meditation Practice and Mindful Living.* New York: Bell Tower, 1992.

Nye, Naomi Shihab. *Words Under the Words: Selected Poems.* Portland, Ore.: Eighth Mountain Press, 1995.

O'Reilley, Mary Rose. *Radical Presence: Teaching as Contemplative Practice.* Portsmouth, N.H.: Boynton/Cook, 1998.

Oliver, Mary. *House of Light.* Boston: Beacon Press, 1990.

Oliver, Mary. *West Wind.* Boston: Houghton Mifflin, 1997.

Paley, Vivian. *You Can't Say You Can't Play.* Cambridge, Mass.: Harvard University Press, 1992.

Palmer, Parker J. *The Active Life: A Spirituality of Work, Creativity, and Caring.* San Francisco: HarperSanFrancisco, 1965.

Palmer, Parker J. *To Know as We Are Known: Education as a Spiritual Journey.* San Francisco: HarperSanFrancisco, 1971.

Palmer, Parker J. *The Courage to Teach: Exploring the Inner Landscape of a Teacher's Life.* San Francisco: Jossey-Bass, 1998.

Palmer, Parker J. *Let Your Life Speak.* San Francisco: Jossey-Bass, 1999.

Remen, Rachel Naomi. *Kitchen Table Wisdom: Stories That Heal.* New York: Riverhead Books, 1996.

Rilke, Rainer Marie. *Letters to a Young Poet.* New York, 1908.

Rose, Mike. *Lives on the Boundary: The Struggles and Achievements of America's Underprepared.* New York: Free Press, 1989.

Rose, Mike. *Possible Lives: The Promise of Public Education in America.* Boston: Houghton Mifflin, 1995.

Resources That Honor and Sustain the Teacher's Heart

Sarton, May. *The Small Room.* New York: Norton, 1961.

Sarton, May. *Collected Poems, 1930–1993.* New York: Norton, 1993.

Shepard, Odell. *Pedlar's Progress: The Life of Bronson Alcott.* New York: Little, Brown, 1937.

Suskind, Ron. *A Hope in the Unseen: An American Odyssey from the Inner City to the Ivy League.* New York: Broadway Books, 1998.

Uchiyama, Kosho. *Opening the Hand of Thought: Approach to Zen.* New York: Arkana, 1993.

Whyte, David. *Fire in the Earth.* Langley, Wash.: Many Rivers Press, 1992.

Whyte, David. *The House of Belonging.* Langley, Wash.: Many Rivers Press, 1997

FILM AND VIDEO RECOMMENDATIONS

Dead Poets Society. St. Paul, Minn.: DVS Home Video, 1992.

Finding Forrester. Culver City, Calif.: Columbia TriStar Home Video, 2001.

How We Feel: Hispanic Students Speak Out. Falls Church, Va.: Landmark Films, 1991.

Joseph Campbell and the Power of Myth. Montauk, N.Y.: Mystic Fire Video, 1988.

RESOURCES THAT HONOR AND SUSTAIN THE TEACHER'S HEART

The Editor

Sam M. Intrator began his teaching career as a substitute teacher at Abraham Lincoln High School in Brooklyn, New York, in 1987 when he took over the classes of a heroic English teacher named Lenore Braverman who was called to jury duty. He then taught high school English in Brooklyn's Sheepshead Bay High School and in public schools in Vermont and in California, where he was also a high school administrator. He is now an assistant professor in the Department of Education and Child Study and the Program in Urban Studies at Smith College in Northampton, Massachusetts. A W. K. Kellogg National Leadership Fellow, he has received the Distinguished Teacher Award from the White House Commission on Presidential Scholars and the Faculty Teaching Award at Smith College. In 2003, Yale University Press will publish his book examining meaningful and memorable classroom experiences from the perspective of high school–aged youth. He says, "I feel most alive and triumphant as a teacher when I witness students becoming engrossed in understanding ideas, each other, and the world in which we live. Watching students recognizing and experiencing their own special strengths and capacities has always been a thrill for me."

About the
Courage to Teach Program

Under the guidance of Parker J. Palmer, the Fetzer Institute created Courage to Teach, a seasonal program of quarterly retreats for the personal and professional renewal of public school educators. The retreat program primarily serves K–12 educators, administrators, and educational leaders on whom our society depends for so much but for whom we provide so little.

Courage to Teach employs an approach to vocational renewal called "formation." The formation process invites educators to reclaim their own wholeness and vocational clarity and makes connections between the renewal of a teacher's spirit and the revitalization of public education. This approach to personal and professional renewal is rooted in the belief that good teaching flows from the identity and integrity of the teacher.

The Center for Teacher Formation was established in 1997 to develop, deepen, and expand the work of teacher formation nationally. The center provides information and consultation to individuals and communities that wish to initiate Courage to Teach programs. The center is also responsible for the selection and preparation of formation facilitators.

For more information about the Center for Teacher Formation and Courage to Teach, please see our Web site: www. teacherformation.org.

Index

328

INDEX

New York City Board of Education, strike against, xxix
New York Times, xliii
Newness, spirit of, 120–124
Nieto, S., 64, 65–71, 75–77
Nietzsche, F., 31
Nodell, R. S., 269n
Nonviolence, 264
Nouwen, H., 251
"Now I Become Myself" (Sarton), 300
Nozick, R., xxxvi
Nye, N. S., 224

O
"Ode" (Wordsworth), 112
Oliver, M., 224
Opening circle, 284
O'Reilley, M. R., 108, 109–115
Out of the Silent Planet (Lewis), 111
Overwhelmed feeling, xliv–xlv

P
Palmer, P. J., xvii, xxxiii–xxxiv, l, li, 3, 30, 31, 45, 51, 101, 102, 103, 137, 188–189, 203, 210, 272, 280, 287–288, 309
Pangburn, L., 225, 227
Paradox: concept of, teaching, 303; flowering of, 292; and formation space, 295–297; lens of, viewing through, 24–25, 45, 49; making use of, 238
Parallel process, 258
Paraprofessionals, inclusion of, in staff development programs, 199
Peace, leadership of, 274–276
Peer coaching, 199
Personal and professional development, addressing, 74–75, 219–228, 282–307

Personal safety, student concern for, 257–258
Phonics, teaching, xxxiv
Piercy, M., 270, 271, 293
Plague, The (Camus), 274
Poetry Through Music, 69
Poets, comparison to, contrast in, 1, 2–3
Political blaming, effect of, 195–196
Poor communities, situation in, 196
Powell, L. C., 254, 255–267
Pragmatism, 60
Prayer, school, 265
Presence. *See* Teaching presence
Pride and Prejudice (Austen), 86
Principals: admonishment from, 169, 170, 193–194; reform effort by, 246; 247–252; repercussion of test scores on, xliii
Principles of Learning initiative, 162
Problem storytelling, 214–215
Process bound up with product, 275
Professional boundaries, balancing, with making connections, 90, 91
Professional and personal development, addressing, 74–75, 219–228, 282–307
Projective processes, 258–259, 260, 263
Public Agenda survey, xxxvii
Public confidence, erosion of, xxxi–xxxii
Public Enemy, 69
Public support, lack of, for urban schools, 66, 67

Q
Quakerism, 112, 297, 301

R
Racial intolerance, addressing, 101–106
Racism, experiencing, 127–128

Schutz, A., 154

Scientific management, notion of, xxxii

Scott, M. A., 34, 35–40

Seasonal metaphors, 291–292, 293, 303

Seeing Calvin Coolidge in a Dream (Derbyshire), 46–47

Self Knowledge Symposium, 40

Self-disclosure, vulnerability from, 90–91, 92

Self-discovery, space for, 275, 276. *See also* Reflection

Selfhood: expression of, xxxvi; knowing and trusting one's, xxxiii; questions involving, 294; rediscovering, story of, 29–32

September 11, 2001, tragedy, aftermath of, li

Servant Leadership School (SLS), 263

"Seven of Pentacles, The" (Piercy), 293

Shakespeare at Winedale program, 167–168, 176

Shakespeare, W., 24, 69, 86

Shared work and common purpose, newness of, 123–124

Shulman, L., xxxi

Silence, 263–264, 294–295

Small things, significance in doing, 35–40, 114

Social environment, 269–271

Social typecasting, avoiding, 309–310

Sovereignty of Good (Murdoch), 44

Soviet Union space program, xxxi

Spelling curriculum, change in, group effort toward, 226

Spencer Foundation Practitioner Research and Communication Mentoring Grant, 219–220

Spiritual realm, 51

Spiritual starvation, 259, 265

Splitting processes, 258, 260

Staff development programs, inclusion of paraprofessionals in, 199

Stafford, W., 15, 224

Standardized methods, prescribing, advent of, xxxii

Standardized testing: preoccupation with, effect of, xli–xliv, 284, 310, 314–315; resisting, 161, 163, 164; understanding, and making useful, 194–195

Standards of Learning (SOL), xliii

Status quo, guarding, 274

Strassberger, J., 315

Stretch, versions of, 155

Strikes, xxix

Stromberger, C., 158, 159–177

Student perspectives: devaluing, 238; importance of, 230, 232–233, 237; on listening circles, 180–191; on literature circles, 235–236; obtaining, 233–238

Students: anger of, 14; attentive love toward, 49; believing in, 69–70, 130; birthright gifts of, 303–304, 310–311; concern of, over personal safety, 257–258; identity of, affirming, 68–69; listening to, need for, 311–312; masks worn by, seeing beyond, 310–311; responsibility of, letter addressing, 73–74

Substitute teachers, approach to, 198

Success and failure: discerning, uncertainty in, xlix; measure of, questioning, 14

Suffering, inevitability of, 312–313

Sufis, encounter with, 109–110

Super, D. C., 58

Supplies, spending on, xli

Swaim, M. S., xliv–xlv

The Courage to Teach:
Exploring the Inner Landscape
of a Teacher's Life
Parker J. Palmer

$23.95 Hardcover   ISBN: 0787910589

"This is the best education book I've read in a long time. Palmer provides a powerful argument for the need to move from our over-reliance on technique toward a learning environment that both honors and truly develops the deepest human capacities in children and teachers. It's about time we remember that it's the person within the teacher that matters most in education, and Palmer makes the case eloquently."—*Teacher Magazine*

"This book is for teachers who have good days and bad—and whose bad days bring the suffering that comes only from something one loves. It is for teachers who refuse to harden their hearts, because they love learners, learning, and the teaching life."—Parker J. Palmer

Teachers choose their vocation for reasons of the heart, because they care deeply about their students and about their subject. But the demands of teaching cause too many educators to lose heart. Is it possible to take heart in teaching once more so that we can continue to do what good teachers always do—give heart to our students? In *The Courage to Teach,* Parker J. Palmer takes teachers on an inner journey toward reconnecting with their vocation and their students, and recovering their passion for one of the most difficult and important of human endeavors. "This book builds on a simple premise: good teaching cannot be reduced to technique; good teaching comes from the identity and integrity of the teacher." Good teaching comes in myriad forms, but good teachers share one trait: they are truly present in the classroom, deeply engaged with their students and their subject. They possess "a capacity for connectedness" and "are able to weave a complex web of connections among themselves, their subjects, and their students, so that students can learn to weave a world for themselves."

PARKER J. PALMER is a highly respected writer who works independently on issues in education, community, spirituality, and social change; he offers lectures, workshops, and retreats across the country. He has inspired a generation of teachers and reformers with evocative visions of community, knowing, and spiritual wholeness. He lives in Madison, Wisconsin.

[Price subject to change]

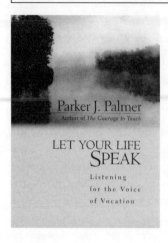

Let Your Life Speak:
Listening for the Voice of Vocation
Parker J. Palmer

$18.00 Hardcover   ISBN: 0787947350

Parker Palmer's writing is like a high country stream—clear, vital, honest. If your life seems to be passing you by, or you cannot see the way ahead, immerse yourself in the wisdom of these pages and allow it to carry you toward a more attentive relationship with your deeper, truer self.—John S. Mogabgab, Editor, *Weavings Journal*

"Is the life I am living the same as the life that wants to live in me?"

With this searching question, Parker J. Palmer begins an insightful and moving meditation on finding one's true calling. *Let Your Life Speak* is an openhearted gift to anyone who seeks to live authentically. The book's title is a time-honored Quaker admonition, usually taken to mean "Let the highest truths and values guide everything you do." But Palmer reinterprets those words, drawing on his own search for selfhood. "Before you tell your life what you intend to do with it," he writes, "listen for what it intends to do with you. Before you tell your life what truths and values you have decided to live up to, let your life tell you what truths you embody, what values you represent."

Vocation does not come from willfulness, no matter how noble one's intentions. It comes from listening to and accepting "true self" with its limits as well as its potentials. Sharing stories of frailty and strength, of darkness and light, Palmer shows that vocation is not a goal to be achieved but a gift to be received. A compassionate and compelling meditation on discovering your path in life with wisdom, compassion, and gentle humor, Parker J. Palmer invites us to listen to the inner teacher and follow it toward a sense of meaning and purpose.

PARKER J. PALMER is a highly respected writer who works independently on issues in education, community, spirituality, and social change; he offers lectures, workshops, and retreats across the country. He has inspired a generation of teachers and reformers with evocative visions of community, knowing, and spiritual wholeness. He lives in Madison, Wisconsin.

[Price subject to change]

Courage to Teach: A Guide for Reflection and Renewal
Rachel C. Livsey
Parker J. Palmer

Foreword by Parker J. Palmer

$8.00 Paper ISBN: 0787946451

Teaching From the Heart: Seasons of Renewal in a Teacher's Life
with Parker J. Palmer
Sponsored by the Fetzer Institute

$79.95 Video ISBN: 0787946443

To go on this journey with Parker Palmer into the uncharted territory of "the self" in teaching is not only to experience the joy of viewing teaching from a thrilling new perspective. It is also to be in the presence of a great teacher who, by sharing himself so openly and honestly, engages us in the very kind of teaching he so eloquently describes.—Russell Edgerton, director of educational programs, Pew Charitable Trusts, and past president, American Association for Higher Education

From the best-selling author of *The Courage to Teach: Exploring the Inner Landscape of a Teacher's Life* comes two new resources for reflection and renewal.

The guide will help teachers, individually and in groups, reflect on their teaching and renew their sense of vocation by exploring the "inner landscape" of their lives along Palmer's three dimensions—intellectual, emotional, and spiritual. The guide will raise questions, examine ideas and images, and suggest practices that emerge from the many insights in *The Courage to Teach*.

The inspiring documentary follows one hundred K–12 teachers in four cities around the United States as they take part in the two-year Courage to Teach program. Gain valuable insight as you follow them through a sequence of seasonal retreats where they explore—in solitude and community—their gifts, their needs, their pains and joys, and move closer to the intersection of "soul" and "role" in their work as teachers. They, and we, find courage as they return to their classrooms with a renewed sense of caring, commitment, creativity, and calling.

PARKER J. PALMER is a highly respected writer who works independently on issues in education, community, spirituality, and social change; he offers lectures, workshops, and retreats across the country. He has inspired a generation of teachers and reformers with evocative visions of community, knowing, and spiritual wholeness. He lives in Madison, Wisconsin.

[Price subject to change]